INDIAN CINEMA AND THE URBAN EXPERIENCE

EDITED BY PREBEN KAARSHOLM

LONDON NEW YORK CALCUTTA

Seagull Books

Editorial offices:

1st Floor, Angel Court, 81 St Clements Street,
Oxford OX4 1AW, UK

1 Washington Square Village, Apt 1U, New York,
NY 10012, USA

26 Circus Avenue, Calcutta 700 017, India

Seagull Books 2007

ISBN 1 9054 2 236 9

British Library Cataloguing-in-Publication Data
A catalogue record for this book is available from the British Library

Typeset by Seagull Books, Calcutta, India
Printed in the United Kingdom by Biddles Ltd, King's Lynn

CONTENTS

ACKNOWLEDGEMENTS

The majority of essays in this volume originate in presentations made to a seminar and researcher training course held at Filmhuset in Copenhagen from 20 to 24 September 1999 on 'Representations of Metropolitan Life in Contemporary Indian Film: Bombay, Calcutta, Madras' which brought together the 'stars' of Indian film studies and criticism represented here with Danish colleagues, critics and Ph.D students.

The meeting was accompanied by the showing of a series of films, including Nimai Ghosh's *Chhinnamul*, Satyajit Ray's *Mahanagar* and *Jana Aranya*, Ritwik Ghatak's *Meghe Dhaka Tara* and *Subarnarekha*, Mira Nair's *Salaam Bombay*, Mani Ratnam's *Bombay* and Rituparno Ghosh's *Dahan*—an enterprise which was extremely difficult to arrange, delayed the occasion by more than a year, and demonstrated how incredibly difficult, for reasons of bureaucracy and preservation method, it is to actually get to see screenings of what can only be regarded as absolute highlights in the modern cultural history of India.

The idea for the Copenhagen seminar arose at a Cultural Studies workshop organized in Mysore in November 1995 by the Centre for Studies in Social Sciences, Calcutta, on the theme 'Cultural Studies for India' at which Tejaswini Niranjana, Ashish Rajadhyaksha and Ravi Vasudevan gave presentations, and which took place while the debate in India around Mani Ratnam's *Roja* was at its peak. Other presenters at the workshop included Susie Tharu, Gyan Pandey, S. V. Srinivas, Partha Chatterjee, Tapati Guha-Thakurta and Vivek Dhareshwar, and the workshop became the first in a series of annual cultural studies workshops arranged by the CSSSC at different venues in India, offering training to Ph.D students from India and other countries of the South.

The Indian cultural studies workshops have been planned in collaboration with the Graduate School of International Development Studies at Roskilde University, and Roskilde scholars have contributed lectures and discussion inputs. In this process, the Danes have certainly learnt no less than the Indians, and the purpose of the Copenhagen seminar on 'Representations of Metropolitan Life in Contemporary Indian Film' was to bring some of the inspiration and excitement of the workshops in India to Denmark. Another intention was to stimulate a Danish interest in the rich, strange and wonderful world of Indian film which is already growing, as shown by the popularity of Indian movies at the 'Films from the South' festivals which have been held in Copenhagen and other Danish cities in recent years, and by the Indian film series shown by Danish TV 2 in July 2003 (including *Devdas* and Mani Ratnam's *Dil Se*).

The Copenhagen Indian film event in September 1999 was financed with contributions from the Danish Council for Research in the Humanities, 'Det lange Udvalg', the Graduate School of International Development Studies at Roskilde University, the Department of Film and Media Studies and the Department of Comparative Literature at the University of Copenhagen, the Danish Ph.D Network for Development Studies and International Relations, and, finally, the ENRECA programme under Danida, which had also funded the Mysore cultural studies workshop in 1995.

The venue for the event as well as indispensable practical and logistical support was provided by the Cinematheque and the Danish Film Museum at Filmhuset in Copenhagen. Successive Indian Ambassadors to Copenhagen—Mrs Neelam Deo and subsequently Mr Shashank—gave moral support, and helped in locating the whereabouts of copies of film.

The contribution of Madhuja Mukherjee to an earlier version of Manas Ray's essay which was titled 'Bollywood in Diaspora: in the tracks of a twice displaced community' is gratefully acknowledged.

Apart from the contributors to the present volume, I should like to thank the following individuals for having in different ways helped to bring the project to fruition—Dan Nissen, Katrine Høyberg, Amrit Gangar, Stig Hjarvard, David Hanan, Ritaban Ghatak, Amiya Bagchi, Mrinal Sen, and Peter Madsen—whose lecture to the September 1999 gathering has been published separately in a collection of essays on *The Urban Life World* (Madsen and Plunz, 2001).

Special thanks are due to Anjum Katyal for the care with which she prepared the Seagull edition of the book, and to Moinak Biswas for advice and assistance in the process of editing.

INTRODUCTION

UNREAL CITY: CINEMATIC REPRESENTATION, GLOBALIZATION
AND THE AMBIGUITIES OF METROPOLITAN LIFE

PREBEN KAARSHOLM

The growth of Indian film production and of the significance of
movies in Indian society since 1947, closely associated with the rapid
expansion of Indian cities and of urbanism as a lifestyle which has
taken place concurrently, has been colossal. Indian films have not only
portrayed the process of urbanization as a struggle towards coming to
terms with and formulating agendas for modernity, but also as reactions to and counter-programmes against this process.

Movies and cinemas have in themselves been central rallying
points, symbols and institutions of modernization, and battlefields for
the understanding of, for formulations and appropriations of, the
conditions of the new life as against 'what used to be'. The production
and reception of film is a crucial arena for negotiating and asserting
control over the parameters of modern urban culture and politics. At
the same time, the urban landscape has been inscribed with cinematic signs to such an extent that it is hard to form a mental image of an
Indian city without a bombardment of both sight and sound from
movie posters, film advertisements, tannoys, radio and tapes of
soundtrack music.

In conditions of widespread poverty and illiteracy, movie spectacles
in India have fulfilled a role supplementing that of literature and

print culture in making modernity popular—creating images representing the challenges of change, the threat to old orientations, the emergence of new forms of dominance, as well as of new fields for manoeuvre.

Debates over modernization in India since 1947 have been closely linked to debates over nation-building and nationalism, and films have contributed significantly to such debates, formulating visual agendas for a new coherent, modern and secular national life as well as criticizing and undermining such agendas by giving visual representation and soundtrack voice to notions of cultural and communal autonomy.

Indian cinema has been an important icon of the modern, both nationally and globally. Images of urban modernity have been carried by movies from metropolises into smaller towns and the countryside, and in other parts of the world showings of Indian films have represented rallying points for notions of Indian-ness as well as institutions of cosmopolitanism and globalization. Thus, in many African countries, the presence of Indian film is a distinguishing and spectacular feature of modern urban culture (cf. Larkin, 1997).

Modernity and Metropolis

In a variety of ways, more generally, the association of modernity and metropolis has been a commonplace in critical discourse. The big city has been a recurrent and flexibly faithful metaphor of modern life, and it has been assumed that particular characteristics of perception, psychology and consciousness are integral parts of metropolitan life: that urban dwellers represent either refinement, politesse and gentility at a higher level, or else, as members of 'the urban crowd' as envisaged by Gustave le Bon and Simmel in Europe at the turn of the 19th and 20th centuries, represent decadence and a nervousness of disposition which threaten to undercut the foundations of civilized social behaviour (cf. Kaarsholm, 2001: 125).

In the great 19th century novels of European critical realism, the metropolis stands out as a spectacle of a life world in the making, to the shock, despair and exhilaration of those who enter it from the backwaters of the provinces. In Balzac's *La comédie humaine*, Paris is the stage which modernity requires to unfold itself—a universe of fascinations, rapidly and hypocritically changing surfaces, cynicism, betrayals and constant movement where everybody watches everybody else like in a theatre, through binoculars or a lens. Until recently a provincial, Lucien—in *Lost Illusions*—finds his eyes 'glued to the curtain' of the boulevard theatre and feels

> so much more vulnerable to the enchantments this kind of life offered with its alternations of lightning flashes and clouds because it was as dazzling as a firework display after the profound darkness of his own laborious, inglorious, monotonous existence (Balzac, 1971: 293).

Similarly, in the novels of Charles Dickens, London represents a wholly new kind of life, which is like an 'earthquake' and characterized by perpetual motion, rush, simultaneity, coincidences, fog and slipperiness, written about by Dickens in ways which, to 20th century readers, seem to anticipate Eisenstein and motion picture techniques of representation. The urban world in Dickens's narration is one of

> such continual kinetic distraction of the eye as the *kinematograph's* "animated pictures" would bring ... We do not have to wait for film's *avant-garde* 1920s for the spirit that gave birth to urban evocations like *Berlin, the Symphony of a Great City* (Rutmann 1927) or Vertov's *Man with a Movie Camera* (1928) (Marsh, 2001: 76. Cf. Williams, 1975: 189-201).

This metropolitan world is one of necessarily mixed feeling in which values are being continuously overturned, the highest beauty found in the most lowly surroundings; and the *flaneur* who moves restlessly through alleys and boulevards represents the only possibility for authentic experience—'in Baudelaire's mercurial and paradoxical sensibility, the counter-pastoral image of the modern world generates a remarkably pastoral vision of the modern artist who floats, untouched, freely about it' (Berman, 1983: 139). The ambiguity of experience is so strong that

> to be fully modern is to be anti-modern: from Marx's and Dostoevsky's time to our own, it has been impossible to grasp and embrace the modern world's potentialities without loathing and fighting against some of its most palpable realities ... the deepest modern seriousness must express itself through irony (Berman, 1983: 13ff.).

In parallel terms, social theorists have used the panorama of life conditions in the city to demonstrate both what was horrible about the modern condition—its satanic mills and generalized prostitution—and also as a counterpoint of liberation and the opening of possibilities to what Karl Marx famously and brutally called 'the idiocy of rural life'. For Marx, the metropolis was the embodiment of those highest stages of western capitalism in which—like a mirror—other parts of the world might gain a vision of their own futures.

A not unrelated evolutionist perspective can be found in the modernization theory and development studies discourse of the post-World War Two period, where 'tribesmen' would become 'townsmen in the making' (Southall and Gutkind, 1957), and in the process overturn their dispositions, the structures of their dreams, and their capacities for mobility and for 'empathy'—for envisaging the possibility of difference and change. 'Transitional individuals' would undergo a 'characterological transformation', become 'participant persons' and experience a 'massive growth in *imaginativeness*' (Lerner, 1964:411; italics in original)—spurred on by the 'mobility multipliers' of 'mass media of print, film and radio' (Lerner, 1968: 391).

The modernity of big-city life has been seen to bring with it a reflexivity which is different from what existed earlier. In *The Consequences of Modernity* (1990), Anthony Giddens represents the emergence of such reflexive modernity and 'disembeddedness' as something both universal and unique, and as the outcome of a particular avenue of historical development. It represents an 'institutionalisation of doubt' whose beginnings can be attributed to a particular phase in the development of capitalism and the formation of nation states, but whose effects in the process of becoming globalized are not culturally specific—'Progress becomes emptied of content as the circularity of modernity takes hold' (Giddens, 1990:177).

This view, however, of the outcome of a particular historical trajectory becoming a universalized condition has for a long time through colonialism been tied to notions of progress which were far from emptied of content, and which identified 'modernization' with 'westernization'. In this way, a dualism was established and consolidated between 'modernity' and 'tradition' which disregarded internal struggles, debates and contradictory dynamics in the life worlds of non-western colonies, and reduced them to homelands of custom into which European progress and modernity could only gradually be introduced. Thus— through systems of indirect rule—European colonial powers came to consolidate paradoxically gerontocratic and traditionalist forces, and undercut indigenous forms of and agendas for modernization, the metropolis defining its periphery:

> ... a model of city and country, in economic and political relationships, has gone beyond the boundaries of the nation-state, and is seen but also challenged as a model of the world... in a new and universal sense, this was the penetration, transformation and subjugation of the 'country' by the 'city'... (Williams, 1975:334, 343).

As an alternative to such a colonialist unilinear and dualist view, a possibility would be—as Raymond Williams suggests in *The Country and the City*—a perspective which sees the contrasting of the urban with the countryside rather as a pattern of representation and understanding that has come around repeatedly like an 'escalator' moving, and has occurred at widely different times and places to give expression to widely different meanings:

> ... what seemed a single escalator, a perpetual recession into history, turns out, on reflection, to be a more complicated movement: Old England settlement, the rural virtues—all these, in fact, mean different things at different times, and quite different values are being brought to question. We shall need precise analysis of each retrospect, as it comes. We shall see successive stages of the criticism which the retrospect supports: religious, humanist, political, cultural. Each of these stages is worth examination in itself (Williams, 1975: 22).

In this more complex perspective, modernities and experiences of the breakdown of the old come to the fore in the plural—as historical conjunctures and life situations which are not the outcomes of a single evolutionary logic, but rather as battlefields of contestation between different forces of development and different cultural and political agendas.

Movies and the Urban Experience

The special capacity of film to represent the experience and life world of urban modernity has been pointed out often enough from

Chaplin's sentimentalism and breathless pursuits through Eisenstein's montage and Vertov's moving camera to Fritz Lang's futuristic horrors and under-earth paranoia in *Metropolis* and *M*.

In his essay in the present volume, Peter Larsen discusses a corresponding set of assumptions put forward in early film theory of the comprehensibility of film and moving pictures being in return dependent on forms of perception peculiar to an audience with experience of big-city life. Like people making sense of a cubist painting, movie spectators must be able to 'integrate single disjointed pictures into a coherent scene.' But discussing the assumptions, Larsen gets on to an 'escalator' moving much like Raymond Williams's—the 'cognitive fundamentals of film comprehension' put forward by, for example, Kracauer and Benjamin do not hold water empirically; modern as well as old ways of seeing can be found in both the metropolis and rural backwaters. What the theorists propose makes sense rather as 'utopian visions about the connections between film language and urban modernity.'

The experience of urban modernity as something peculiar depends on its being seen through a lense of alienation or difference—in this sense Chaplin's urban scenarios cannot be separated from the perspective of music-hall and melodramatic vaudeville in which they are framed, and which belong to an earlier world. Similarly, Ashish Rajadhyaksha has argued that the theatricality and 'neo-traditionalism' of early Indian silent films are rooted in the ways in which they understood and dialogued with the audiences to whom they were representing experiences of modernity and urbanism, and who were assumed to need such theatricality of address in order to understand (Rajadhyaksha, 1987).

Furthermore, debates in India around representations of modernity have been particularly complex and intense because of the ways in which they have been bound up with issues of colonialism and nationalism; as Ravi Vasudevan writes,

> the power-laden circumstances in which modernity was introduced caused culturally defensive reactions against it; but... the 'inner' or 'traditional' stance which developed in response inevitably employed modern perceptual, technological and organizational developments to institute itself (Vasudevan, 2000: 11).

As colonialism—in spite of oppression and segregation—identified itself as a programme for modernization and progress, strategies to counter it relied on the elaboration of alternative notions and programmes of modernity that might not simply reject Europeanness as modernity per se, but situated Indian experiences and agendas against it. And which developed their own diagnoses of the malaises and possibilities of a modern life world whose ambiguities were intensified by its colonialist framing.[1]

Debates around the constitution and contradictions of modernity were re-directed and fuelled further by conditions of national independence and post-colonialism after 1947. In his contribution to this volume, Moinak Biswas discusses Nimai Ghosh's film *Chhinnamul* from 1949-50 in which the experience of big-city modernity is shown from the perspective of a group of East Bengali peasant refugees who arrive in Calcutta after having been forcefully removed from their homes during the Partition of 1947. Dramatically and effectively, the film shows village life in almost stilted theatrical fashion and within sets that do not attempt to hide their artificiality. By contrast, the world of the metropolis—as it erupts on the refugees when they arrive at Calcutta's Sealdah station—is shown as 'documentary' reportage.

In Ghosh's film, classically, modernity is shown in the form of the big city as seen through the eyes of new arrivals, but here also within a general setting of catastrophe and upheaval—with the nation as the modern coming into being through the foundational violence of the Partition.[2] This vision of modernization as tragedy is expanded as the original cohesion—politically and culturally—of the refugee community eventually cracks up in Balzacian fashion, with individual members seeking their own selfish luck. In this way, *Chhinnamul* and its refugee world of south Calcutta 'colonies' foreshadows the suggestive later political-existentialist exposés of modern life by Ritwik Gathak, whose *Meghe Dhaka Tara* 1960 plays in the same urban landscape.[3]

The focus on big city life as incarnating the loneliness and alienation of capitalist modernity is continued in later Ghatak films and in *Subarnarekha* (1962) is given further depth by the looming of a potential nuclear war apocalypse. It also becomes a prominent theme in the production of Satyajit Ray—the best internationally known representative of Bengali art cinema—whose critical realist *Mahanagar* (1964) and Calcutta trilogy of *Pratidwandi* (1970), *Seemabaddha* (1971) and *Jana Aranya* (1976) explore the liveliness of the big city, but also the depths of moral corruption to which human beings can be reduced, and situates these in a context of contemporary politics.

Another Calcutta trilogy was produced almost simultaneously with that of Satyajit Ray by Mrinal Sen, consisting of the films *Interview* (1970), *Calcutta 71* (1971) and *Padatik* (1973). Here the urban vision is a much more directly political one and aims at interacting with the revolutionary left wing and social movements at the time of the Naxalites and the Emergency proclaimed by Indira Gandhi's government. Sen 'deployed a wide variety of influences from Glauber Rocha's early work to Truffaut . . . and from Augusto Boal's *Theatre of the Oppressed* to Solanas and Getino,' and at the same time 'evoked the radical currents of Bengali theatre and folk forms' in collage-like combinations, providing a counterpoint to the moral approach of Ray—a contrast that became the focus for intense public debate (Rajadhyaksha and Willemen, 1999: 211).

Cultures High and Low

In later Bengali film production, the distinction between 'high' cultural art cinema and popular cultural entertainment has been upheld, though popular film has suffered in competition with the booming industry of Hindi film production with a base in Bombay, and art cinema has lost some of its critical edge and ambition. In Rituparno Ghosh's *Dahan* (1997), the urban and moral focus of earlier art films is continued, but has become a much more narrow one of a middle-class south Calcutta, threatened by street crime and collapsing notions of respectability. In its mode of presentation, *Dahan* incorporates techniques from television drama and—by doing this—manages to balance its metropolitan street scenes with penetration into a sphere of privacy not usually put on show, but screened off, a breach of decorum almost equal to the intense kissing scenes of Ghosh's later movie *Bariwali* (1999).[4]

A similar interest in urban middle-class life as the home ground of Indian modernity is cultivated in the work of the Tamil filmmaker Mani Ratnam whose *Bombay* (1995) along with its scenes of violence and communalist mobilization presents images of an urban world of globalized affluence and smoothness. This is a world which points beyond the strife and misery of the streets, and revolves around values of individualism and personalized love relationships, while at the same time showing these as not irreconcilable with other values of family loyalty and respect, thereby reconciling conflict and naturalizing lifestyles of globalized modernity in their Indian setting. In an earlier Mani Ratnam film, *Roja* (1994) which deals with marital love and obligation against a contemporary background of the Kashmir conflict, the nationalist character of Indian middle-class modernity is asserted even more strongly (for debates on *Roja* and Mani Ratnam, see Niranjana, 1994, Vasudevan, 1994 and Prasad, 1998: 230-7).

Related gestures of reconciliation and naturalization are exhibited in Mira Nair's *Monsoon Wedding* (2001) which shows an Indian modern everyday as the life styles of a metropolitan middle-class family with wealthy globalized extensions. In this film also individualist feelings of love versus the constraints of an arranged marriage are at the centre of contestations, but the ensuing conflict is resolved by the benevolence and decency of the central characters involved. While the film with its marriage focus pays loving tribute to recurrent features in popular Bombay cinema, its side story of family incest dialogues with international cinema (including Thomas Vinterberg's *The Celebration* (1998), and—to a much greater extent than the films of Mani Ratnam—*Monsoon Wedding* is directed at an international audience and circuit of screening.

What above everything represents the notion of 'cinema' as a specific cultural genre in India is Bombay-based Hindi cinema. It is interesting that in his contribution to this volume—reflecting on how in his West Bengal childhood strands of literary 'high' culture would clash with those of popular culture as incarnated by film and movie songs—Sudipta Kaviraj does not think of Bengali films, but of Bombay and Hindi cinema. This, obviously, was what 'cinema' meant as something unique and something peculiarly modern in its articulations which could match and live up to (as literary 'high' culture had been unable to do in quite the same way) the moral and existential challenges of the metropolitan life that stood out as the incarnation of modernity—

its ambiguities, despairs and excitements. And which was not just 'representation', but in itself part and parcel of modernity as such.

Kaviraj points to an absence and an irony here, both in the sense of popular movies and film music giving expression to particular structures of feeling (as Raymond Williams would have it) which 'high' literature had not dealt with in serious terms, but only as satire, farce and travesty, the world of the westernized *babus*, and the invasion of the foreign: for Tagore, 'the city cannot find a poetry of its own, because the city in its slovenliness does not deserve poetry.' And at the same time popular cinema as a cultural form remains 'low' and linked to the 'depravity' which urban modernity was seen to represent and therefore bound up in a sphere not considered 'proper' for respectable critics and intellectuals to deal with.

Why is it, asks Ashish Rajadhyaksha in a comment on Sudipta Kaviraj's essay in this volume, that social scientists for long did so little to take cinema seriously, and that intellectuals would have such ambivalent feelings about it:

> My ... question [is one] that I, and many others in the 1970s and early 80s asked, as we struggled to establish a film theory in the Indian context. As we read the work of many social scientists including yourself who were, just about then, working out theories of cultural practice, and as I had an opportunity to meet them, I discovered that practically all of them were intense cinephiles, and music-philes, and especially Bengali intellectuals who were, literally, authorities on the cinema; that after six o'clock, the moment *adda* began,[5] they would intensely discuss and argue about the cinema as animatedly as about politics or anything else. So then I would ask them this question: how come the social sciences in India do not seemingly take the cinema seriously? Why can film not be discussed seriously by them before 6 o'clock, and in more serious forums?[6]

The answer implied in Kaviraj's essay is that the world of popular cinema has related to a quite different set of feelings about the urban than those given expression by the 'high' cultural forms with which middle-class intellectuals had most comfortably identified themselves:

> The city was culturally dominated by the lower middle class, but its experience was obviously more diverse. Ironically, the poor in the city did not necessarily share this gloomy sense of the city and its place in

history... Other classes in the city, even in a relatively stagnant and declining city like Calcutta did not necessarily share the historical melancholy of the educated lower middle class. The city for most people was a far more mixed and complex arena of experience. It certainly produced hopelessness and despair, but it was also a space in which anonymity gave a sense of freedom from restrictive village customs, and it was enjoyed by most characters in the films as a context in which genuine love could be experienced against the obstacles of deprivation, parental objection and vicious neighbours (Kaviraj, in this volume).

The cultural studies approach to film represented by the Indian contributors to this volume therefore represented an innovation and a break-through vis-à-vis this ambiguity by taking popular cultural forms seriously and submitting them to analysis and theory, while at the same time trying to understand the processes through which 'high' and popular forms of culture become differentiated and institutionalized as separate idioms.

These endeavours were pursued in contributions to the *Journal of Arts and Ideas* (edited by Geeta Kapoor, Ashish Rajadhyaksha and others), in Rajadhyaksha's and Paul Willemen's *Encyclopaedia of Indian Film* whose first edition was published by the British Film Institute in 1994, by Ashis Nandy and younger scholars such as Ravi Vasudevan at the Centre for the Study of Developing Societies in New Delhi, at the Department of Film Studies, Jadavpur University in Calcutta, where Moinak Biswas is based and the *Journal of the Moving Image* published by M. S. S. Pandian and colleagues at the Madras Institute of Development Studies, at workshops organized by the Centre for Studies in Social Sciences in Calcutta and the Central Institute for English and Foreign Languages in Hyderabad, and more recently by scholars such as Tejaswini Niranjana, Ashish Rajadhyaksha and M. Madhava Prasad at the Centre for the Study of Culture and Society in Bangalore (cf. Vasudevan, 2000:3). A major systematic contribution has been M. Madhava Prasad's *Ideology of the Hindi Film: A Historical Construction* which came out in 1998 and on which much in the following section is based.

'Bollywood'

The popular Bombay-based or 'Bollywood' Hindi film comprises of many varieties, some of which are not easily distinguishable from other genres within the sprawling world of Indian cinema in languages like Tamil, Telugu, Kannada, Malayalam, Bengali and so forth, whose most successful products—such as the Mani Ratnam films—are often also distributed in Hindi versions. But what has come to be identified most commonly with Hindi or 'Bollywood' film both in India and increasingly also internationally is a particular type of montage-like product, which in its tendency and development aims at being the 'all-inclusive film'.

In such movies the coherence between elements in the montage is flimsy and full of clashes, the action proceeds slowly with many interruptions and through a mixture of narrative sequences and more tableaux-like scenes, shifting between scenes of realism, dream sequences and flash-backs, and including elaborately choreographed dance incidents and powerful songs, aimed at becoming hits in their own right. The songs are an especially important ingredient, having been written especially for the film, recorded for the sound track by dubbing artists with a status as stars almost equal to the actors, and calculated to bring in—through sales of records and tapes etc.—perhaps up to 30% of the film's earnings. The importance of star actors in the films is tremendous, and inconsistencies between elements can sometimes be explained by a movie's being predominantly a vehicle for the promotion of its stars, who may also well have (together with their commercial sponsors) invested in the production of it.

If the 'all-inclusive' version of the package is a post-Independence development, the characteristics of the genre can be traced back to the beginning of the 1930s and the introduction of 'talkies'. In India this led to an escalation of film development in the different national languages, and aimed at establishing idioms of cinematic representation which were specifically Indian and contrasted with existing colonial, British and American iconographies in the field—e.g. by turning episodes from 'national' epics such as the Ramayana and the Mahabharata into film. It also led to the unfolding—already in the 1930s—of a range of genres such as 'socials, mythologicals, devotionals, and stunt, costume and fantasy films' which all included song and dance as integral elements:

> The social has always been the broadest and, since the 1940s, the largest category and loosely refers to any film in a contemporary setting not otherwise classified. It traditionally embraces a wide spectrum, from heavy melodrama to light-hearted comedy, from films with social purpose to love stories, from tales of family and domestic conflict to urban crime thrillers (Rosie Thomas, 1987: 304, quoted in Prasad, 1998: 46)

Critics have attempted to see the emergence of the fragmented, 'all-inclusive' film as an expression of Sanskrit dramaturgical principles winning through, but according to Madhava Prasad, the main explanation is a more pragmatic and materialist one, relating to the logic of film production and finance which meant that cinemas and chains of distribution gained hegemony over studios, and that the basic modern production unit in Indian cinema became the individual film. Thus, what in economic terms Prasad describes as the 'heterogeneous form of manufacture' operating in the Hindi film industry shows itself at the level of representation as a victorious rebellion of components against the whole:

> The different component elements have not been subsumed under the dominance of a cinema committed to narrative coherence. The heteronomous conditions under which the production sector operates are paralleled by a textual heteronomy whose primary symptom is the absence of an integral narrative structure (Prasad, 1998:45. Cf. Vasudevan, 1999: 117).

To this is added the influence and inspiration from different dramatic and performance traditions—in Bombay cinema not least from Parsi theatre and from various forms of European and American popular acting dating back to the early 19th century. This placed forms of melodrama at the centre of what was filmic, and made 'feudal family romance' a prominent component in movies from the 1940s to the present. Such melodramatic forms can be either aristocratic or democratic, depending on how the struggle between rank and 'the power of the modern to destroy' is shown to be resolved (Prasad 1998: 55, 66-7), and represent, rather than an idealized conflict between tradition and modernity, one between two different ideologies of modernity, which has then again sometimes overlapped with one between '*masala*' and 'realist' film-making (Prasad, 1998:31).

In the light of the above, Ashis Nandy has argued that the popularity of Hindi cinema relies on its giving expression to

> traces, however distorted, of affiliation to forms of community, cultural languages and concerns endangered by the homogenizing imperatives of modernisation (Vasudevan, 2000: 5, paraphrasing Nandy, 1995).

Nandy has also argued that it is the neo-traditionalism of Indian movies—and especially their melodramatic qualities and representations of 'large, extended families', and of women as mother figures—which accounts for their popularity in particularly 'developing countries', because to audiences in the Middle East, for example, 'India's family values are more familiar . . . than the dysfunctional families often featured in American films' (interview in Fuller, 2000).

Madhava Prasad, on the other hand, argues that popular film works in cahoots with modernization and accommodates 'desires for modernity':

> While often anchored in familiar narratives that reinforce traditional moral codes, the popular film text also offers itself as an object of the desire for modernity. The fragmentary text of an average popular film is a serial eruption of variously distributed affective intensities whose individual effects are not subsumed in the overarching narrative framework. As an effective medium of propagation of consumer culture, popular cinema has managed to combine a reassuring moral conservatism with fragments of utopian ideology and enactments of the pleasures of the commodity culture. The very familiarity of the narrative makes it a useful non-interfering grid within which to elaborate the new (Prasad, 1993: 85).

As compared to Hollywood, the unitarian principles of Aristotle get to suffer much more radically in 'Bollywood' movies because of production techniques where the brilliance and appearance of the individual component become decisive, and where such components are developed and produced separately and individually, and only brought together through a process which is often highly improvised, and where a master script has not been finally developed before the beginning of shooting.

While coordination is weak, and the relationship between a film's individual parts may be varied endlessly, the production of components is delegated out to highly specialized experts, whose sense of craft drives them to adhere to strict regulations of form. For example, film songs are bound by rigid conventions of genre as to theme, stylistic devices and the use of metaphors, and film song writers—as is also discussed by Kaviraj—in their 'real' lives would often be 'high' cultural, particularly Urdu, poets, and inspiration would come from *ghazals, qawwalis, thumris* as well as from Hindu wedding songs (cf. Prasad, 1998: 45). On the same pattern, there are inflexible criteria deciding what constitutes a good or bad script, a good or bad fighting scene, and so on. Which means that the 'all-inclusive film' must have everything—the best action, the best songs, the biggest stars, the most exquisitely choreographed dancing scenes, etc., but as a series of perfected components, rather than as a unified whole, and with production logics being underpinned by those of finance, aiming for each film to be an investment with quick and maximum returns.

Examples of 'All-inclusiveness'

As recent examples of 'all-inclusive' movies, we may briefly compare a production which was a success story inside and outside India, *Kuch Kuch Hota Hai* (directed by Karan Johar, 1998), and one which was a flop both in India and with diaspora audiences—Aziz Mirza's *Phir Bhi Dil Hai Hindustani* from 2000—both vehicles for the superstar and Pepsi Cola icon, Shah Rukh Khan.

Kuch Kuch Hota Hai broke new ground internationally, because it became an international success, not only with Hindi-speaking Indian diaspora audiences and with African and other third-world audiences who have traditionally appreciated Bollywood films even if the dialogue component was inaccessible, but also—in sub-titled versions—with audience groups who saw it as a new global trend, rather than something localized and exotic: a variety of 'world cinema' to match 'world music', or a more general dislocation and incoherence which is felt to be 'post-modern' or 'a show for the 21st century' (Goldbæk, 2002) .

The reason for the success of *Kuch Kuch Hota Hai* may be sought in the particular mix of components represented by the film which is generally accommodating to a wide range of viewers' desires and characterized by high production values, though a few individual components are strangely miserly, primitive and embarrassing. This goes for the scenario of the nationalist children's holiday camp in the countryside to which Rahul—the Shah Rukh Khan character—sends his child in the last part of the film after the death of its mother. This is also where he meets again by accident his long-lost childhood tomboy girl friend played by Kajol, who is destined to become the child's new mother, and help reconcile at last the tensions experienced by the modernizing middle-class male protagonist in the face of the confusingly disharmonious aspects of contemporary womanhood he has been up against.

This is an absolutely central episode within the plot structure of the film, but is played out in sets that are strangely shoddy and reminiscent of amateur theatre—something which is not uncommon, but contrasts oddly with what has otherwise become a standard expectation for Bollywood films: to include lavishly spectacular locations, most often with scenes from the Himalayas thrown in, and nymphs of various extractions going though choreographic motions in the fountains of Mysore's Brindavan Gardens. In *Kuch Kuch Hota Hai* such extravagance is represented by the sequences played out in the Scottish highlands, representing a trend which has led to European competition for the custom of the Bombay film industry and, recently, to a campaign in Indian newspapers on behalf of the Austrian national tourism agency to suggest that more Indian movies must have their action placed in the Alps, Tyrol and Kärnten.

More seriously, at least for some Indian audiences, such scenes seem to represent the opposite of dislocation, more a placing of Indian middle-class experiences as belonging naturally with and constituting part of the modern global—an effort at 'glocalization' which is an important part of the function which the surrealist mix of components in *Kuch Kuch Hota Hai* is meant to fulfil. Such appropriation of the global by the local is played out most importantly in the film in its incorporation of the youth, life style and consumption culture represented by American youth soaps such as *Glamour* and *The Bold and the Beautiful*, Indianized and transplanted on to the national body by satellite networks like Star-TV and MTV.

In the film, this is symbolized by the possibility of the protagonist reconciling his love for the cosmopolitan beauty returning home (who becomes his first wife and the mother of his child) and for Anjali, the locally rooted Kajol character; a scenario in which hip-hop and *gangsta rap* are mutated into work-out exercises for well-nourished specimens of the Mumbai bourgeoisie, and one which naturally and effortlessly leads to an extravagant, traditional Hindu wedding as its conclusion and rounding-off. In this sense, the film very successfully represents a dream universe in which the local succeeds, is marked by progress and middle-class prosperity, and assumes its obvious place within a globalized modernity.

In *Phir Bhi Dil Hai Hindustani*—whose point of departure for its 'all-inclusiveness', like that of *Kuch Kuch Hota Hai*, is the 'social' film— the local is to a higher degree represented by a national and political problematic, possibly inspired by the success of Mani Ratnam's films, and related in self-contradictory and messy, but extremely interesting ways, to a discussion of terrorism and authoritarian state excesses.

The action of *Phir Bhi Dil Hai Hindustani* comes to a halt almost before it starts, because it has to give equal prominence to elements from the genres in which its three stars—who are also the producers of the film—have excelled, and from there disintegrates into scraps of comedy, political thriller, action movie and melodrama, which undermine and sabotage each other. Thus, the extremely effectively choreographed and tableau-like dancing sequences—which at regular intervals interrupt the unfolding of the different plots—stand out as the most dynamic elements in the movie, to which the spectator eagerly looks forward.

Shah Rukh Khan plays a successful journalist chasing a story about the involvement of top politicians with a gangster mafia, but also acts as clown and a romantic lover, as he charms and flirts his way into the favours of a female reporter colleague, employed by a competing television station. They eventually get to collaborate in the hunt for a very Muslim-looking terrorist who has shot and killed a strongman of one of the top politicians, but find out that he is being framed, and that his violent action is not terrorism, but the justified revenge of an outraged and honest patriarch for the gruesome rape of his daughter, relived in the movie through a series of flashbacks.

All this is played out in a scenario of metropolitan modernity as represented by a highly idealized Bombay—advertising liberalization and the consumption of a multiplicity of commodities, which here as in *Kuch Kuch Hota Hai* are posited as belonging naturally and obviously in the urban Indian world, obliterating all aspects of reality contradicting this in the experience of audiences. What is particularly interesting in the film is its populist manner of demonizing everything that has to do with the state and institutionalized politics, contrasting this with the healthy energy and solidarity of groups of individual citizens and their families.

At the conclusion of the movie, a force of such sane and liberalized citizens go marching in demonstration through the city, braving the assaults and prevention of a brutalized police force, to liberate from prison the patriarch-cum-liquidator-of-villainous-politicians just as he is about to be hanged—the prisoner already clad in his execution outfit covered with commercial advertisements, and the TV cameras ready to shoot as he drops.

The confusion of the messages relayed by *Phir Bhi Dil Hai Hindustani* is striking; it seems to be critical of both Hindu-Muslim communalist antagonism and of the State. The 'people'—represented in the film by middle-class families—are the essence of a 'true' India, betrayed by politicians, but who these politicians are, and the exact direction of the film's populism, remains unclear.

Another noticeable aspect is that the film, in spite of not having done well in terms of box office income, seems to have made a profit and been a financially viable venture. An explanation for this—other than the earnings from songs—is that *Phir Bhi Dil Hai Hindustani*, much more unashamedly than *Kuch Kuch Hota Hai* and in spite of the cynical satire of its execution scene, is saturated with 'hidden', i.e. extremely visible advertisements, for Swatch watches, Pepsi Cola, Hyundai cars, and other global brands directed in particular at consumers with adolescent lifestyles. Owners of such brands are extremely active and willing to invest large sums in India which, like China, represents a giant future marketplace, and one which is in the process of being dramatically changed from conditions of plan economy, regulation and cultural 'autonomy' to liberalization and globalized media culture. In this sense, there is something particularly decadent about *Phir Bhi Dil Hai Hindustani* as a movie, since in financial terms it seems to be able to afford to disregard its reception and the response and concerns of its audience completely, at least as far as these extend beyond commodity brand differentiation.

The Globalization of Indian Cinema

If it is difficult to make head or tail of the message of a film like this from an Indian perspective and vis-à-vis Indian cinema-goers, what meanings can then be made of it among spectators abroad? What accounts for the tremendous capability to 'travel' which Indian film— and 'Bollywood' cinema in particular—has demonstrated, and which seems to have been increasing and appealing to new and expanding audiences over recent years?

The globalization of Indian cinema is not new; as Vashna Jagarnath's contribution to this volume shows, it has followed Indian diasporas into their settlements around the world, and has been a source enabling them to confirm, rejuvenate and debate their Indian identities. In this capacity it has also provided powerful inspiration for other forms of cultural activity—in Jagarnath's Durban and South Africa, a shortage of films shown in Tamil led to the production of theatre shows among Tamil-speakers, who represent the majority of Indians, descendants of the indentured sugar-cane cutters who arrived in Natal in the late 19th century. According to Jagarnath's research, such drama performances would imitate the structure of the films shown in Durban's segregated Indian cinemas: their length, their incoherence, the supremacy of components over unity. In this respect, they were similar to the Ugandan drama shows which came into existence in Kampala in the 1970s after Idi Amin's expulsion of the Ugandan 'Asians'—which led to the closure of the city's cinemas which had been owned by Indians.

The globalization impact of Indian films from early on went beyond the diaspora communities and on to the cultures and societies in which they were settled. Brian Larkin has described the process of this in Northern Nigeria and interpreted the meanings made of Indian cinema among West African Muslims in the special issue of the journal *Africa* on 'Audiences' which Karin Barber edited some years ago (Larkin, 1997); a story Larkin extends in his contribution to the present volume on cinemas and the urban space of Kano. My own enthusiasm for 'Bollywood' film took off in a cinema in Zanzibar in 1989, watching dance scenes, gods and goddesses, averted kisses, and heroes and heroines rolling joyfully singing down the slopes of Himalayan mountain sides, in the company of an Afro-Arab audience of Swahili-speaking Muslims who understood as little of the Hindi dialogue as I, but were as effectively hypnotized, eagerly whistling the songs and debating what had been going on after the show.

In recent years, the globalization of Indian popular film has taken other forms in moving beyond the diaspora, as movies have become available, distributed with English sub-titles, and marketed internationally more ambitiously than before. In Vashna Jagarnath's post-apartheid Durban, for example, major Indian films like *Kuch Kuch Hota Hai* or Santosh Sivan's historical 'epic' *Asoka* (2001)—also starring Shah Rukh Khan—are now shown, not in 'Indian' cinemas, but in subtitled versions in the major middle-class, mainstream—i.e. formerly white—halls (like the prestigious Ster-Kinekor in the Musgrave Centre).

Karan Johar's mega-star 'family values' follow up to *Kuch Kuch Hota Hai, 'K3G'* or *Kabhi Khushi Kabhie Gham* (2001), with not only Shah Rukh Khan and Kajol appearing again as characters called Rahul and Anjali, but also with Amitabh Bachchan as father figure (and his wife Jaya Bachchan as mother!) with Hrithik Roshan as Rahul's younger brother and Kareena Kapoor as Anjali's sister Pooja—was launched through a major international campaign directed both at an expanding range of international cinemas (and managing to enter British and US box office top tens), but also at a booming VHS and DVD market for subtitled versions. And 'Bollywood' seems to have surpassed itself in Aamir Khan and Ashutosh Gowariker's historical cricket romance *Lagaan* (2001) which was Oscar-nominated and made a major breakthrough into more general international circulation.

Thus 'Bollywood' aesthetics are experiencing a popularity peak as a globalized trend and fashion, illustrated also by the 'Indian Summer' festival in London of 2002 which included a wide range of screenings of Hindi films, a simultaneous retrospective of Satyajit Ray films in copies restored for renewed circulation by the Merchant-Ivory company, as well as the launch of A. R. Rahman and Andrew Lloyd Webber's musical *Bombay Dreams* paying tribute to 'Bollywood', and moving on to be produced in New York, Canada, Japan (cf. Bedell, 2002 and Spencer, 2002).

All this was supplemented during May 2002 by thematically laid-out show-rooms at Selfridge's in Oxford Street celebrating the world of Indian cinema—some of them by Nitin Desai, who did the sets for *Lagaan*, others 'a faithful reproduction of an entire floor of [film personality and socialite] Dimple Kapadia's house in Mumbai which was designed by Abu Jani and Sandeep Khosla. Both designers use a blending of traditional Indian designs and crafts with a thoroughly contemporary environment.' The idea was promotion of empathy—to make people feel that they could be living there themselves:

> Customers will be able to experience the Bollywood lifestyle and meet the artistes [sic!], enjoy live performances of dance and music, film screening, exclusive fashion shows, specialist food in the food hall and cooking in the restaurants by India's leading chefs from the Taj group of hotels, as well as choose from an array of precious objects and designs for the home (Basu, 2002).

While the empire is thus seemingly striking back, and the West learning to be most fashionably modern or post-modern by being 'Bollywood' eastern, it will be interesting to see what impact such new varieties of cultural globalization will have on the future development of Indian cinema.

On the one hand, the outreach of Indian movies to a more international market coincides with liberalization and new legislation in India which will make the entry of Hollywood and other types of western films onto the Indian market much easier than before. This will mean both intensified competition, and an interference of transnational capital and production interests with the world of Indian film, which may affect the lay-out of its genres and modes of expression.

On the other hand, there also remains a huge domestic Indian market for films that are 'peculiarly' Indian and do not travel well or translate into international successes, as demonstrated by some of the films discussed by Ravi Vasudevan and Tejaswini Niranjana in their essays in this volume. Also in the diaspora worlds of non-resident Indians (NRIs) the effects of globalization and the impact of new international media are not unambiguous and necessarily homogenizing. They carry with them not only new possibilities for confirming belonging and feeling at home, but also for disagreement and new types of political involvement and identity differentiation. What was called by the late Claude Aké the enormous 'explosion of monopoly'— and monotony—which the global spread of capitalism sets off, is accompanied by re-defined differences, the production of new localities, new forms of metropolitan life, and new challenges to make sense of modernity which will require a variety of forms of cinematic representation to make themselves understood.

Notes

1 Such debates are the subject of discussion in Raychaudhuri, 1988, Chatterjee, 1994, and Chatterjee, 1997: 193-210. Cf. also Sudipta Kaviraj's monograph on Bankimchandra Chattopadhyay (Kaviraj, 1995).

2 Though this disaster, as Biswas shows, was preceded by that of the 1943 famine to which the villagers' dialogues refer, and during which—like in 1946-47—masses of people were also forced off the land.

3 In *Chhinnamul*, Ghatak plays the role of the village goldsmith who becomes one of the individualist opportunists.

4 For taboos on scenes of kissing, see chapter 4, 'Guardians of the View: The Prohibition of the Private', in Prasad, 1998: 88-113.

5 *Adda* is often presented as the central institution in Calcuttan intellectual life—intense informal conversation, discussion, criticism, joking and being together.

6 From an e-mail to Sudipta Kaviraj (and the other contributors to this volume) of 29 October 2001.

References

Balzac, Honoré de (1971), *Lost Illusions*, translated by Herbert J. Hunt, Penguin Classics, Harmondsworth (French original published 1837-43).

Basu, Shrabani (2002), 'Dimple's Designer Home on View at Selfridge's', *The Telegraph*, Calcutta, 8 February 2002.

Bedell, Geraldine (2002), 'World Wide Webber', *Indian Summer* special issue of *Life: The Observer Magazine*, 7 April, 10-12.

Berman, Marshall (1983), *All That Is Solid Melts Into Air: The Experience of Modernity*, Verso Editions, London (first published 1982).

Chatterjee, Partha (1994), *The Nation and Its Fragments: Studies in Colonial and Postcolonial Histories*, Princeton University Press, Princeton.

— (1997), 'Our Modernity' in P. Chatterjee (ed.), *The Present History of West Bengal: Essays in Political Criticism*, Oxford University Press, New Delhi, 193-210.

Fuller, Thomas (2000), 'Indian Movies Speak to a Global Audience', *International Herald Tribune*, 20 October (Hague edition).

Giddens, Anthony (1990), *The Consequences of Modernity*, Polity Press, Oxford.

Goldbæk, Henning (2002), 'Nye drømme—postmoderne æstetik', *Dagbladet Information*, 25 July, Copenhagen (review of A. R. Rahman and Andrew Lloyd Webber's *Bombay Dreams*).

Kaarsholm, Preben (2001), 'The Jungle of the City: London and the Imperialist Imagination c. 1900' in Martin Zerlang (ed.), *Representing London*, Spring Publishers, Copenhagen, 122-36.

Kaviraj, Sudipta (1995), *The Unhappy Consciousness: Bankimchandra Chattopadhyay and the Formation of Nationalist Discourse in India*, Oxford University Press, New Delhi.

Larkin, Brian (1997), 'Indian Films, Nigerian Lovers: Media and the Creation of Parallel Modernities', *Africa*, 67:3, 406-40.

Lerner, Daniel (1964), *The Passing of Traditional Society: Modernizing the Middle East*, The Free Press, New York (first published 1958).

— (1968), 'Modernization: Social Aspects' in D. L. Sills (ed.), *International Encyclopaedia of the Social Sciences* 9, The Free Press, New York, 386-395.

Madsen, Peter and Richard Plunz (eds.) (2001), *The Urban Life World: Formation, Perception, Representation*, Routledge, London.

Marsh, Joss (2001), 'Recreating London: Dickens, Cinema and the Imagined City' in Martin Zerlang (ed.), *Representing London*, Spring Publishers, Copenhagen, 74-121.

Nandy, Ashis (1995), 'The Intelligent Film Critic's Guide to the Indian Cinema' in *The Savage Freud*, Oxford University Press, New Delhi (first published 1987-88).

Niranjana, Tejaswini, P. Sudhir and Vivek Dhareshwar (eds.) (1993), *Interrogating Modernity: Culture and Colonialism in India*, Seagull Books, Calcutta.

Niranjana, Tejaswini (1994), 'Integrating Whose Nation? Tourists and Terrorists in *Roja*', *Economic and Political Weekly*, 29: 3, 15 January.

Pandey, Gyanendra (2001), *Remembering Partition: Violence, Nationalism and History in India*, Cambridge University Press, Cambridge.

Prasad, M. Madhava (1993), 'Cinema and the Desire for Modernity', *Journal of Arts and Ideas*, 25-26, December.

— (1998), *Ideology of the Hindi Film: A Historical Construction*, Oxford University Press, New Delhi.

Rajadhyaksha, Ashish (1987), 'The Phalke Era: Conflict of Traditional Form and Modern Technology', *Journal of Arts and Ideas*, 14-15, July-December.

— and Paul Willemen (1999), *Encyclopaedia of Indian Cinema*, second edition, British Film Institute, London (first edition 1995).

Raychaudhuri, Tapan (1988), *Europe Reconsidered: Perceptions of the West in Nineteenth Century Bengal*, Oxford University Press, New Delhi.

Southall, Aidan and Peter C. W. Gutkind (1957), *Townsmen in the Making: Kampala and Its Suburbs*, East African Institute of Social Research, Kampala.

Spencer, Neil (2002), 'Bollywood Blockbuster', Indian Summer special issue of *Life: The Observer Magazine*, 7 April, 16-22.

Thomas, Rosie (1987), 'Mythologies and Modern India' in W. Luhr (ed.), *World Cinema since 1945*, Ungar, New York.

Vasudevan, Ravi (1993), 'Shifting Codes, Dissolving Identities: The Hindi Social Film of the 1950s as Popular Culture', *Journal of Arts and Ideas*, 23-24, January.

— (1994), 'Other Voices: *Roja* against the Grain', *Seminar*, 43, November.

— (1999), Review of M. Madhava Prasad, *Ideology of the Hindi Film* in *Journal of the Moving Image*, 1, Autumn, 117-27.

— (2000), *Making Meaning in Indian Cinema*, Oxford University Press, New Delhi.

Williams, Raymond (1975), *The Country and the City*, Paladin Books, London (first published 1973).

URBAN LEGENDS

NOTES ON A THEME IN EARLY FILM THEORY

PETER LARSEN

True Stories

'A Russian friend told me the following true story,' writes Béla Balázs, the Hungarian filmmaker and film theorist, in 1930 in his book *Der Geist des Films*:[1]

> Somewhere in the Ukrainian countryside, hundreds of kilometers from the last railway station, there lived a man who formerly owned and after the revolution managed an estate. For fifteen years he had not been to a city. He had kept up with world history, but he had never seen a film. A highly educated intellectual who sent for all new books, newspapers, journals, who owned a good radio set, who was in continuous contact with the world and up to date with all things intellectual. Only he had not yet been to a cinema (Balázs, 1984:52).

Then during a visit to Kiev he sees his first movie, 'a very simple, naive Fairbanks story'. The cinema is full of children enjoying themselves. Our man is concentrated, shaking with excitement and effort. All in vain:

> He had not understood the film. He had not grasped the *story* that children could follow without difficulty. For it had been a new language which all town-dwellers mastered with ease, and which he, the highly educated intellectual had not yet understood (Balázs, 1984:52).

Almost twenty years after he wrote these lines, Balázs summed up his views on film culture in the book that was later published in English under the title *Theory of the Film* (Balázs, 1948).[2] Large parts of the book consist of excerpts from his earlier works, but at the place where one would expect the Russian steward to appear there is instead a story about an English colonial administrator 'who, during the first world war and for some time after it, lived in a backward community' (Balázs, 1972:34). He 'knew of films, and had seen pictures of the stars and had read film reviews and film stories; but he had never seen a motion picture' (Balázs, 1972:34). Then he finally comes to a city, he goes to the movies, sits down among interested children, watches a very simple film—and the story of the Russian steward is repeated: The Englishman did not understand the film, 'because he did not understand the form-language in which the story of the film was told, a form-language every town-dweller already knew at that time' (Balázs, 1972:34).

The colonial administrator has company: A Russian friend has told Balázs about a certain cousin who arrived in Moscow 'on a visit from a Siberian collective farm—an intelligent girl, with a good education, but who had never seen a motion picture (this of course was many years ago)' (Balázs, 1972:34-35). Then, obviously, they send her to the movies; she sits down, watches 'a burlesque', and does not understand a thing. She is indignant and agitated. 'I can't understand why they allow such dreadful things to be shown here in Moscow!' she says. But what was so horrible then? 'Human beings were torn to pieces and the heads thrown one way and the bodies the other and the hands somewhere else again' (Balázs, 1972:35).

A Ukrainian steward, an English colonial administrator, a girl from Siberia: three people who did not understand 'the form-language in which the story of the film was told'. In order to understand 'the new picture language', Balázs writes, you must be able to 'make visual associations of ideas', you must 'integrate single disjointed pictures into a coherent scene' (Balázs, 1972:35). The steward, the colonial administrator, and the girl from the Siberian kolkhoz had not learned to do that.

Fictions

Are these stories true? Of course not. There are far too many odd-ities here—the steward's transformation into a colonial officer, the sudden appearance of a Siberian cousin, not to mention some peculiar discrepancies between the German and the English versions of *Theory of the Film*.[3] The almost identical sequences of events should be enough to make one suspicious: First some hazy remarks about how the narrator came to know about the incident—a 'true story' told by 'a Russian friend'; another one told 'by a friend in Moscow', and 'there is a story about an English colonial administrator . . .' Then an explanation about why the protagonist happened to be so isolated—hundreds of kilometers from the last railway station; a world war, chance circumstances; the incident lies many years back. Then the unsuccessful visit to the cinema. And finally the punch-line: The protagonist did not understand what he or she saw.

These stories are obviously constructions, fictions, three variations of one and the same narrative—told in order to support, if not to prove, one and the same point: that film is a language, a language that has to be learned. They do, however, also make another point. If we were to read only the first story we would probably miss it, but everything becomes clear as soon as the Ukrainian steward is replaced by the English/Siberian duo in the *Theory of the Film* version: read in sequence these two stories suspend all traditional distinctions regarding gender, age, nationality, and social status. A male British government official living in a foreign colony reacts just like a young peasant girl from a Siberian kolkhoz. Only one crucial distinction, common to all three stories, remains: that between urban and rural areas.

The steward lived 'in the Ukrainian countryside', 'had not been to a city' for fifteen years, and had to go to Kiev in order to see his first film. The Englishman 'lived in a backward community' and did not understand the 'form-language every town-dweller already knew at that time'. The cousin came 'from a Siberian collective farm' and was horrified at what she saw in Moscow. These stories are stories about cities. Film belongs to the city, they tell us—thereby articulating and illustrating a central theme in early film theory.

Film in the City; Film and the City

Within the time frame of Balázs' stories—'during the first world war and for some time after it'—film was an urban phenomenon in many important respects. First of all it was an urban *institution* in terms of social space, audience, and function: In these first decades of the 20th century most films were shown in urban movie theatres—not necessarily in large cities, but in cities nevertheless. As soon as film production became industrialized movies were aimed at mass distribution, the socially heterogeneous urban audience being their prime target. From the very start movies were designed to cut across cultural and educational barriers in the modern cities.

Furthermore most of the early films were city films in terms of basic *narrative material*. With their representations of life in the big city they became powerful socialization agencies, indirectly educating their audiences in the ways of the world, emphasizing the rules and norms of urban life, presenting model situations, model forms of behaviour, etc.

Balázs' three stories tell us that film comprehension is something you learn, not on an estate in Ukraine, not on a farm in Central Africa, not on a kolkhoz in Siberia, but in a city. This was how he and his contemporaries saw it; this was a central theme in the film theory of his time. However, according to the most radical, and also the most influential, version of this theme, film comprehension must be learned not only *in a city*, but *by living in the city*—not just because movie theatres happen to be located in cities for technical and financial reasons, or because most movies try to catch city audiences by telling them stories about city life, but because movies, on a more fundamental level, are constructed to match basic urban *forms of perception and experience*. The language spoken by the film is not just a new 'form-language', as Balázs' stories suggest; it is the language *of* the city. In order to read the film, you must be able to read the city.

Urban Experiences

What is urban experience? The early sociologists tended to give rather abstract answers to this question. An often quoted example is Georg Simmel's famous essay on the metropolis and mental life

(Simmel, 1903). Money economy and intellectualism are closely connected phenomena, he argues, and since large cities are the very centres of modern market economy, urban life is by necessity characterized by a high degree of rationalism expressed in a multitude of phenomena—for example, in how people organize their personal life, how they react to each other, which aesthetic preferences they develop, etc.

Another example is the American anthropologist Louis Wirth who in 1938 in a seminal essay, 'Urbanism as a Way of Life', echoes Simmel by arguing that the characteristics of an urban population affect how individual members experience their social world, how they deal with each other etc. (Wirth, 1964). The mere size of the population prevents people from establishing close social relationships and leads to a rational, calculating view of social interaction. People tend to orient themselves from visual cues as a result of the population density; the social heterogeneity leads to psychological instability and insecurity, and also to a certain blasé attitude.

The radical argument about the connection between film comprehension and urban experience is based on general observations of this kind, often directly inspired by Simmel. A summary of the argument may sound like this: In order to read a film the spectator must be able to connect dissociated images into a unified and continuous narrative whole, or, in Balázs' words, to 'integrate single disjointed pictures into a coherent scene'. This particular type of mental activity presupposes a distanciated attitude to the sequence of images and an ability to perform the logical, rationalist operations normally associated with urban life. Balázs' fictitious Siberian girl is written into his text in order to support this view: Where the urban cinema audience saw a story, a coherent narrative, the poor girl merely saw unrelated fragments.

The film–city argument appears in many variations and disguises in early writings on film and film theory, often intimately connected with radical political visions and expectations. Perhaps the best known examples are Siegfried Kracauer's and Walter Benjamin's reflections on their experiences in the Berlin cinemas of the 1920s and 1930s.[4]

Cinematic Languages

According to Kracauer and Benjamin, film is connected with urban experience in a variety of ways. Both of them consider the film medium to be a social institution that answers the need for stimulation created by the general stress of urban life. The films are not only the reverse, the negative expression as it were, of monotonous work processes, they themselves bear the stamp of the workplace. As Benjamin argues: 'That which determines the rhythm of production at the assembly line, is the basis of reception in film' (Benjamin, 1977:208). Thus, the film speaks the *Language of the Factory*, one might say.

Second, film may function as criticism of the very same urban conditions. Both Kracauer and Benjamin argue that the medium can be used as an aesthetic means of developing and organizing knowledge of the contradictions of modernity, and that it can indicate how the social situation can be changed. With its duality of fragmentation and montage, the medium offers aesthetic expressions of urban mass existence which are more adequate than most traditional art forms: On the one hand, the cinematic sequence of shots presents a fragmented view of the world which matches the actual disorder of urban reality; on the other hand, the disorder may be solved by means of an interpretative montage producing insights into the historical situation and preparing the spectators for the inevitable, radical change. For Kracauer the film *could* produce the insight that 'all this will suddenly burst apart', but as he concludes: 'Most of the time it does not' (Kracauer, 1995: 327). Benjamin is more optimistic: he is certain that film by virtue of its fragmentation has the redeeming power necessary to help the urban masses break the spell of modernity, to blow up 'our taverns and our metropolitan streets, our offices and furnished rooms, our railroad stations and our factories' (Benjamin, 1977:161). Thus, the film speaks the *Language of Utopia*.

Third, both Kracauer and Benjamin agree that there is a direct, immediate connection between cinematic montage and the everyday experience of urban reality. According to Benjamin, the same perceptual techniques are needed in the cinema as in metropolitan traffic:

The film corresponds with profound changes in the perception apparatus—changes which the man in the street experiences on an individual scale as he tries to cope with big-city traffic, and which all present-day citizens experience on a historical scale (Benjamin, 1977:165).

Several decades later, Kracauer presents a similar point of view in his *Theory of Film*. The film medium is particularly well suited for catching the transient impressions characteristic of urban experience, he argues, pointing to 'the city street with its ever-moving anonymous crowd' where

kaleidoscopic sights mingle with unidentified shapes and fragmentary visual complexes and cancel each other out, thereby preventing the onlooker from following up any of the innumerable suggestions they offer (Kracauer, 1965:72).

Thus, according to Kracauer and Benjamin the film speaks the *Language of the City*, and should be read just like one reads the city. Here we are relatively close to Simmel's general argument as sketched above: In order to cope with the city as well as with the film, the spectators have to shield themselves by adopting a distanciated, blasé attitude and by performing certain rationalist mental processes.

Kracauer's and Benjamin's observations remain inspiring and thought-provoking to this very day. On the other hand, it is hard to deny that their basic arguments have a rather tentative and speculative character. Reading these texts today one gets the feeling that they are to a large extent based on local and/or personal experiences and impressions, and that the suggested connections between film and urbanity are ideological constructs shaped by predominant political and artistic notions of urbanity, modernity, and avant-garde aesthetics.

It is true that the invention of moving pictures coincided historically with the explosive urbanization in the last decades of the 19th century, and there is, as indicated above, a whole range of obvious connections between the new medium and urban modernity, especially in terms of narrative material, but also with regard to film experience as compensation for and critique of urban conditions. Thus, it is probably correct to say that films spoke the *Language of the Factory*, and in some cases even the *Language of Utopia*, in the early decades of the 20th century. However, the connection between film language and basic forms of urban perception is quite another matter. Did the films then—or do films in general—speak the *Language of the City*? Benjamin's answer to this question is particularly problematic, based as it is on a series of seemingly superficial, textual analogies between cinematic montage and random urban phenomena like traffic, office buildings, railway stations etc.[5]

Learning Processes

At about the same time as Kracauer and Benjamin wrote about going to the movies in Berlin, the Soviet psychologist A. R. Luria travelled from Moscow to Central Asia. The account of his observations throws an interesting light on the argument about the connection between film and urban experiences and may also be read as a commentary and a correction to Balázs' anecdote about the Siberian girl who is said to have travelled in the opposite direction.

In 1931-32, in a period of radical restructuring and social change in the Soviet Union, Luria performed a series of psychological tests on peasant populations in remote villages in Uzbekistan and Kirghizia (Luria, 1976). The intention was to study the historical shaping of cognitive processes.

During their stay Luria and his staff were able to make comparative studies of 'underdeveloped illiterate groups (living in villages)' on the one hand, and 'groups already involved in modern life' on the other (Luria, 1976:14). Among the latter were women who attended short-term courses in the teaching of kindergarteners, active kolkhoz workers who had taken short courses, and women students admitted to a teachers' school after two or three years of study.

The study indicated substantial differences between these two sections of the rural population. The groups 'involved in modern life' scored significantly higher in all tests concerning perception, conceptualization, logical reasoning, self-awareness and so on, a fact which, according to Luria, indicates that changes in the social and practical forms of activity, and especially the introduction of formal schooling, even in the form of short term courses, produce 'changes in the basic structure of cognitive processes and result in an enormous expansion of experience and in the construction of a vastly broader world in which human beings begin to live' (Luria, 1976:163).

As it appears, the decisive feature in Luria's study was the difference within the rural community itself between a traditional lifestyle and what he calls 'modern life', meaning a life situation characterized by complex, collective work processes, new forms of social relations, and the acquisition of rudimentary theoretical knowledge. Luria's findings are in line with innumerable later studies in the tradition of Jean Piaget, showing that basic cognitive abilities with regard to conceptualization and logical reasoning are developed by all individuals at a certain, relatively precisely defined stage in their life, given the right conditions, i.e. provided these abilities are needed in order for the individual to function adequately within the given social context, be it urban or rural.[6]

Applied to the radical version of the film/urbanity question, Luria's study strongly suggests that the mental processes said to be characteristic of film comprehension are not necessarily associated with or developed within an urban context: People in rural areas do not have to go to the big city in order to learn the distanciated attitude necessary for making generalizations and abstractions, the ability to perform logical or rationalist operations. A 'modern life' situation including formal training programmes and participation in complex work processes is sufficient.

Visual Literacy

This leads us back to Balázs and his *Theory of the Film*. Immediately after the stories about the Englishman and the girl from Siberia he recalls the situation twenty years ago, 'when we ourselves would probably not have understood films which are quite obvious to spectators to-day' (Balázs, 1972:35). He remembers seeing a film in which a man is hurrying to a railway station to take leave of his beloved. She has already boarded the train, and the scene ends with a close-up of the man's face, showing his changing expressions as light and shadow crosses his face more and more quickly. Balázs writes:

> When I first saw this film in Berlin, I did not at once understand the end of this scene. Soon, however, everyone knew what had happened: the train had started and it was the lamps in its compartment which had thrown their light on the man's face as they glided past ever faster and faster (Balázs, 1972:36).

By introducing this new anecdote Balázs in a way neutralizes the city/country distinction which the two previous ones have served to articulate: At some earlier point in time he and his fellow Berliners had been in the same situation as the English administrator and the Siberian girl. The Berlin audience who understood the language of the city was not able to understand the language of the film.

Balázs' heading to this part of the text is, 'We have learned to see'. Benjamin thought that the cinema taught people how to adjust themselves to the dangers of everyday life in a modern city. Balázs, on the other hand, suggests that the most important thing people learn in the cinema is how to watch movies. 'We have learned to see': As time went by, people learned to master the new language.

Thus, the English/Siberian duo and the film/city equation notwithstanding, the real point of Balázs' anecdotes seems to be that film comprehension is a question of time and of basic learning processes— a point which obviously places him in a less radical position than both Kracauer and Benjamin on the question of film and urban experience.

However, even this position may be a bit too radical. Several later studies suggest that it is doubtful whether film comprehension per se is something you have to learn at all. In an overview of the available literature on the question, Paul Messaris discusses Balázs' story of the colonial administrator several times (Messaris, 1993).[7] Each time he tries to take it at face value, but is forced to conclude that in the light of current empirical and theoretical knowledge the Englishman seems to have reacted in a highly unlikely way.

First, there is no reason to believe that a person unfamiliar with the medium should have problems in understanding moving images *as images*, i.e. as visual representations. On the contrary, most studies support the view that there is a significant connection between perception of images and the ordinary use of the faculty of vision in real-life situations. These studies further indicate that moving images are actually easier to understand for an inexperienced spectator than ordinary still photos.

Second, it seems highly unlikely that this inexperienced spectator should be unable to understand what Balázs calls 'the new picture language', i.e. be unable to make 'visual associations of ideas', to 'integrate single disjointed pictures into a coherent scene' etc. It is true that most early filmmakers doubted their audiences' visual reading skills, and that most of the classical editing procedures were developed with the purpose of helping untrained spectators understand the narrative—which means that if Balázs' Englishman actually went to a movie theatre in the mid-1920s he would probably have seen a film in which every possible precaution had been taken in order to make the story intelligible. Whether such precautions were really needed is, however, an open question. Studies of first-time television viewers in Kenya and studies of children's understanding of basic editing practices indicate the opposite, namely that inexperienced spectators are perfectly able to understand a story even if it is presented in a fragmented, unedited format (Hobbs et. al., 1988). On the basis of such studies and other available literature Messaris argues that it is not a spectator's prior experience with the medium, but his or her general cognitive development which determines if a film is understood or not.

Against the Grain

It is probably a bit unfair to introduce psychological and anthropological studies of this kind into what started as a discussion of the film/city theme in early film theory. Obviously, the cognitive fundamentals of film comprehension was not the main point for radicals like Kracauer and Benjamin when they wrote their utopian visions about the connections between film language and urban modernity. Neither was it a decisive point for Balázs. Although he repeatedly stressed that film is a new 'form-language' which has to be learned, his prime interest was film aesthetics and his prime concern was to study and discuss what makes film 'a specific independent art employing methods sharply differing from those of the theatre and using a totally different form-language' (Balázs, 1972:30).

Nevertheless, it is hard to resist reading Balázs' stories against the grain, interpreting them in the light of Luria's work or later empirical studies. Take for example the cousin of his Russian friend: If she actually was 'an intelligent girl, with a good education', if she actually came 'from a Siberian collective farm', she would probably have reacted just like Luria's women students 'already involved in modern life' or like the first-time television viewers in Kenya discussed by Messaris, i.e. she would have had no difficulties at all in understanding the film they sent her to see—even if this was the first film she ever saw.

And, ironically, this seems in fact to have been the original point of Balázs' three stories—or rather of their original source. Helmut H. Diederichs, the editor of Balázs' writings, suggests that the first of the stories, the one about the Russian steward, is actually a paraphrase of an article Balázs had read in 1914 in a German-language Budapest newspaper in which the author Margit Vészi told a story about an educated, highly intelligent 'old gentleman' who lived 'on a lonely estate far away from the Berlin noise'. Though he had never been to the movies before, this old man apparently had no problems in understanding the first film he ever saw. According to Diederichs, Vészi used the story to demonstrate that film is a universal language based on gestures and facial expressions; Balázs did not use the story 'in the same film aesthetic context', Diederichs dryly remarks, adding: 'The way in which Balázs handles supposedly empirical evidence is hardly scientific, but rather poetic' (Diederichs, 1997).

Notes

1 My translations.

2 A German translation, *Der Film. Werden und Wesen einer neuen Kunst,* came out in 1949; it is quoted below from Balázs, 1976 which is the fifth edition of a reprint published by Globus Verlag, Vienna. The English version came out in 1952; it is quoted from Balázs, 1972. Thanks to Melinda Szaloky for sorting out the intricate relations between the Hungarian original and the two other versions.

3 According to the German translation (Balázs, 1972:23f), the colonial officer was stationed, not 'in a backward community', but *auf einer zentralafrikanischen Farm*, i.e. on a farm in Central Africa, and the Siberian girl was actually not a cousin but a new *Hausangestellte*, i.e. a new maid who had come to work for Balázs' friend (which seems rather strange considering that the incident is supposed to have taken place some time after the revolution—she did after all come to Moscow from a kolkhoz). Helmut H. Diederichs, the editor of Balázs' *Schriften zum*

Film, talks in a lecture of 'the undoubtedly fictitious . . . story of the Russian steward' and regards the transformation of the story as 'a funny example' of how 'Balázs' film theory developed from 1924 to 1948' (Diederichs, 1997).

4 Several central Kracauer texts are reprinted in English translation in Kracauer, 1995—for example 'Kult der Zerstreuung: Über die Berliner Lichtspielhäuser' [1926], 'Die Photographie' [1927], and 'Die heutigen Film und sein Publikum' [1928]. See also the film reviews reprinted in Kracauer, 1974. The central Benjamin texts are 'Das Kunstwerk im Zeitalter seiner technischen Reproduzierbarkeit' [1936] and 'Über einige Motive bei Baudelaire' [1939], both texts quoted below from the German reprint (Benjamin, 1977), my translation.

5 For a more detailed discussion of Benjamin's Artwork essay, see Larsen, 1993. Cf. also the discussion of Benjamin and Kracauer's view of mass culture in Larsen, 1997.

6 For an overview of Piaget's work, see Flavell, 1970. A series of Piaget-inspired anthropological studies of 'primitive thought' comparable to Luria's work in Central Asia are discussed in Hallpike, 1979.

7 See also the introduction to Messaris, 1994.

References

Balázs, Béla (1948), *Filmkultura. A Film müvészfilozofiája*, Szikra Kiadó, Budapest.

— (1972), *Theory of the Film. Character and Growth of a New Art* [1952], Arno Press and *The New York Times*, New York.

— (1976), *Der Film. Werden und Wesen einer neuen Kunst* [1949], Globus Verlag, Vienna.

— (1984), *Schriften zum Film*, vol. 2, Helmut H. Diederichs and Wolfgang Gersch (eds.), Carl Hanser Verlag, Munich.

Benjamin, Walter (1977), *Illuminationen. Ausgewählte Schriften*, Suhrkamp, Frankfurt.

Diederichs, Helmut H. (1997), 'Béla Balázs und sein Beitrag zur for-mästhetischen Filmtheorie' (lecture at Freie Universität Berlin, Institut für Theaterwissenschaften, 20 November 1997, quoted from http://www.sozpaed.fh-dortmund.de/diederichs/texte/balázsvo.html).

Flavell, John (1970), *The Developmental Psychology of Jean Piaget*, Van Nostrand Reinhold, New York.

Hallpike, C. R. (1979), *The Foundations of Primitive Thought*, Clarendon Press, Oxford.

Hobbs, Renee et. al. (1988), 'How First-time Viewers Comprehend Editing Conventions', in *Journal of Communication*, 38:4, 50.

Kracauer, Siegfried (1965), *Theory of Film. The Redemption of Physical Reality*, Oxford University Press, New York.

— (1974) *Kino. Essays, Studien, Glossen zum Film*, Suhrkamp, Frankfurt.

— (1995), *The Mass Ornament*, Harvard University Press, Cambridge, Mass.

Larsen, Peter (1993), 'Benjamin at the Movies. Aura, Gaze, and History in the Artwork Essay', in *Orbis Literarum*, 48.

— (1997), 'Benjamin, Kracauer, Mass Culture', *Working Papers* 26, *Department of Media Studies, University of Bergen*.

Luria, A. R. (1976), *Cognitive Development. Its Cultural and Social Foundations*, Harvard University Press, Cambridge, Mass.

Messaris, Paul (1993), 'Visual "Literacy": A Theoretical Synthesis', in *Communication Theory*, 4.

— (1994), *Visual "Literacy": Image, Mind, and Reality*, Westview Press, Boulder, Colorado.

Simmel, Georg (1903), 'Die Grossstädte und das Geistesleben', in T. Petermann (ed.), *Die Grosstadt. Vorträge und Aufsätze zur Städteausstellung*. Jahrbuch der Gehe-Stiftung, Dresden, Band 9. English translation: 'The Metropolis and Mental Life', in Kurt H. Wolff (ed.), *The Sociology of Georg Simmel*, Free Press, Glencoe, Ill.

Wirth, Louis (1964), 'Urbanism as a Way of Life' [1938], in L. Wirth (ed.), *On Cities and Social Life: Selected Papers*, University of Chicago Press, Chicago.

THE CITY AND THE REAL: *CHHINNAMUL* AND THE LEFT CULTURAL MOVEMENT IN THE 1940s

MOINAK BISWAS

Chhinnamul is one of the first Indian films to show a political consciousness of the reality of the metropolis. In it, the country–city dualism was cast in a mould unknown to Indian cinema till then. As we are invited by the film to witness the city of Calcutta, we are made aware in a quite unfamiliar and urgent way that we are in the midst of an intractable present, a present that cannot be escaped from because it has a special status of reality validated in the film, validated by cinema as a new political practice. Moreover, as the film invites us to witness what can be called the 'present as the city'—it invokes a gaze that belongs to the country that has come to invade it, to lay claim to the reality and the time in question. In order to understand these new cinematic impulses one needs to take a look at the context of the film's production. I will present a brief overview.

I

Chhinnamul was made in 1948-49, and released in 1951. The director and cinematographer was Nimai Ghosh, but to all appearances it was a collective effort of artists who belonged to a movement that has come to be named after the IPTA (Indian People's Theatre Association), an organization launched in 1943. The actors included some of the stalwarts of that movement, and two of them were of crucial importance in the history of the radical arts in India—Bijan

Bhattacharya and Ritwik Ghatak. The first was the author of the play *Nabanna* that ushered in the era of social realism in Indian theatre and signalled off the IPTA; the second was instrumental in shaping a modern cinema for India. In a way both of them as well as Nimai Ghosh were part of an enterprise that started in the 1930s and culminated after Independence—a project of forging a modern culture that would mark a move forward from Tagore and be characterized by a new realism and an internationalized artistic consciousness. Not all writers and intellectuals in question were partisan individuals, but they were increasingly responding to the call for a socially committed art. Japan's Manchuria campaign, Mussolini's attack on Abyssinia, and the Spanish Civil War provided the context for such organized cultural efforts on the part of the left. The Progressive Writers' Association (PWA) was formed in 1936—the year Franco's troops marched on republican Spain—and had the support of Tagore and Premchand among the veteran liberal writers. The leaders were from the political left and it was through their initiative that a large section of the Association members also became a part of the Anti-Fascist Writers' and Artists' Association when it was convened in 1942, right in the middle of the War. A year before that Germany had attacked the Soviet Union and the Indian Communists had adopted the controversial People's War line. 1942 was also the year of the August Movement, one of the bloodiest and most widespread revolts against the British government. A chain of events was set in motion that would continue to rock the country and specially areas like Bengal through the decade. 1943 saw the devastating Famine in Bengal, the death of five million people from starvation, and migration of thousands of peasants to the city of Calcutta. The Famine also brought home the fact that the world is linked into a fateful unity by the forces of modernity even as it exploded the ahistorical illusions that urban educated classes would nurture about the Indian village. The IPTA was formed as a direct response to this in Bombay in 1943. Bijan Bhattacharya's *Nabanna* brought upon the Indian stage completely new protagonists in the form of starving Bengal peasants.

IPTA was led by communist partisans but it mobilized the support of a very wide spectrum of artists. This broad base was maintained till

1953-54 even though a section of the liberals was drifting away from the ranks as the Party adopted a more militant politics around 1948, falling out sharply with the Congress government over peasant revolts and workers' agitations. It is impossible not to take the crucial role of the IPTA into account in understanding the culture of the period, even where the artist in question was not directly affiliated to the organization. One could make a distinction here, following an activist of the association, between IPTA as an organization and IPTA as a movement.[1] The reverberations of the movement could be felt right into the early 1970s when the second wave of radicalism after Independence came to a climax.

As Premchand—a patron of the PWA—pointed out in 1936, progressive literature was committed to 'a rationalist and scientific reflection of social reality' (Premchand, 1979). What Premchand and a host of younger writers of the time would practise in the wake of the progressive movement was a realism of social criticism—a critical realism, as Lukács would call it, distinguishing it from socialist realism (Lukács, 1963). The progressive writers' movement included both the liberal critical stance of fiction writers like Tarashankar Bandyopadhyay, Premendra Mitra, Subodh Ghosh and Narayan Gangopadhyay and the more politicized vision of Manik Bandyopadhyay, Nabendu Ghosh, Manoranjan Hazra, and Gopal Haldar. The doctrine of Socialist Realism was adopted in the Soviet Union at the first Writers' Congress in 1934. But even when the Indian left critics used the term in the 1940s—and they did read Gorky and Louis Aragon on this as well as Mao's Yenan Forum lecture on art— they often confused the word with social realism, a term that was ideologically more loose and inclusive. A play by Bijan Bhattacharya, *Jabanbandi*, was singled out by the critic Dhurjatiprasad Mukhopadhyay as the first instance of socialist realism in Indian drama. In fact, although important thematic changes were visible in the new literature, there was continuity with the realism of the liberal democratic consciousness. As a form realism can be adopted in the context of consensual politics as has been demonstrated often in the course of the 20th century. A theoretical vindication of this was the Dimitrov thesis, which was much discussed within the left at that time.

Presented in 1935 at the Comintern, the thesis argued for a common forum—which Dimitrov called the Popular Front—with the democratic progressive section of the bourgeoisie against fascism and a united front with the national progressive bourgeoisie against colonialism (Dimitrov, 1945). It was as much a matter of cultural cohabitation as of political entente. Bourgeois realist modes could well serve as a radical choice within such compulsions. And looked at from the point of view of a local history of art forms, realism was the mandate of modernity that many Indian forms had yet to fulfil. The IPTA produced a powerful crop in the first years in music, drama, visual arts and performing arts. They were brought thematically into a contact with the lives of the toiling masses and their everyday struggles, to the topical crises of the day, though social realism or the 'progressive' reflection of reality meant different things for each of these forms.

Intervention in film was rare: film could not be brought into the project of non-commercial artistic practice so easily, and the structure of the popular film in India has strongly resisted the impulse of such 'modernization'. This cinema has worked within paradigms that do not conform to realist textual ideals. Themes of social reform were common in the films of the 1930s and 40s, but even where these films adapted regional literary fiction (where realist conventions were fairly well established), they treated the material with typical emphasis on melodrama and moral schematism. A large number of such films fell under the generic description 'social', a term borrowed from the popular stage. The discourse of family romance in these films revolved around the broad 19th century questions of social conflicts around modernity and tradition, the impact of the West, and the dualism of the country and the city. In literature, music and painting avant-garde precedents already existed. Drama and film were organically popular, not yet touched by modernism of the sort that produces a high and low cultural distinction. As the IPTA intervened in these two forms, it was natural that they would come quite close to each other again; they had a similar democratic potential in their social function.

II

Direct involvement of the IPTA in films did not happen before 1946, but the new impulse is already palpable in a film like *Udayer Pathe*. Produced by one of the foremost studios of the first sound era, the New Theatres, *Udayer Pathe* was directed by Bimal Roy. The writer, Jyotirmoy Roy, had an important role to play in the production. Jyotirmoy Roy was a socialist already close to the Progressive Writers' Association; Bimal Roy himself became the President of the IPTA later on. The film comes at the climax of a trend that can be traced back to the 1930s. One can mention Charu Roy's *Bangali* (1936), Nitin Bose's *Didi* (1937) and *Desher Mati* (1938), and Prafulla Roy's *Thikadar* (1940) in this context. When one of the major writers of the period, Premendra Mitra, made *Samadhan* in 1943, he showed the divergence between the kind of realist fiction he had been writing and the compulsions of existing film conventions. It is the familiar story of conflict between workers and factory-owner reduced to cross-class romance and family intrigue. When *Udayer Pathe* repeats the theme a year after *Samadhan* certain marked changes are brought in. The use of the non-star Radhamohan Bhattacharya (speaking lines barbed with political sarcasm); the direct reference to Marx and socialism; the parallel cutting between a strike meeting in the workers' colony and the banquet at the rich factory-owner's; the theme of intellectual exploitation of the trade unionist hero employed to ghost-write for the boss; and most importantly, the romantic climax that brings the couple out into the street, out of the parental family, marching down the Delhi Road to organize a strike in a mining town—all this shows that the IPTA had taken place between *Samadhan* and *Udayer Pathe*. The fairy-tale conflict of the rich and the poor had to be recast in a political mould. Members of the production team of *Udayer Pathe* would often turn up at the rehearsals of *Nabanna,* and there was a rumour that the film was an IPTA venture by proxy (Pradhan, 1982).

The organization got involved in film production in 1945-46. A report of the IPTA says,

> It was decided to produce a picture provisionally entitled *Children of the Earth* with an idea to depict in as realistic a manner as our resources could permit the life of Indian peasants in general and the Bengali

farmer in particular, with special emphasis on the grim tragedy wrought by the recent famine in Bengal' (Pradhan, 1979).

Udayer Pathe ends with the protagonists leaving the metropolis; as they walk into a new dawn they renounce the city in some sense. *Dharti ke Lal*, the film that IPTA produced, would draw upon the two plays by Bijan Bhattacharya mentioned above (*Nabanna* and *Jabanbandi*), and a novelette by Krishan Chandar, *Annadata*, and bring back into focus the theme of the country coming into contact with the city. But there is a crucial new aspect to this migration from the country—it does not bring into play the gaze of the bumpkin or the morally pure rustic displaying foolish amazement or spiritual disappointment; rather, it is a collective gaze of the peasantry, cast at the city. The famine brings them to the city, which they leave at the end to return to their villages, nurturing the dream of a new harvest. For the urban consciousness, the village erupting into the city was like a sudden revelation of history itself, in its vast and unbearable dimensions. But instituting the body and voice of the peasant masses at the centre of the narrative meant a major shift in representation, and also in discourse. Satinath Bhaduri's *Dhorai Charit Manas* or Tarashankar Bandyopadhyay's *Chaitali Ghurni, Ganadebata* and *Hansulibanker Upakatha* performed the same function more convincingly in literature.[2]

The genre of the 'social film', which set itself in the contemporary in terms of the perennial conflicts and family romance, and the studio-style of filmmaking, provided a framework that *Udayer Pathe* could still make use of, but that a film such as *Dharti ke Lal* was obviously uncomfortable with. In parts, both *Dharti* and *Chhinnamul* owned up to the inadequacy of the system of the studio 'social'—the mode of acting, mise-en-scene and shooting style that became fairly common in the 'socials' of the period across the studios—and were drawn to the radical theatre in search of models. The commonly held film-history belief is that though these films were moving towards a stark realism of content, something like a 'neo-realist' language was still beyond their reach; the realism of form was jettisoned by the persistence of the studio style. Among other things, it implies theatricality as a primitive trace in these films, something that Indian cinema had to wait till Satyajit Ray's work to overcome completely. If one moves away from this notion of the linear destiny of realism one can discern that the films in question—and I would add films like Ritwik Ghatak's *Nagarik* (1953) and Debaki Bose's *Pathik* (1953) to the group—were incorporating a new theatrical influence often quite distinct in character from the New Theatres films. They were using the elements that proved successful on the stage in the plays by Bijan Bhattacharya, Binoy Ghosh, Tulsi Lahiri or Digindra Bandyopadhyay.

Dharti was directed by Khwaja Ahmad Abbas and the method of production was widely different from that of the industry. It was a collective effort from the script to post-production stages and involved a large number of artistes from the IPTA—Balraj Sahni and Sombhu Mitra, Ali Sardar Jafri and Prem Dhawan, Ravi Shankar and Shanti Bardhan. Many of the performers reappeared in *Chhinnamul*. The hunger marchers came from the Kishan Sabha, the peasant wing of the Communist Party; members of the Students' Federation appeared as the organizers of relief kitchens for the famine victims. Abbas and his team shot in a farm near Pune, but also used indoor sets for most of the locations. The lighting, art direction, dialogue and acting are close to the realist stage; they do not conform to the conventional realist filmic codes known to us. Along with the people, the streets of the city were supposed to come alive as part of documentary evidence, but this spatial articulation, like everyday speech, is avoided for a more schematic, commentary-like exposition. Abbas writes in his autobiography that he could not shoot on the streets of Calcutta because of the wartime regulations (Abbas, 1977). But the distinctively theatrical conventions he and his team adopted from the political drama would not require such treatment. There is even a shadow play within the film, performed in the style of certain stage items that the radicals were using for relief and propaganda at the time. The IPTA report on the film called it the 'first documentary feature film in India' (Pradhan, 1982). Even *Nabanna* was often described as documentation. The visual and performative idioms of the film are shared with a number of films made through the early 1950s. One can mention here the unique history of a print of the film reaching the quarters of Mao's Eighth Route Army in Yenan.

In *Chhinnamul*, made five years later, a more curious combination of conventions takes place: conventions of the studio 'social', of the IPTA stage and visual arts, and the seemingly non-fictional sections which did not have a precedence in Indian cinematic practices. The actors— Bijan Bhattacharya, Ritwik Ghatak, Charuprakash Ghosh, Gangapada Bose, Sova Sen, Shanti Mitra, et al—were from the IPTA and the rest were non-actors, sometimes actual refugees enacting this migration of a group of villagers from East Pakistan to the city of Calcutta. The most memorable from the latter group is an old widow who clings to the bamboo pole of her hut, refusing to budge when her neighbours urge her to leave with them. Nimai Ghosh considered it an 'experiment', a film that would not fit into the conventional framework of cinema of that time at all, a film deliberately aimed at breaking the logic of enter- tainment and consequently, that of dramatic organization. He points out six principles of the 'experiment': not to use professional actors, not to use make-up, to shoot at low cost within 10,000 ft. of film, not to use song sequences, using candid camera, and using dialectal, natural speech.[3] Similarities with what Cesare Zavattini later outlined as char- acteristics of Italian neo-realism are apparent. The neo-realist films were not seen in India before the International Film Festival of 1952. But Ghosh, with Ray and others, was part of the Calcutta Film Society (founded in 1947), which did give him and some of his associates an exposure to the European realist films, besides the Soviet avant-garde. He said in an interview that he had read about the Italian films in *Film Review*, seen stills of them and had got deeply interested in the style (Ghosh, 2003). Pudovkin and the actor Cherkassov were shown the film in Calcutta in 1951. They later wrote to Ghosh: 'It seems to us that in your work you are carrying out a great and noble task in confirming a realistic trend in Indian cinematic art . . . Cling steadfastly to the real- istic path you have chosen. Develop and deepen its foundation' (Pudovkin and Cherkasov, 2003). Ghosh was invited to show the film in the USSR, and Pudovkin wrote a review in *Pravda* elaborating on the point of realism (Pudovkin, 2003).

A cinema of social criticism developed in the period through films like *Aurat* (1941); *Udayer Pathe, Dharti ke Lal, Neecha Nagar* (1946); *Chhinnamul, Babla* (1951); *Pathik, Nagarik, Natun Ihudi, Bhor Hoye Elo*

(1953); *Do Bigha Zamin* (1955) and *Jagte Raho* (1956). But they had a troubled relationship with realism.[4] The full-blown realist aesthetic of Ray's *Pather Panchali* (1955) coincided with the receding of the political engagement of such films to the margins. It is a historical development yet to be studied. But when one looks at the work of Ritwik Ghatak and the specific 'difficulty' it poses for critics, one understands better some of the sources and motivations of his work from this perspective. Ghatak carries over not only the political passion but also some formal characteristics of this era into his films of the 1960s, thereby occupying a position astride the boundaries of what was considered two antagonistic practices from 1955 on: realist art cinema and the melodramatic popular tradition. As the new Indian cinema came into existence, a new popular was also fashioned by the industry—and both of these had to work out in their specific ways an encounter with the modern.[5] The city—urban space—became an increasingly important location for films in the 1950s: the site where survival and change, allurement and search were to be dramatized; it embodied the life-world of a new individual that cinema had to invent in the context of the post-independence modernization. I will take a closer look at *Chhinnamul* in the following section and try to point out the formal elements as well as the thematic and contextual linkages that I have in mind here.

One can easily notice that the principles of filmmaking that Nimai Ghosh points out are not always adhered to in the film. The admixture of idioms in *Chhinnamul* is even more curious than *Dharti*, because to a large extent the two styles in the film are segregated into two episodes and this is based upon nothing other than a country–city dualism. The neo-realist tendencies that are often pointed out become apparent in the second part of the film as the story moves into Calcutta. The village is invoked through the idiom of realist political theatre, whereas the city invokes the documentary form. I am trying to indicate the broad tendencies without suggesting a complete divergence at all levels as I point to the formal division between the two parts. It can be argued that as *Chhinnamul* comes to stand at a juncture of film history in India, it provokes us once again to cover the ground of the old arguments over representation. To the extent that the two locations necessitate two languages in the film, it is perhaps not unprofitable to start from a conception of reality and work through the question of 'reflection'. The theoretical mistrust of reflection is well-founded, but the figure has remained with us in a lot of our descriptive work, and may serve a special purpose in reading the forces at work in texts which emerge out of a radicalizing context, a context where the very urgency of the real, and the instability of the categorical difference between event and form, experience and expression, create the scope for a capture, a portrayal, that can be directly related to the life of the object. The question of the 'referent' has to be reconsidered on these occasions.

III

The film opens with credits and music (by Kalobaran) in a mode that can be clearly linked to contemporary conventions. A title announces it is going to be a 'stark portrayal of the victims of partition'. As it introduces the village Naldanga and its inhabitants, the film adopts a very schematic, almost commentary-like exposition. The river, the mosque, the temple, the villager—the narration traces a linear sequence. We then find the protagonist of the first section, Srikanta, meeting a number of people, a sequence that gives us a view of the various trades—the potter, the goldsmith, the jute farmer. It is like a reconstructed documentary exposition. The land and the life, its imminent crisis, is presented for the knowledge of the outsider to some extent, as an ethnographic documentary is supposed to do. The actual use of voice-over narration in the place of dialogue at least five times in this section would confirm this observation. When these people enter the city this voice-over mode will almost disappear (it is used there only once and briefly), as if the story by then has become theirs, they are in a position to represent themselves and need not be represented any more.

Soon after this, we enter Srikanta's home—the site of the family drama, the story of the couple that will be used to impose a narrative limit on the film. The set is indoors and exhibits the characteristic artifice of the studio era. The road outside the house is also shot in the studio lot, as well as some of the outdoor meeting places of the villagers.

As Srikanta and his wife talk about their conjugal dreams of a happy home, we are taken through images of a bird and its nest. It comes as a straight metaphor but the bird motif is brought back time and again over the rest of the scenes at Srikanta's home, suggesting the existence of an actual nest. The peasants talk about *akal* throughout, which means bad harvest and starvation. On three occasions, the dialogue refers to the 1943 Famine. The shadow of another such devastation looms over their lives. At the same time, they are aware that something of a large-scale historical change is coming about. They look to Srikanta to explain that change to them. Srikanta is a political activist, but like many others in 1946-47, the partition is not yet a concrete reality that he can visualize. He tries to organize the peasants against the local landlords and their oppression. This is the time of the Punnapra Vayalar, Telengana and Tebhaga peasant rebellions and the reference here is clearly to these uprisings, all of which were launched in 1946 in NW Travancore State, Hyderabad State and the province of Bengal respectively. These were struggles that came into confrontation with the independent state and the Congress leadership after 1947, and finally led to the banning of the Communist Party. The presentation of the peasants and their lives in *Chhinnamul* should be understood in the light of a politics that focused on the local reality of exploitation and resistance, not only on the narrative of colonialism/nationalism. If this was shared with socialist literature and theatre of the period, the mode of presentation is also often borrowed from them, specially from the latter. The most schematic, almost allegorical, parts of the film are related to the portrayal of the two landlords— one Hindu and the other Muslim—working hand in glove to make a killing as the peasants are forced off their land. We are told they have done it before, during the great Bengal Famine, and this is how the political games played at the national level translate into local class exploitation. The two landlords are presented as classic villains. In a very literal way they appear to work in collusion. As the police swoop down on the house of Srikanta and arrest him, they are shown for the first time frontally, standing under a tree and leering. The mixture of narrative idioms is quite pointed here. On the verandah the scene of the couple: the wife putting on her vermilion dot, unaware of the imminent disaster, Srikanta sensing the danger and asking her indirect questions about what she would do if something happened to him. As he mentions his own possible danger she gives a start and the dot is smudged—a familiar melodramatic gesture. This also brings on the climax: the door latch shakes, boots stamp on it, the two villains under the tree look on. While the two are presented in the manner of cutouts reminiscent of the contemporary drama, dance drama and agitational pantomime, the police onslaught is more in tune with a certain cinematic rhetoric. The quick cutting back and forth, the oblique angles, the accelerated montage, and the suggestive exposition (where we do not see the police at all but only the boots and the handcuffs) evoke the Soviet films that were shown by the IPTA and then the Calcutta Film Society in the late 1940s.

There are other montage sequences, more conventional to Indian cinema of the period, and these relate to seasonal changes or large-scale time transition. The partition itself is presented in this manner. As the lonely, traumatized Batasi, Srikanta's wife, looks on, there is a series of dissolves and superimpositions of shots of the nest, lightning and storm, a flame from an earthen lamp, two hands trying to guard it. Soon after this a second series: a hand holding a knife stabbing downwards, houses on fire, city streets streaming with people. Apart from such conventional iconography and punctuations, noticeable is the presence of the images of political reportage, illustrations and news photographs, of conventions borrowed from painters like Zainul Abedin and Chittaprasad, from photographers like Sunil Janah, from the visual material that one found in Communist Party publications from Calcutta like *Swadhinata* or *Janajuddha*. The strange cohabitation of a documentary impulse and theatre in this section of the film is most apparent in the use of voice-over narration. At these points in the film, the dramatic exposition stops and a voice narrates what is happening. It is there when Srikanta is found addressing a political meeting in Umeshpur, or when the news of his arrest spreads through the village. Often, as this takes place, the action becomes more schematic and stage-like. The voice-over not only tells us the events, it also mimics the dialogues that are silently enacted on the screen. This helps abbreviate passages of action and also underlines an external narrative agency that realism usually tries to erase from the text. It is a language of propaganda, the idiom of activist art that makes these shifts in narrative agency possible. The instance found here seems peculiar, but the basic principle of external narration is integral to the very aesthetic of popular Indian cinema.

There was nothing in that cinema, though, that could match the starkness of the image as the villagers arrive in Calcutta as refugees. As they board the train they come out of the indeterminate location of Naldanga, the name given to the village in the film, to real places on the map of a burning country. We catch a glimpse of the station 'Darshana' on the way, conjuring up the fateful route of the refugees who came in through murder and mayhem to the city. The arrival at the Sealdah Station in Calcutta—the top angle shot of the maze of tracks and the low angle shot of the platform roofs—has almost a dream-like quality as a new reality dawns on the characters, invades the film's frame. They land in a sea of humanity, many of them displaced people, on the railway platform. They will now have to forge a new community with other refugees. For decades afterwards, this community would be politically an extremely important demographic entity. They have neither come to marvel at the big city as peasants, nor to climb the ladder of individual success as we find in countless popular plots. They are here to take part in a reconstruction of the city. Already, in 1951, *Chhinnamul* carries a vision of that future. It places the refugees as protagonists in the city and also institutes a refugee gaze at the city. As we suggested earlier, these characters can now appear to represent themselves so that the ethnographic exposition and the commentary mode almost vanish from the text.

Chhinnamul could place the fictional characters of villagers right in the middle of a present time—a time coincident with the film's activity itself—because of its engagement in a certain politics. This politics was trying to make visible another reality undercutting the chronicle of colonialism and nationalism. The riots, the partition and the massive uprooting contribute to a tragic view of the moment of independence, to a political vision that sees this moment of the founding of the nation-state as the beginning of a struggle rather than an end to a course of destiny.

The city as it appears on the screen is an entity in formation, a place that has just woken up to history itself. In a sense the village episode was still tucked away in some timeless place; these people have entered time now as an immediate experience. No escape from its course is possible. The Famine had shocked the urban artist into a new consciousness as the villages burst upon the cityscape like a nightmare. In fact, the metaphor of the phantasm—people without food, without clothes, shorn almost of their very physical reality—haunts the literature of the period, the most memorable being Manik Bandyopadhyay's short stories. But the intense workers' and peasants' movements since 1944-45 worked towards a new image of the awakening village, of the peasants becoming agents of history.

The refugees, some of whom actually appear on the scene now, extended the city's limits. Only a handful of the well-off came and bought property; the rest took the urban authorities by surprise. The Calcutta authorities, like their Delhi counterparts, were not prepared for the waves of migration. People just encroached upon vacant land on the outskirts, eventually stretching the city borders. The humbler section built squatter colonies on public land. The poorest flocked to relief camps, like the one shown in the film. The 1951 census puts the population of Calcutta at 2.7 million. In 1961, the slum population was estimated at 650,000. A large number of the immigrants flocked to the informal sector, many of them finding work—if at all—in areas which were dramatically different from their traditional trade and ethos. Contemporary literature and art seemed to grasp the new reality much more sensitively than the urban planners and other specialists, as one demographer points out (Chakrabarty, 1991). The theme of an overall moral crisis generated by a violent uprooting and the compulsions of survival appeared often in contemporary literature. Manohar, the goldsmith played by Ritwik Ghatak in the film, is shown peddling 'American combs for four paisa each' on the street, and he is the one who secrets some money away for his own family. People like him moved out of the group to set up on their own, to the progressive weakening of the original community.

When Srikanta finally finds them, Bishu and Prasanna tell him that the Naldanga he is looking for has fallen apart. But they are shown living amidst refugees from other villages and districts of East Pakistan. As the groups broke apart under pressure, new groups were formed among the refugees, and the colonies were built upon this new principle of re-creating the village. The refugee colony that Srikanta visits shows an inhabitant trying to nurture his little plants. He says, 'If I had the land I could produce gold on it.' As the refugees built these new villages in the city, they also created little plots of vegetation, schools and 'clubs'. They would have their own distinctive culture of humour, folk music, civic life. One is reminded of Ishwar, the protagonist of Ghatak's *Subarnarekha* (1962) getting a job and moving out of the 'Nabajiban Colony' which he has himself struggled to build. His friend Haraprasad calls him a 'deserter'. His downfall is related to this loss of engagement with fellow sufferers. But the vision has become bleaker in *Subarnarekha*. Haraprasad himself ends up failing even more miserably. Ishwar's sister Sita cannot escape the reality that Ishwar was running away from in his search for the 'Natun Bari', the new home. Ghatak brings her back to the city; it is another colony that she ends up in. The earlier film *Meghe Dhaka Tara* (1960) is of course almost wholly set in a colony; these grew up mainly on the southern fringes of the city and were named after the nationalist heroes— Netaji, Chittaranjan, Bagha Jatin, Gandhi.

It was no coincidence that through the political upheavals between 1967 and 1977, the 'colony' areas proved a stronghold of radical politics in and around Calcutta. They still constitute a support base for the left. That is part of the history of how the homeless who form that impossible crowd in the Sealdah railway station organized themselves into a cultural and political entity, not merely a population to be brought under governance.

But *Chhinnamul* concentrates on a point where the crowd, an explosion of faces and bodies, of tongues and expressions, hits the streets of the metropolis. The great achievement of the film was to animate that crowd into a people. The film does not render them passive objects for documentation of poverty on the streets, like photo reportage has often done. Nor is it the story of one of the hapless embarking upon a private odyssey, as the standard narrative treatment would have it. The migrants from Naldanga become a collective focus of action. One feels that the film is interested in a record of their tryst with a moment in history, not so much in the conceivable end of their story.

Srikanta is released from jail and comes to Calcutta searching for his wife and fellow villagers. His search provides an elementary linear form to a description that is otherwise too broad in canvas and too unpredictable in development. It is a compromise, an inevitable one, with the logic of the institution of narrative, but the film does not appear to be rounded off around his search and Srikanta's final meeting with his wife. Forces of scattering are far too strong in the narration. This is another sign of what we see as the city invoking a form. Srikanta's narrative is narrative in the traditional sense—where the sense of being 'told', of experience already belonging to a kind of past, would work towards textual integration. But the sheer possibility of scattering, of the unexpected happening to them any moment, that looms large in these lives, evokes the sense of a place and time that are relatively free. We know that the film looks disorganized because of this freedom, this sense of being 'not yet told'. True to the habit of socialist fiction and films, Srikanta's union with his wife coincides with her death and the birth of their child. This is the climax of the story of the couple that began in the first part of the film, but Srikanta hardly remains the focus of the film once the great journey of the people begins.

The film was responding to a time when the city itself became the protagonist for a new generation of poets—Jibanananda Das and Samar Sen being the most important among them—and we come across this image of a face in the crowd, a face that is anchored in a sea of humanity out on the streets, in the poetry of Subhash Mukhopadhyay or Sukanta Bhattacharya. This is the time when Calcutta became the city of *michhils*, political processions and rallies. A wave of protest marches and barricades started in the city around the time of the INA trials. Millions came out on the streets in organized protests that often took the nationalist leadership by surprise. This leadership would often straightaway betray the movements. People would fraternize on the streets, braving murderous police attacks. November 21, 1945, was a preamble to a series of events that looked like explosions on a revolutionary scale, and that had to be contained through brisk negotiation and transfer of power between the colonial government and nationalist leadership. It came to a climax on Rashid Ali Day in February, 1946. Manik Bandyopadhyay's novel *Chinha* describes a single siege on the streets on 25 November and deals with characters who emerge out of the street. Tarashankar Bandyopadhyay captured the Rashid Ali Day protests in his novel *Jhod o Jharapata*. The workers' and peasants' movements continued to inspire these urban rebellions. There were literally hundreds of these between 1945 and 1950. In 1946 alone workers all over India launched agitations more than a thousand times. The first workers' strike (and the police attack on it) in West Bengal came only eight weeks after independence. Against the experience of the communal riots that ravaged the city between 1946 and 1947, these events demonstrated remarkable solidarity between religious communities and presented the other, surging face of the multitude in search of a utopia. And they were not only voicing local demands but showed a vibrant internationalism of concern: In January 1947, five months after the Great Calcutta Killing, the students laid siege to the Calcutta Airport to protest against the French Air Force using the place for sending warplanes to Vietnam.[7]

Srikanta's reunion with his people in the end is of course a coincidence. But it is a coincidence that should probably be considered with the historical context in mind rather than as an unreconstructed convention. The partition is an event on a scale that cannot be approached through simple rationalities. Too many people were thrown overnight into the nightmare of death, separation and loss. The logic of such violence and dispersal is meant to generate accidents—unforeseen separations and meetings that are the stuff such times are made of. One could see this end to *Chhinnamul* not simply as a melodramatic one but as melodrama invoked by a certain consciousness of reality. This could give us a point of entry into the work of Ritwik Ghatak. In his films of the 1960s—*Meghe Dhaka Tara, Komal Gandhar* (1961) and *Subarnarekha*—conventions I have tried to trace in the body of *Chhinnamul* would come together in the most forceful combination. When the refugees from Naldanga land in Sealdah there is a close-up of Ghatak looking at the sordid life of the city. He is looking at scenes of pavement dwellers that seem to have come straight out of the contemporary drawings of Zainul Abedin. One cannot but remember the scene of the play that opens *Komal Gandhar*: the old refugee on the city street cries out, 'Even the sky is covered in smoke here.' Ghatak would work through plays, songs and slogans from the IPTA and would sometimes be deliberately 'theatrical' in his treatment of the theme of partition, which he saw as an embracing symptom, both historical and civilizational in significance. In *Subarnarekha* he uses a number of coincidences in the plot and suggests to the critics who attacked him for lapsing into melodrama that the film is 'about coincidences' (Ghatak, 1987).

The city that we see in *Chhinnamul* seems to lack memory. The drunken Haraprasad says as much over the shots of passing street lamps in *Subarnarekha* as he takes a taxi ride with the protagonist, Ishwar: 'Never. Haven't seen the War, haven't seen the Famine, haven't seen the riots, haven't seen Partition . . .' This city is caught in the grip of the present. It is the place to which memory must be restored. Coincidences will continue till then to bring people into profoundly new encounters.

Notes

1 Hemango Biswas makes this distinction in Biswas, 1998.

2 Pradyumna Bhattacharya discusses the question of the peasants' gaze in the novels of Bandyopadhyay in Bhattacharya, 1976 and 1998.

3 Cited in Samik Bandyopadhyay (Bandyopadhyay, 1991).

4 Taking a cue from Raymond Williams (Williams, 1977), one can think of a framework where it would be possible to trace a quantitative as well as a qualitative 'development' of realism in this period. Realism was developing within the 'social' film and appears till 1953 or so in various combinations with the elements of conventional social melodrama. After the moment of *Pather Panchali*, the diffusion of realism takes another dimension, again calling for a mapping of realism across the genres rather than solely in the new 'art cinema' that *Pather Panchali* inaugurated. The conceptual point that I would like to make is that so far as we think in terms of smaller sets within this history, realism can indeed constitute a measure of advance in a specific case. Discarding

the linear development of realism as a measure of progress does not mean that this local historical question of securing an advance in language and form should become an irrelevant question.

5 The point to suggest is that firstly, the popular cinema developing from around 1955 was not the old popular now coming into conflict with the modern art cinema—an assumption tacit in most discussions of Indian cinema. And secondly, the popular cinema of the period was essentially a modern practice, not a traditional foil to modernity. It had to make its own negotiations with the modern. On the latter point see Prasad, 1998.

7 See for a spirited account of the decade, Sengupta, 1989. For surveys of art and literature of the period, see Das, 1992. For a general historical account, see Sarkar, 1983.

References

Abbas, Khwaja Ahmad (1977), *I Am Not an Island: An Experiment in Autobiography*, Vikas Publishing House, New Delhi.

Bandyopadhyay, Samik (1991), 'Calcutta Cinema: The Early Years', in S. Chaudhuri (ed.), *Calcutta: The Living City*, Oxford University Press, Calcutta.

Bhattacharya, Pradyumna (1976), 'Samajer Matra Ebong Tarashankarer Upanyas: *Chaitali Ghurni*', *Ekshan*, n/a

— (1998), 'Rajnaitik Upanyas: Swarupyer Sandhane?', in *Tika Tippani*, Papyrus, Calcutta.

Biswas, Hemango (1998), 'Gananatya Andolon o Loksangeet', in *Ganer Bahirana*, Papyrus, Calcutta.

Chakrabarty, Satyesh C. (1991), 'The Growth of Calcutta in the 20th Century, in S. Chaudhuri (ed.), *Calcutta: The Living City*.

Das, Dhananjay (ed.) (1992), *Banglar Sanskritite Marxbadi Chetanar Dhara*, Anustup Prakashan, Calcutta.

Dimitrov, Georgi (1945), *The United Front against Fascism: Speeches at the Seventh Congress of the Communist International, August 1935*, Current Book Distributors, Sydney.

Ghatak, Ritwik (1987), 'On Subarnarekha', in A. Rajadhyaksha and A. Gangar (ed.), *Ghatak: Arguments/Stories*, Screen Unit, Bombay.

Ghosh, Nimai (2003), 'Prasanga *Chhinnamul* o Anyanya: Nimai Ghosher

Sakshatkar', in S. Basu and S. Dasgupta (ed.), *Chhinnamul, Nimai Ghosher Prabandha Baktrita Sakshatkar, Ebong Tar Jiban o Kaj Samparke Alochona*, Cine Central and Monchasha, Calcutta.

Lukács, György (1963), 'Critical Realism and Socialist Realism', in *The Meaning of Contemporary Realism*, Merlin, London.

Pradhan, Sudhi (1979), *Marxist Cultural Movement in India: Chronicles and Documents*, vol. 1, Santi Pradhan, Calcutta.

— (1982), 'Bharatiya Gananatya Sanstha Ebong Bharatiya Chalachitra', *Chitrakalpa* (July).

Prasad, M. Madhava (1998), *Ideology of the Hindi Film: A Historical Construction*, Oxford University Press, New Delhi.

Premchand, Munsi (1979), 'The Nature and Purpose of Literature', in S. Pradhan (ed.), *Marxist Cultural Movement in India: Chronicles and Documents*, vol. 1.

Pudovkin, V. I. (2003), 'The Uprooted', in S. Basu and S. Dasgupta (ed.), *Chhinnamul, Nimai Ghosher Prabandha Baktrita Sakshatkar, Ebong Tar Jiban o Kaj Samparke Alochona*, Cine Central and Monchasha, Calcutta.

— and Cherkasov, N. (2003), 'A Letter from V. I. Pudovkin and N. Cherkasov', in S. Basu and S. Dasgupta (ed.), *Chhinnamul, Nimai Ghosher Prabandha Baktrita Sakshatkar, Ebong Tar Jiban o Kaj Samparke Alochona*, Cine Central and Monchasha, Calcutta.

Sarkar, Sumit (1983), *Modern India 1885-1947*, Macmillan, New Delhi.

Sengupta, Amalendu (1989), *Uttal Challish: Asamapta Biplab*, Pearl Publishers, Calcutta.

Williams, Raymond (1977), 'A Lecture on Realism', *Screen*, 18:1.

READING A SONG OF THE CITY—

IMAGES OF THE CITY IN LITERATURE AND FILMS

SUDIPTA KAVIRAJ

In this essay I shall take an autobiographical line. As my experience of viewing Hindi films is very limited, the only sensible contribution I can make to this discussion is by comparing the filmic representation of the city with literary ones. Secondly, even the limited filmic evidence that I can draw upon, episodically and anecdotally, from my own personal experience, is limited to a few Bengali films. Though why people like me saw so few Hindi films is itself an interesting cultural question. I shall begin by continuing a line of argument made in an earlier paper (Kaviraj, 1998).

I should like to begin by presenting that argument in a fuller form. I began my lecture on the culture of democracy by analysing a song from a film about the city of Bombay. The argument I was making there was that in the 1950s there was a clear, very widespread, *spatial* translation of the rupture between the modern and the traditional. The villages constituted the space of tradition—of caste oppression, of stagnant customs, of poor and undeveloping lives, of religious superstitions. The city, by contrast, was the space of the modern. And since democracy, or rather the democratic principle, was distinctively modern in this view of history, democracy lived in the city.

I used the example of a song taken from a film called *CID* [Criminal Investigation Department] which I had not seen, delivered in the film, I am authoritatively told, by a very popular comedian, Johny Walker, who had a typical city dweller's image to his audience. It was sung by Mohammad Rafi, the most popular playback singer of Hindi films of the Nehru era, in an enunciative style that took great pains to communicate in its lightness of utterance a typical urban knowingness. In spite of using it often in my social science arguments, I have not seen that particular film on the screen. Yet the song is one I have heard since my childhood, my schooldays, in a small religious town, Nabadwip, about sixty miles north of Calcutta.

Since I have chosen an autobiographical line, the circumstances in which I heard the song ought to be analysed in some detail. Significantly, Nabadwip was a historic religious centre for Bengali *vaishnavas* as the place of birth of the 15th century *bhakti* saint Chaitanya. Nabadwip in the 60s was a strange but lively mixture of the traditional and the modern. The town's main reputation came from its association with Chaitanya's birth. Though others with deeper knowledge of Bengali cultural history would have known that it was the great centre of Sanskrit knowledge—particularly in *Navyanyaya* logic and in *Smriti*. It was a major centre of *vaishnava* pilgrimage, particularly on significant occasions of the *vaishnava* calendar—like the ceremonies of the *jhulan purnima*, the *raslila* or *janmashtami*. Like other great religious centres, it was a centre for thriving commerce, and the modern railway made it more accessible to pilgrims.

Its second claim to fame as the traditional centre for esoteric Sanskrit learning, and the seat of a highly specialized system of ritual legality, was by then completely dwarfed, almost forgotten by its ordinary people. Few inhabitants of the city felt any pride in great logical schools. Also unnoticed by its pilgrims, and behind the spectacular religious aspect, it was by this time a considerable centre for the production of cotton sarees. The commercialization of its religious life fed directly into modern developments like cinemas, and a booming business in speakers/tannoys, which local shops and businesses used for advertising their wares, or announcements of upcoming films by cinemas, of public meetings by political parties, and municipal announcements by the local authorities. Aurally at least, the tannoys and their blaring sound were, in a literal sense, an inescapable part of our existence.

This sociological structure produced a very specific economy of sounds in the town—of various, different, often conflicting parts—and in this the tannoys played an indispensable role. That was the ubiquitous technological link between the blandishments of commercial advertisements, the enticement of the romantic films, and the exertions of the police to control the vast crowds streaming through the narrow streets at times of festivals. But this sound was distinctively modern, demonstrating the power and the vulgarity of modern things. In a crowd of other sounds, they always pushed their way through. Because, there were many other sounds in the town. Nabadwip was among other things a city of unceasing music. The *vaishnava* sect around Chaitanya had developed a new communal form of worship, which took two unusual forms. On festival days, there were religious processions in which devotees sang, played a drum called the *khol*, and collectively danced on the streets, which set this sect apart from most other Hindu worshippers. When Chaitanya first initiated this form of collective dancing and singing, it created a scandal among the orthodox brahmins of Nabadwip who had complained to the Qazi, and implored him to suppress the uproar. But more routinely, in the hundreds of small local temples, all round the year, lower level performances, called *palakirtan*, went on. In these, a small troupe of *kathaks* (literally, tellers of tales) or performers enacted segments of the stories of the love of Krishna and Radha through a fascinating combination of simple narration, mimed enactment, sung passages recounting their famous trysts or verbal exchanges, and dancing.

It was an immensely powerful aesthetic economy—a combination of various narrative and interpretative media, held together tightly by a single theme, animated by a *rasa* aesthetic that the audience knew intimately and enjoyed in endless re-enactments. The average *vaishnava* was strongly urged by his religious sensibility to use aesthetics—visual images, narrative forms, music and dance—to enliven and ennoble his quotidian existence; in other words, to have a fundamental attitude towards life that was aesthetic.

A part of this aesthetic reception of everyday life was a simple custom of singing a standard tune early in the morning. Except in the rainy season, despite its transcendent connections, the town experienced an acute shortage of municipal water supply; but that was offset by the 'divine' supply of water from the Ganga. Most people, for most of the year, went for a bath in the river early in the morning, as later in the day, especially in summer, the sand on the wide banks of the river became unbearably hot. One interesting technique of communal worship in the *vaishnava* religion was that most of the songs sung in the morning had identical or very similar tunes, generically called *prabhati* (from *prabhat*, early morning). Early in the morning from sunrise to mid-morning, the town hummed with this general melody of morning worship—gentle, pastoral, expressing a sense of restrained and elegant joyfulness.

Those were Nehruvian times, and the ability of authorities to enforce legal rules had not crumbled. Apparently, the municipality had a rule that banned the use of tannoys before eight in the morning. (I might be wrong about the exact hour; it could be half past eight or nine. But in that town eight in the morning was quite late in the working day); at that exact hour, all the 'mike shops' (*maiker dokan*) on the main street started their tannoys, which usually carried the currently fashionable Bengali and Hindi popular music, instantly re-ordering the aural economy. It immediately introduced a different music with a very different reading of the nature of human existence.

Hindi film songs used to be vastly popular, despite the widespread belief among the elder family members that they were corrupting. In some ways this was rather strange. The Radha-Krishna stories were often deeply erotic; compared to them, the Bengali *adhunik* (literally, modern) songs and the Hindi film lyrics simply expressed a vague sense of romantic longing, in most cases narratively frustrated by immovable and unforgiving family obstacles.

Yet these songs were considered dangerous precisely because they were romantic. Eroticism of a kind was a recognized part of traditional culture. Romantic love was a modern moral ideal. Against the iron laws of arranged marriages, these songs advocated, however vaguely, the individualistic principle of romantic choice of partners, and described this as a state of divine emotional fulfilment. Family elders might be faulted for their moral principles, but they acted on a highly accurate perception of the sociological implications of this relatively pedestrian poetry. Our own family did not even have a radio through which such moral enticements might infiltrate into our home. Listening to songs from Hindi films was disapproved of even more strongly because the disapproval against romantic behaviour was compounded by the Bengali disdain about the general lowliness of north Indian culture. They came under three degrees of prohibition—they were romantic, they were from films, and they were Hindi. I first heard this song in that context. Ironically, just as the religious music had a compelling repetitiveness, coming back to your hearing every morning, so that it was impossible to forget that that was the proper way to start the day (in a gentle and subtle attitude of thankfulness), this film music also had its own answering repetitiveness. Since the songs were immensely popular among the young, the shops played them often, many times a day, often during the festivals when the individual marquees would hire an individual tannoy with a supply of gramophone records. They were additionally often carried by popular music channels of the Delhi-based AIR [All India Radio] and for some curious reason, by Radio Ceylon. Thus these songs were not an episodic musical experience; they had their own structures of repetition, which made it impossible to forget them. In a sense, they also came back every mid-morning or afternoon to remind you how to face life in the city. Long before I encountered sociological theories of modernity and tradition or heard of Max Weber, I learnt, vaguely but vividly, through this undeniable line across the musical experience of my everyday, that these two types of tunes represented two immense principles of organizing experience, or the life-world.

There are some other peculiarities to this hearing. The first interesting fact was that I heard these songs, and this one in particular, hundreds of times, without watching the film in which it figured. This indicates two important things. First, songs like these had a strangely dual character: they were both contextual, and freestanding. Of course, in the context of the narrative of a specific film, the song enhanced a situation, carried and amplified a mood, inserted a twist or did something of immediate narrative import: within the film it was inextricably connected to the story. Indeed, in extension of an argument Mukund Lath makes, the underlying aesthetic of popular Hindi films had some distinct similarities to the aesthetic of the classical *Natyashastra* and he argued that in the *natya*, i.e. a play/film, several primary modes came together to form a more complex form of aesthetic enjoyment, in which each mode enhanced the other (Lath, 1998).

But apart from the contextual meaning in this immediate narrative structure, many of the most popular songs were capable of achieving a freestanding meaningfulness as a literary, musical object, as a rhetorical comment on life. They were also part of a story, but in a different sense, not the story of this particular love, but the essential story of love in general. They had an ability to transcend the narrative frame in which they were conceived. There could be several reasons for this. A simple reason could be that some of the most popular songs from better Hindi films were composed by Urdu poets of considerable standing who were slowly drawn into the capacious network of the film industry in Bombay. Composing for films probably gave them a highly remunerative but relatively undemanding occupation, leaving them free thereafter to simply be poets, rather than overworked office drudges.

In many cases, I can believe that the creative urges of these writers went into the composition of even rather mundane film songs. In many cases, these songs survived after they performed their more limited, contextual purpose of advancing a particular story. Afterwards, they achieved something like a cult status as free-standing cultural items, only slightly humbler than Urdu ghazals, or Tagore songs—but vastly more popular. In part, this was helped by the loose structure of the average popular Bombay film. Although the various parts formed an interconnected whole, as a film, some of these parts could also be enjoyed as independent artefacts, de-linked from the connectedness of the film structure. The need for an aesthetic of the crowded, teeming, fast-moving city was deeply rooted in the circumstances of Indian modernity. Such songs gave to people who lived rather impoverished lives a lilting language that achieved a miraculous 'transfiguration of the commonplace'.

There is a second, related, point, which is linked to larger questions. The fact that items like this song could subsist as freestanding cultural objects—like poems, or songs in a superior artistic culture—was precisely because through these aesthetic processes a new aesthetic structure was being formed. This was an aesthetic structure in a narrower, technically structuralist theoretical sense—a stock of resources which were like elements for improvising acts of recombination—a cultural combinatory of the modern sensibility which managed to find a strangely joyous description of the grim city while recognizing its sordidness.

Thus the song could be said to have two entirely different contexts of meaningfulness. It emerged from a more immediate, closed context of the film narrative, which imparted to it its meaning, and in which the song in turn contributed to the total structure of meaningfulness of the film's signifying success as a complex structural form. But it was also part of a second structure of meaningfulness—more relevant for our present discussion—about the aesthetic perception of the city in films. This song formed part of an entire repertoire of popular songs, mostly taken from the films, in which each song with its idiosyncratic sequencing of words, internal economy of images, mood, became a supporting neighbour to others of a similar kind. This poetry and these songs were not from the same films, or from identical narratives, or composed by the same poets. But taken together, each of them advanced by slow and peculiar steps an aesthetic description and elaboration of the experience of modernity, and at its centre, of the taste of city life. They were linked—not as parts of a single narrative, but rather of a single aesthetic.

I shall now turn to the song in greater detail to substantiate my point, and then go on to argue that this aesthetic interpretation of the city has important points of distinctiveness, and its collective 'sense' of the city is vastly different from the more self-consciously artistic aesthetic of modern poetry. It is through these songs, forming an aesthetic series or combinatory, that the inhabitant of the modern city formed an expressive language of his emotions and moods, and his ultimate reception of this life-world. Most significantly, as I shall argue later on, they made it possible to view the modern city as a place of joy—limited, contradictory, yet in an ultimate sense pleasurable.

The text of the lyric runs as follows:

Yeh hai Bombay meri jaan
Ay dil hai mushkil jina yahan (refrain)
Zara hatke zara bachke yeh hai Bombay meri jaan.

Kahin building kahin tramen kahin motor kahin mill
Milta hai yahan sabkuch ik milta nahi dil.
Insan ka nahin naam o nishan,
Zara hatke zara bachke yeh hai Bombay meri jaan,
CH: *Ay dil hai mushkil jina yahan . . .*

Kahin satta kahin patta kahin chori kahin race,
Kahin daka kahin faka kahin thokar kahin thes.
Bekaron ke hain kayi kaam yahan,
Zara hatke zara bachke yeh hai Bombay meri jaan,
CH: *Ay dil hai mushkil jina yahan . . .*

Beghar ko awara yahan kahte hans hans,
Khud katen gale sabke kahe isko bisnes (business).
Ik chiz ke hai kayi naam yahan,
Zara hatke zara bachke yeh hai Bombay meri jaan,
CH: *Ay dil hai mushkil jina yahan . . .*

(feminine voice)

Bura (?) duniya voh hai kahta aisa bhola to na ban,
Jo hai karta voh hai bharta, yeh yahan ka hai chalan.
Dadagiri nahin chalne ki yahan
Yeh hai Bombay, yeh hai Bombay, yeh hai Bombay meri jaan,
(male voice)
Ay dil hai mushkil jina yahan,
Zara hatke zara bachke yeh hai Bombay meri jaan.
(female voice)
Ay dil hai asan jina yahan
Suno bandhu, suno Mister, yeh hai Bombay meri jaan.

CH: My heart, it is difficult to live in this place,

Move aside, watch out, this is Bombay, my love.

Buildings, trams, motors and mills—
Everything's here but a human heart.
Not a trace of a human being
Move aside, watch out, this is Bombay, my love.

CH:

Speculation, gambling, thieving, racing
Robberies, skipping meals, kicks, blows.
The jobless have a lot to do here,
Move aside, watch out, this is Bombay, my love.

CH:

People laugh at the homeless as at madmen
They themselves cut everyone's throat, that's called business.
Every single thing here bears many names . . .
Move aside, watch out, this is Bombay, my love.

CH:

(feminine voice)

He calls the world bad, don't be so childish
Here the law is: you reap what you sow.
Bullying will not do here
This is Bombay, this is Bombay, this is Bombay, my love.

(male voice)

My heart, it is difficult to live in this place,
Move aside, watch out, this is Bombay, my love.

(female voice)

It is easy to live here
Listen friend, listen Mister, this is Bombay, my love.

The two most striking aspects of the song are its lyrics and its tune. Since I am not qualified to comment on it musically, my analysis will remain restricted mainly to its poetic elements. As I had pointed out in the earlier essay referred to (Kaviraj, 1998), there is considerable poetic artifice in the lyric. Even for a song, it starts with a pleasing abruptness, and its first sense of the city is almost a tactile feeling of its bustling, crowded dynamism. It instantly communicates the bodily rhythms of a person walking through a crowded Indian city—full of unruly, jostling crowds on the pavements and traffic on the streets.

Yet its crowdedness is unthreatening: it creates an atmosphere of anonymity within which the romantic couple can enjoy the strange seclusion of a romantic exchange. The enunciator of the song says you have to twist, turn, stop, give way—because this is no ordinary town: *yeh hai Bombay meri jaan* (this is Bombay, my love), instantly creating a sense of the incomparability of Bombay, the paradigmatic metropolis. And Bombay's incomparability is constantly followed by the refrain stating: my heart, it is hard/difficult to live here (*ay dil hai mushkil jina yahan*).

The life-world of modernity turns into a struggle—not to live well, just to live—'un-adjectived' living, which should be the simplest activity of all. The song goes on immediately to set up a deliberate contrast between the modern and the natural. In the city there are buildings, trams, cars and mills, and it is hardly an accident that these are all referred to by their English names—*kahin building, kahin tramen, kahin motor, kahin mill.* Evidently, these are things not available outside the magic world of Bombay—they are absent in the countryside.

This is followed instantly by a sharp comment on the heartlessness of the city—*milta hai yahan sab kuch, ik milta nahi dil.* Everything is available here except the human heart. And this heartlessness is matched by the city's general deceptiveness—*ik chiz ke hai kayi naam yahan*—every single thing goes by several names. The city's defining characteristic is the difference, in paradigmatically Marxist terms, between appearance and reality, and its deep deceptiveness. Here people deceive each other smiling all the while, merchants cut throats and 'call it business', and those without homes or shelter are accused of being feckless tramps. In some Hindi films, particularly those by Raj Kapoor, the figure of the tramp in Chaplin is taken up with modifications as the 'natural' carrier of such an outsider's vision.

There is also a subtle exchange between the two figures in the song, though in the dialogical structure, the presence of the feminine voice is asymmetric. She says very little; but brevity is compensated by the enormous power of her interjections. She cuts into the dolorous recitation of the city's lack of faith only twice. The first occasion is a triumph of composing technique: when we expect her to simply repeat the refrain 'it is difficult to live in this place', she says with unexpected, wonderful, sparkling irony, a sense of luminously optimistic surprise —*ay dil, hai asan jina yahan* (my heart, it is easy to live here). When we expect her to confirm the repetitive theme that it is hard to live here, she unexpectedly says the opposite. The sharp and brief sentence is not amplified. We are left to surmise: is this precisely because of the thousand excuses and occasions for deception? Is the city a great unbounded space of a lowly form of freedom, but freedom all the same, for a De Certeu-esque game of disappearance from social invigilation and political control, the sordid pleasure of 'tactics'? Does the city allow people to hide—to fall in love in its vast and comforting anonymity? Does it make it possible to find a living, using its many opportunities? The second time, the same voice cuts into the song, taking the element of levity even further. I am sure the intended meaning here is to convey a certain streetwise intimacy: the woman calls her man *suno Mister, suno bandhu* (pal/buddy), *yeh hai Bombay meri jaan.*

What is remarkable in the lyric is a kind of critical sensibility of the city which sympathizes with the downtrodden, the fallen, the destitute. One suspects that this is the view of no common poor man, but the highly educated, high-cultured, lower-middle-class protagonist of modern Indian literature, the central, dominating figure of its poetry and novels. He is a strange and potent mixture of achievement and misfortune—educated, cultured, highly sophisticated in his social and aesthetic sensibility, yet always short of money, and acutely sensitive to the constant threat of indignity. He does not face the city with the numbness, despair and deceit associated with the ordinary poor. He faces the city with indignation and a highly refined sense of cultural violation. Both these features—moral indignation and aesthetic distaste—are conditional on possession of standards by which to judge the world; only a possessor of clearly defined moral principles, and equally clear aesthetic standards would feel these emotions against the modern city. Therefore, he uses a strange set of 'weapons of the weak': not foot-dragging, stealth, shortchanging; his weapons are high principle, irony, aesthetics. He has the great rare gift of turning his humiliation into poetry. He has the unmatched weapon, as long as the conflict is in the arena of culture, of middle-class eloquence.

Purely textually too we find an interesting structure of consciousness in the lyric. Remarkably, the lyric does not counterpose the city—the space of deprivation, deceit and defilement—with an idealized space of the pastoral idyll of the village unspoilt by history.[1] The subtler current of thought running through the song is closer to a kind of humanist Marxism. Its imagic economy is very similar to Marx's analyses in the *Economic Philosophical Manuscripts*, in the famous sections on alienated labour and the power of money in bourgeois society. The 'badness' of the city is contrasted not to the 'goodness' of the village, which Marxists would have found reactionary and nostalgic, but with a 'natural' condition of man. Interestingly, from this natural condition of fullness and un-alienation both the poor and the rich are estranged: the poor are ground into degradation, the rich are mired in deceit.

Accordingly, the song demonstrates a suitably popular version of what Marxists would have called a Feuerbachian general humanism. What it misses in the city is not a rural, traditional ethic, but a general humanistic sympathy: there is no sign of the general sign of 'man' (*insan ka nahin naam o nishan*); and man in this naturalist sense is marked by the heart, which is the only thing that Bombay cannot offer (*milta hai yahan sabkuch, ik milta nahi dil*). The reason I associate this critical sensibility with the wide genealogy of Marxist thought is due precisely to its absence of a nostalgic relation with a rural past—it spurns that route as sentimentality, and firmly contrasts the degrading present of rising capitalism with a natural condition of humanity.

There is also a startling presence of the voice, which if not directly radical, carries a suspicion of subalternity, all the more surprising because it is a feminine voice, which turns the usual expectation of roles upside down. Literary studies have shown conclusively that in the artistic literary reflection of the colonial world, the voice of rational control, or of rational understanding of the external—particularly city—world, is a male voice. Rationalistic figures are primarily male figures. Women are generally associated with sentimentality and sustenance, occasionally with an invincible instinct for survival or protection of their children. But women are usually not the carriers of a sly knowledge of the city and its vast world of power and opportunities. They are never at home in the modern.

Here the feminine voice in the film song is refreshingly different— not merely from the standard enunciations of the literary values of femininity, but also from the disillusion expressed by the primary male voice about Bombay itself. Her four lines therefore deserve more careful analysis. The city produces a new, soiled kind of intelligence: and in some strikingly exceptional instances, at least in literature, this sly street wisdom is carried by women characters.

This stanza expresses some fairly complex judgements: unfortunately, the world we are thrown into is a bad world. But its ways, at least in the fallen city of Bombay, lays down that those who do the work reap the benefits, and fate does not rule people's lives. In the startling concluding turn, the woman declares a great and paradoxical truth about the city—*hai asan jina yahan*—this makes it easy to live here. And the two words of 'Mister' and *bandhu* are also characteristic urban words of address. So the woman's lines in a sense agree with what the main voice of the song says about Bombay, but also asks the man to see the city as a space of contradiction, and to get reconciled to its other side—learning to live in this city, not by compromising his principles. To my sensibility, shaped no doubt by the tastes of Bengali *bhadralok* high literature, the two words of address appear a bit odd; but their meaning is unmistakable.

I now wish to take this reading in a more general direction. My reading of the lines has been frankly excessively literary, in fact, literary in two senses. First, I read it outside the narrative frame of the film, which I never saw. Second, I also read merely the words, in effect analysing what I converted from a song into a poem. But even as a lay listener, I find some features of its musical composition interesting. First, the tune contains a subtle parodic element. If we listen carefully, we begin to hear the familiar western song, 'O my darling Clementine'. This opens up a potentially vast and interesting subject—of imitation, mimicry, modification, and appropriation, and the meanings of all these different cultural acts. Is this an act of borrowing, stealing, imitating? Does this signify exaggerated respect, an inability to produce one's own art? Or does this demonstrate a strange assurance which can deftly pick up a well-known piece of artistic creation and displace its meaning by highly deliberate modification? Does this demonstrate dependence of the cultural imagination, or a playful and confident creative subjectivity?

The composer has employed a technique that is not rare in Hindi film music. He has quickened the tempo and changed the tune ever so slightly, to yield a very different rasa—structure of feeling. Despite obvious similarities, users of rasa theory would not find it hard to demonstrate that the rasa-sensibility is different. The mood of the song is quick, witty, there is a sense of joyous enjoyment of the city's crowds and the rapid rhythms of its street life. By the change of pace, he has miraculously changed the meaning and the predominant colour of feeling. I call this relation 'parodic' in the sense that it picks up a very well-known cultural object, takes it out of its settled, familiar context, and by making it do something unusual, changes its meaning completely. Yet the fresh meaning is not an unsuccessful pretence: it is a successful creation of a new meaning which is grasped, as the vast popularity of the tune showed, by the ordinary filmgoer across the entire country.

There is an equally impish and daring example of similar parodic appropriation of a famous European tune in Salil Chowdhury's com-position of another film song: *itna na mujhse tu pyar badha* which is taken from Mozart's Symphony no. 40 in G Minor and altered in tempo. Anyone familiar with the original tune cannot escape a sense of wondrous enjoyment of the displacement of meaning.[2]

However, I am not an ideal listener for the song; let us bring the appreciation of the song closer to a more standard understanding of its ideal audience, made up of people who are habitual Hindi filmgo-ers, who know the actors, and the playback singers. What would they make of this song? How would they receive its various aspects? The reception of the song is a fairly complex affair. The narrative charac-ters in the films performed their task of artistic enchantment by a deft combination of the familiar and the unfamiliar. Narrative characters are evidently recognized as belonging to types. Their power of aes-thetic signification is at least in part drawn from this fact. Yet every story, however conventional and following narrative formulae, in the modern literary context, must have a quality of unrepeatedness, of being told for the first time, and contain a sense of surprise. The sur-prise operates within a general structure of recognition. We may have seen many films of revenge, but a particular story is different in par-ticulars, though we can, from the structure of the plot, from the way the actions are arranged in its narrative composition, deduce fairly accurately what the resolution at the end is likely to be.

The enjoyment of narrative is a strange combination of the reassurance of such iterative patterns and surprise of the particular. In addition to these literary-narrative features of reassurance, or what can be called aspects of recognition, in films, there are other techniques of recognition. The specific characters of the story are new to the audience, but they fall into recognition by the casting of the actors. Acclaimed heroes and heroines of the Hindi popular films perform this function very strongly and very often. Even before the spectators have come into the film theatre, the simple association of an actress with a particular role creates a structure of fore-meanings and narrative expectations, which the actual unfolding of the film plot hermeneutically changes and confirms at the same time. The actress's association with a certain standard type of role is created by a long and repetitive association with roles whose characteristic attributes she is acknowledged to bring out particularly well. Thus the complex narrative experience of the filmgoer is not the sensation of being open to an unfamiliar, entirely unpredictable run of events, convolution of plots, forming of characters. It is a more complex sensation of enjoyment in which along with these elements of unpredictability and surprise, there are equally strong elements of recognition or aesthetic repetition—seeing the same face, meeting one's favourite actor or actress—and above all a confirmation in the coloured, charged, heightened universe of imagination of the moral structure of the social world.

A second element of recognition occurs in film songs. The lyrics and their narrative frame of course are new—which offer the element of surprise. But the fact that a well-known playback singer like Mohammed Rafi or Mukesh sings it balances it with recognition—producing the peculiar work of aesthetic enchantment in the song itself.

Finally, I would make a large and speculative suggestion about this entire series of elements of recognition in the cultural universe of Nehruvian India. The films in their generally recognized and well understood interconnection with supporting structures like the narrative economy of the world of novels, the poetic universe of lyrics, the imagic economy from assorted visual sources, produced a whole structure that acts as a complex but single aesthetic unity. I shall call it loosely an aesthetic of the city—the general sense of what 'the city' is.

This aesthetic sense is produced in various ways: first, it is produced by this combination of the single narrative, specific song, individual actors, etc. inside the single film. Each single film sends a message to the audience about what life in the city is as a possibility. But I am concerned with making a larger structuralist point. It is not merely the signifying relations between its dissimilar elements—the story, the acting, the songs, the stream of images inside the film—which constitute a unity. Each song forms a link, a part of a syntagmatic chain with other songs that speak about the joys and frustrations of urban love, forming a musical aesthetic of the city. Equally, this is done by the lyrics and the images. Eventually, since the spectator or the recipient is a repetitive consumer of separate but linked aesthetic discourse, the collective, iterative, total impact creates a general, overarching common aesthetic.

I wish now to briefly compare this aesthetic of the city in the popular Hindi films with the aesthetic in high literature. My comparison has obvious difficulties. The Hindi film has a particular cultural habitus—a combination of the cultural styles from North Indian poetry and theatre combined with an experiential perception of the city drawn primarily from the bustling commercial metropolis of Bombay. The poetic aesthetic I am comparing it with is from Bengali literature, produced by poets of the generation after Tagore, a poetry of a deep moral scepticism and disillusionment. But there is some justification for this contrast, as both groups of people are artists engaged in thinking aesthetically about India's modernity, and they are living at roughly the same historical time.

From its inception, Bengali high literature developed a contradictory relationship with the city. In some ways, the modern life of the mind required the environment of the city as its condition of production. Most of the great literary writers—Bankimchandra Chattopadhyay, Rabindranath Tagore, Saratchandra Chattopadhyay—were city dwellers. It was clearly the new kind of social and intellectual life of their city, Calcutta, which gave them the intellectual, moral and social sustenance from which their literary work emerged.

Yet, dwelling in the city did not always convince them that the colonial form of modernity offered by the city was above criticism.

Bankimchandra did not write disparagingly of Calcutta in his novelistic writings, but in one of his long and influential humorous pieces,
Muchiram Guder Jibancharit—the satirical life of a scoundrel who rose
irresistibly to eminence in colonial society—Calcutta and other towns
figure prominently. The satire is primarily about the inversion of values in colonial public life and institutions, but as these institutions—
the courts and government offices—are mainly located in cities, these
get an indirect lashing of the sarcasm of Bankim's humorous writing.

And although indirect, and secondary, the narrative establishes a
central theme of Bengali writing about the city. The city is a space of
travesty. It is the space in which modern principles, values, institutions, modes of life, unfold, but always in a travestied form. They are
never true to their abstract principles, or even the institutional or
practical form these values acquire in Europe's modernity. The forms
these principles, values and the characters embodying them have in
Calcutta are in some ways a caricature of the original—just as Bengali
modernity is a caricature of the modernity of the West.

In doing this, Bankim was in one sense continuing an earlier satirical tradition in Bengali writing, and in other ways transforming it.
From the rise of the modern city of Calcutta, the social and moral con-
duct of the modern elites and middle classes who resided in the city—
referred to by the collective appellation 'babu'—was a target of traditional farcical forms. In early Bengali literature, some highly talented
authors like Kaliprasanna Sinha extended this tradition of satirical
sketches and comments into a literary tradition of acerbic comment on
the imitative excesses of the new parasitic urban elite.

Although this kind of comment always implies social criticism, the
early writing on the city was mainly marked by its sense of fun at the
expense of the babus and its general tone of light-heartedness. In
Bankim's hands, the lightheartedness is continued, and the babu
remains a butt of fun; but underlying that surface sparkle of gaiety, a
new highly serious historical judgement is subtly introduced. This
judgement indicates that it is wrong to repose great faith in the future
achievements of Bengali modernity, because the relation between its
European exemplars and their Bengali re-enactment is one of travesty. Evidently, this already forms a sufficiently dark background out of

which more deep-lying and melancholic critiques of the modern city could emerge.

Tagore's relation with the city was predominantly one of aesthetic rejection. In his mature works, on many occasions, writing about the city in his poetry, he tries to show that the city cannot find a poetry of its own, because the city in its sordidness does not deserve poetry. His poems are therefore written with their back turned on the city they are talking about: their dominant urge is one of escape into nature, into the countryside, less frequently into a highly coloured romantic past. He is capable of writing wonderful poetry about the hazy cities of the past in which Kalidasa's heroines lived their lives, of a wonderfully mythical Ujjaini; but Calcutta was undeserving and incapable of a lyrical celebration of itself.

In poetry after Tagore, several highly talented poets continued this tone of negative reflection on the city, but with one highly significant difference. In Tagore, escapes from this city were primarily of three types—into imagination and dreams, into the unspoilt nature of the countryside, and into nostalgia. The new poets of the 40s cut off all these routes of escape. They consequently forced the reading public to face the dirt and meaninglessness of the city quite squarely—not as a passing phase, not as a small part of a larger green, beautiful world, but as the undeniable, inescapable present, as the only world there is.

This sense of a claustrophobic space gradually finds two types of poetic enunciation. The more aesthetically sophisticated presentation of this new aesthetic of the city came in the wonderfully colourful imagery of despair in Jibanananda Das, whose visual sensibility constantly prowls the city, specially at night when it is deserted and exhausted, when the crowds have disappeared, when the city gives up, in a sense, its vast, dark, despairing truth. Das's poetry is an aesthetic wonder, because his weaving of words makes this despondent nightmare as beautiful as dreams. But despite everything, despite the immensely exciting craft, the amazing surprise of his imagery, the subtle, tired cadence of the understated meter, the city remains a space of despair.

To take a single typical example, which raises a complicated question about love and fulfilment, one of Das's best known poems,

'Banalata Sen', is about a woman once met in the past, now lost. In painting her face, Das wrote the unforgettable lines: *'chul tar kabekar andhakar bidishar nisha, mukh tar avantir karukarya'*—'her hair the ancient darkness of the night in Bidisha city, her face the sculpture of the past city of Avanti.' She is eventually lost, and constantly returns in memory—not, like a similar figure in Tagore ('Kshanika') to comfort but to hurt.

The present, the immediate, is entirely enclosed in the claustrophobic space of Calcutta with its subtle and ineradicable curse, where everything beautiful is transient, awaiting decomposition and death. Death, decay, the corpse eaten by birds of prey, is a constant theme in Jibanananda, as in the other famous image in his poetry—deer playing in a forest clearing in the improbably bright light of stars; but these deer are destined for slaughter; what eventually ends the idyll is the sharp, final, snap of a rifle shot ringing through that enchanted night.

In Das's poetry, love is constantly present, constantly stalked by a stealthy, confident, unavoidable death. In the themes we found in Tagore, images of love are always linked in a great tenderness of words to the past, to memory, to nature which lives serenely outside the city, and to dreams. But clearly, all these things—the past, the unspoilt countryside, nature—are transient, threatened, ultimately brought to submission by the city.

A second strand of poetic reflection on the city developed alongside this one, animated by a powerful induction of communist ideology into Bengali culture. But the communist poets' sense of the city is not very different from the gloomy despair of Jibanananda. To take a characteristic example, Samar Sen, an acclaimed young leftist poet in the 1950s, saw the city very similarly—as a space of inevitable unfulfilment. And since love is such a shining emblem of fulfilment in earlier poetic aesthetics, this poetry shows a strangely perverse delight in soiling these traditional themes, images and at times even well-known lines taken straight out of Tagore, continuing the tradition of parody, but with a further twist. The parody does not remain a vehicle of laughter as in Bankim, it turns vicious and primarily bears a print of melancholy. Women, still carriers of a remembered beauty in

Jibanananda, become simply objects of lust; in Sen's poetry the space of Calcutta is surprisingly teeming with prostitutes. Some of Sen's lines show the working of the social sensibility behind this aesthetic with exceptional clarity: the figure of the *ganika*, the woman who can be bought, returns endlessly to haunt the poetic imagination, in the final travesty of love—she 'loves' him for the precise minutes for which the price has been paid. Samar Sen's poetry is also admirably explicit about the subject of this poetic enunciation and this sense of the city: this is the *madhyabitta*, the highly educated lower middle class male who is equipped with a cultural sensibility which can never find fulfilment in Calcutta's economic and social world.

By the 1940s, this educated lower middle class had grown to a considerable size; and they were in any case the primary audience, the aesthetic consumers, of this poetic discourse. By the 1950s both the sociological and cultural developments conspired to ensure the utter dominance of this 'sense of the city' in Bengali literature to the exclusion of others. However, this connection between the sociological structure of the city and the enjoyment of its poetic aesthetics also restricted the frontiers of this sensibility. The city may have been culturally dominated by the lower middle class, but city experience was obviously more diverse. Ironically, the poor in the city did not necessarily share this gloomy sense of the city and its place in history. In economic terms, the income of different classes is a dominant consideration; but in the sociology of economic life it is the direction of movement of economic fortunes that is more important in creating a certain kind of collective sensibility. Other classes in the city did not necessarily share the historical melancholy of the educated lower middle class. The city for most people was a far more mixed and complex arena of experience. It certainly produced hopelessness and despair, but it was also a space in which anonymity gave a sense of freedom from restrictive village customs; it was enjoyed by most characters in the films as a context in which genuine love could be experienced against the deterrents of deprivation, and social and cultural taboos.

It is interesting to contrast these two sharply different rhetorical pictures of the city, and reflect about their different social and aesthetic associations. Descriptively, some of the associations are obvious.

First, there is the contrast between a self-consciously 'high artistic' language and comportment of the literary poetic writing. Writers like Jibanananda were engaging in a highly reflexive artistic enterprise in which the attention to form, the crafting of language and mood were paramount; whether the poetry was generally intelligible was a far lesser consideration. Some of the poets, engaging in self-interpretation, pointed out, quite rightly, that the intelligibility of poetry was a matter of familiarity of conventions. Complaints of unintelligibility against modern, post-Tagore poetry often stemmed from the fact that the new poetic form or diction was unfamiliar rather than inherently obscure. Once used to the new diction (in Bengali often they used the term *uccharan*), the audience would begin to enjoy the new poetry and its unconventional linguistic surprises.

The rhetoric of the popular Hindi films, precisely because they were a constituent part of popular culture, entirely dependent on commercial success, could not take such high risks in terms of formal characteristics. That does not mean that there was not considerable craft in the making of the different aspects of these films. The literary elements of the films, in particular, though less visible and subordinated to commercial-popular elements, retained an aspiration to relative autonomy. Poets contributing to them wrote serious poetry independent of the films, and sedulously cultivated their literary reputations. It is not surprising that their general poetic reflection on subjects close to their heart often found expression in these compositions as well.

A second contrast between the two images of the city is probably of greater significance. Both poetry and popular films gave rise to specific aesthetic structures with very different readings of the meanings of city life. For the high artistic poetic discourse the image of the city is a dark one, where lives are unfulfilled and people go through the subtle defilement of their everyday existence. This is reflected in the strange delight that some poets have in the defilement of earlier objects of high art. Samar Sen, for instance, constantly brings up celebrated lines and images from Tagore to mock, to parody, and to defile. This sense of the city could not be a general, universal rhetoric precisely because of its narrow, partial focus on the city's deprivations.

It could only be a poetic sense which was appreciated by a relatively highly educated, middle class minority, who had the cultural skills to understand its subtleties and the social position to experience the nearness of this particular despair.

By contrast, the cinematic image of the city is more complex; it contains the dark image, but this is constantly relieved by an opposite image of hope and optimism—as in the counterpoint of the feminine statement that it is easy to live in the city, in the lift of the pleasurable, optimistic tune of the song, in the general narrative structures of urban love. The filmic representation might be less self-consciously artistic, prone to a melodramatic simplification of emotions, but, from a different point of view, its image of the city was of a space of contradictions—where different things took place—not just of constant, unremitting despair. Unlike the high artistic portrayal of Calcutta, the Bombay of the films was, in this respect, in subtle, important ways, a city of joy.

Notes

1 For a similar discussion about the pastoral idyll of the village in Bengali partition literature, see Chakrabarty, 2002.

2 Salil Chowdhury's song occurs in a film called *Chhaya* and was sung by a very popular singer, Talat Mahmood.

References

Chakrabarty, Dipesh (2002), *Habitations of Modernity*, Chicago University Press, Chicago.

Kaviraj, Sudipta (1998), 'The Culture of Representative Democracy', in P. Chatterjee (ed.), *Wages of Freedom: Fifty Years of the Indian Nation-State*, Oxford University Press, New Delhi.

Lath, Mukund (1998), *Transformation as Creation*, Aditya Prakashan, New Delhi.

REALISM AND FANTASY IN REPRESENTATIONS OF METROPOLITAN LIFE IN INDIAN CINEMA

M. MADHAVA PRASAD

Literature on cities has since the 19th century been centrally preoccupied with one grand theme: the ceaseless conflict of interests between two opposed energies, embodied, on the one hand, in the transparent city that planners and administrators, architects and utopianists dream of bringing into being, and on the other, in the dense, obscure, opaque lived city of human experience. The spaces of the city are a site where struggles between opposing forces and desires, hopes and projections, are played out—confrontations between a governing will and a resistant population or between classes, rulers and ruled. Michel de Certeau, looking down at New York from the top of the World Trade Center, contrasted the Concept City, seen from a godly perspective, and characterized above all by its high visibility, to the city of experience which lies just on the other side of visibility, in the activities of what he calls the ordinary practitioners of the city who live down below, below the thresholds at which visibility begins. 'They walk . . . they are walkers . . . whose bodies follow the thicks and thins of an urban text they write without being able to read it.' The great 19th century novels portray this living city, capturing in an exuberant prose, as in Dickens, the density and confusion, the impenetrable complexity of the city, in tales that are often premised on the idea that this is a moral confusion, a failure of reformist will. The anxiety produced by this metropolitan excess gives rise to the figure of the detective, a la Sherlock Holmes, who is capable of seeing through the London fog and reasoning his way through the indecipherable, dangerous neighbourhoods inhabited by criminals, the unemployed and the outcast. It also gives rise to the figure of the Baudelairean *flaneur*, who revels in the city's sights and spaces, acceding to its overpowering sensual effects and thereby gaining room for a private enjoyment of its disorder. Holmes represents the vertical, penetrating, controlling, organizing gaze of governance,[1] whereas the *flaneur* resides on the same plane as the others, charting a horizontal, zig-zag course through a diversity of signs and activities that he takes in with a detached eye but makes no attempt to control or clarify.

Another theme that figures equally often in the literature is that of the country and the city, the relationship, both complementary and conflictual, between rural and urban. Here the city's own internal complexity is bracketed away in order to highlight its position within a larger economic, social, cultural and political geography. This is the city as an expansionary force, devouring the other and reconstructing it in its own image. In Henri Lefebvre's words, 'Urban life penetrates peasant life, dispossessing it of its traditional features: crafts, small centres which decline to the benefit of urban centres . . . Villages become ruralized by losing their peasant specificity.' (Lefebvre, 1996:119).

Two perspectives, internal and external: (i) the city in itself, internally split into a rational grid aspiring to a universal rationality, and the everyday life, with its teeming diversity, which defies this logic. And (ii) the city in its external aspect, in its relation to its other, again has two dimensions: firstly, the city as site of attractions, exercising what social scientists call the pull factor, a place to go to, an object of imagination and fantasy; and second, the city as a logic of urbanization, which extends beyond the territorial limits of the city proper and transforms the other—the country—into an extension of itself, giving rise, as Lefebvre puts it, to a ruralized countryside.

Since we are dealing with narrative cinema and its representations of metropolitan life, it is appropriate that we should focus, at the outset, on what appears to be an intimate relation between the city and the logic of fictional representation. James Donald, writing on cities and cinema, remarks: 'The modern(ist) metropolis and the institutions of cinema come into being at about the same time' (Donald, 1995). Even if it is not immediately clear precisely what significance Donald attaches to this coincidence, I believe it is possible to posit a certain logic of fictional representation, not confined to the cinema but also applicable to it. Simply stated, this is a logic which manifests itself as a limit to representability, i.e., fictional tales can be located in real cities, but not in real villages. Indeed, the vast majority of fictions which take place in urban settings employ the spaces of existing cities, except in utopias which are anyway imagined as alternatives to existing reality. The city, by nature, is capable of containing, without loss of credibility, an infinity of fictional characters and events. This is because a city is experienced as a space inhabited by a *population*, whose numbers can be counted more or less accurately, but whose mutual relationships cannot be easily specified. In urban spaces, individuals encounter each other as strangers, reified entities, whose position in a social network cannot be known immediately. A face in the crowd can be substituted by any other.[2] A village, where every individual's position in the social network is clearly marked, has no dummy places, no empty seats where fictional characters can be placed. The fictional village has to be invented wholesale. Conversely, even if one were to present all the details of a particular existing village in a fictional account, the same logic would make us read it as a fictional one, as a metaphor for the village. One of the consequences of what Lefebvre terms ruralization and the resultant loss of peasant specificity could be that the village too becomes a stretchable entity, equipped with transferable places, occupied by substitutable individuals: fictional characters. But by and large, this constraint still governs fictional representation, making the village a metaphorical entity and the city a space of infinite metonymy. Modern fiction—whether as novel or narrative film—has a congenital intimacy with the urban.

Thus the city is the pre-eminent space of representation(s). It is the seat of power, from where political representation realizes itself, it is where the last word on justice is spoken, where the complex economic activity of the surrounding territory is sought to be represented, with more or less accuracy, in the speculations of the marketplace. The city is also, in one of its figurations, a parasitical organism,[3] feeding off the village but by the same token, it is also a superstructural phenomenon, a representation in itself, functioning as the consciousness of the land, a consciousness which the peasants ('a sack of potatoes') cannot have. That is what explains the common sense, productive of many narrative situations, that the village cannot *know* the city in the way the city can know the village. Modifying Marx's famous remark, we might say that 'the village cannot represent itself, it must be represented.' In two senses: (i) it must be represented by/in the city and (ii) (in fiction) it must be represented by another village.

For popular Hindi cinema the metropolis of choice has always been Bombay.[4] From *Miss Frontier Mail* (dir. Homi Wadia, 1936) to *Satya* (dir. Ram Gopal Varma, 1998), Hindi cinema's narrative geography, which is otherwise extremely unspecific, incorporates, as a significant turn in the plot, the event of 'going to Bombay.'[5] The city itself figures with varying degrees of specificity, a variance that can be explained in terms of both technological developments making possible a greater investment in realism, as well as the particular genre of film that is in question. A standard device involves showing a montage of Bombay's famed tourist spots and other landmarks as the protagonists enter the city (e.g. *Nau do Gyarah*, dir. Vijay Anand, 1957) or a more disturbing montage of the city's dangerous seductions, for which, naturally, what could be more effective than a quick scanning of a series of film posters and banners accompanied by a loud and fast-paced [Mohammed] Rafi song (as in *Guddi*, dir. Hrishikesh Mukherjee, 1971). The cinema's constant and overwhelming presence, in the form of posters, of songs blaring from a variety of sources everywhere, of crowds in front of theatres—these are as crucial to the cinematic evocation of the big city as anything else.

Paradoxically, the choice of Bombay as the default metropolis in the popular Hindi cinema is indicative of, among other things, the *metaphorical* status that the 'city' occupies within an imaginary that always, compulsively, invokes the city as part of the city-country dyad. Wherever this paradigm prevails, the term 'Bambai' serves to signify the generic metropolitan other, rather than the specific entity that the city of Mumbai is. The location of the film industry there also contributes to the consolidation of this association, as if reinforcing the metaphorical, symbolic dimension by a self-referential twist. It is as if any other city, even Delhi, would be too specific, too resistant to the symbolic logic involved in the representational practices of popular cinema: to say that someone upped and went to Bombay seems self-explanatory: it simply means that they migrated from the country to the city; to say they went to Delhi or Calcutta is to immediately beg the question, 'Why there?' Bombay is Bombay plus The City. Other cities lack this double status as far as the Hindi cinema is concerned.

Leaving aside such standard minimal references to 'going to Bombay' which are a staple of the Hindi film, we could possibly identify two significant cinematic Bombays which have a more than perfunctory presence. These two Bombays have much in common but their difference lies both in their visual quality and narrative functionality. Let us simply call them the Bombay of the 50s and that of the 70s and after. The relationship of characters to the cityscape, the way the city figures, as metaphor as well as site of unfolding of events, in effect the city as horizon of a representational project: all undergo a significant transformation as we move from one to the other, a shift that must be assumed to relate to the changing aesthetic concerns of the Bombay cinema as much as to the social transformations that have altered the image of the city in public discourse.

The first Bombay, which the song *'yeh hai Bombay meri jaan*—'this is Bombay, my love' (*CID*, dir. Raj Khosla 1956)—immediately evokes for the average Hindi film viewer, is a city of pleasure and danger, of a thrilling anonymity as well as distressing inequality, both joyous and fearsome (see Kaviraj, in this volume), a space where class conflict is a dominant thematic concern. We may include here the well-known examples like *Shree 420* as well as the films of a group of filmmakers—Guru Dutt, the Anand brothers, Raj Khosla—who specialized in a *noir*-ish cityscape that defined one of the distinctive sub-genres of the 50s. Sudipto Kaviraj's essay on the culture of representative democracy offers an interesting reading of the song where he argues that it 'evokes the culture of the first historical stage of modern Indian democracy' (Kaviraj, 1998:154), showing the *'representativeness* of the

Nehruvian democratic experiment' (Kaviraj, 1998:155), contrasting representation in this sense with the more risky (for the elites) prospect of delegation. The politics of representation, with reformist members of the elite constituting the leadership, is indeed a dominant thematic focus of many of these films, even though the Guru Dutt–Anand brothers tendency probably portrayed a less easily reformable world. One can see the reformism at work in *Shree 420* obviously, where the stranger who comes into town becomes a friend of the people. Here representativeness also reveals its double nature: one should not necessarily seek, within the film, thematic confirmation of the elite status of the leadership, since the star system can take care of that requirement when the character in question is a subaltern. But the more lighthearted versions of representativeness, of which the comedian Johny Walker is an emblematic figure, go a long way and can sometimes even function outside city limits as the gaze of representation, as it were: consider the film *Naya Daur* (dir. B. R. Chopra, 1957), where Johny Walker goes as a journalist to the village where a conflict is brewing between the working people and the zamindar's capitalist-minded son. Here, he becomes a friend of the workers and villagers, their means of access to the national press, his sympathy for their cause being somehow reinforced by his song : '*Mai Bambai ka babu naam mera anjana, English dhun mein gaaun main Hindustani gana.*' ('I'm a gentleman from Bombay, no one knows my name/I sing Hindustani songs set to English tunes') The anonymous 'citizen' is here sought to be embodied in the figure of the comedian, witnessing the drama on behalf of the Big Other, the Nation. Thus the benign, representative face of Bombay was always present in the imaginary of the 50s, even as the Nehruvian socialist thematics unfolded in reformist tales of class conflict.

This strain does not disappear with the 50s, but with the advent of a new narrative form in the 70s, a new Bombay makes its appearance, more vivid, dense, naked, disorienting. This Bombay can be seen in a variety of guises in films ranging from *Deewar* (dir. Yash Chopra, 1974) to *Nayakan* (dir. Mani Ratnam, 1987), *Parinda* (dir. Vidhu Vinod Chopra, 1989) and *Hathyar* (dir. J. P. Dutta, 1989), in the 80s to the recent *Satya*. It also includes films like *Gaman* (dir. Muzaffar Ali, 1978),

Chakra (dir. Rabindra Dharmaraj, 1980), *Albert Pinto ko Gussa Kyon Aata Hai* (dir. Saeed Mirza, 1980), *Ardh Satya* (dir. Govind Nihalani, 1983), *Dharavi* (dir. Sudhir Mishra, 1991) and other films usually assigned to the category known as art or 'middle cinema'. Kumar Shahani's *Tarang* (1984), where the thematics of class conflict acquire an epic dimension and are inscribed into larger national-allegorical and civilizational frameworks, nevertheless manages to evoke the concrete historical presence of working-class Bombay more vividly than other films of a sociological realist kind. Saeed Mirza has elaborated a distinctive cinematic portrait of Bombay through a series of films all set in the city. The 70s and 80s were a period in which Bombay inscribed itself into the cinematic register of urban life in its own right, coming out of the shadow of the city–country equation where the concreteness of urban existence tended to be smothered under a symbolic representation of opposed values.[6] The urban, contrasted to the rural in the nationalist schematism of, say, *Upkar* (dir. Manoj Kumar, 1967) is recovered as an independently significant object of representation by the filmmakers of these decades.[7]

Thematically, while both these sets of films share a preoccupation with crime, poverty, urban squalor and alienation, there is also a crucial difference. The popular genre deals with the underworld, and unfailingly introduces into this world an outsider, usually coming in from the country, who enters the world of crime by force of circumstance and proceeds to leave his mark on it. He is also affected irreversibly, as with every step his longing to be reunited with the maternal body, the ideal woman, the simple pleasures of village life, etc., recede further into the distance and an inevitable death awaits him at the end. The middle cinema's concerns overlap to some extent with the popular genre, but its world, stamped with the mark of realism, dwells more insistently on the world of the urban poor, their squalid lives and fantasies, the stark contrast between their everyday lives and their dreams of a better life. But here too, the characters seem always to have come from elsewhere. Of course, in terms of the statistics about rural migration to the cities, this is an empirically valid fact, but there is more to it than a straightforward reflection of contemporary realities. It is as if, in both these types of film, narrative agency or centrality of a character hinges on this supplemental datum, as if the memory of a place left behind served in some mysterious fashion to give depth to a character, to provide a crucial interiority without which there would be nothing but a statistical mass of slum-dwellers, indistinguishable from each other and figuring as numbers in some economist's calculations. In a way this little detail testifies to the difficulty that the filmmaker seems to experience in conceiving a meaningful life of the imagination for a second generation slum-dweller or petty criminal, as if when the memory of the original home has faded, the body became emptied of subjectivity.

But it also stands for a stubborn refusal to write off the past, to put it behind once and for all and blend into the new order of the modern state, a refusal to don the so-called 'veil of ignorance'. In *Deewar* a mother and two sons, deserted by the father, and carrying the traumatic memory of the father's humiliation, arrive in Bombay. The move to Bombay is cinematically effected through a calendar photo of Bombay hanging in the home of the family, the street in the photo then coming alive, with the mother and sons now walking along it. The calendar image reminds us that the city, though far away, has a place in the lives of people everywhere, as legend, as utopia, if not a secular variant of those faraway pilgrim centres which everyone hopes to visit at least once in their lifetime. A place known through its reputation and its representations is now the reality that the characters must enter. In *Parinda* (dir. Vidhu Vinod Chopra, 1989) two brothers come to the city. In *Nayakan* (dir. Mani Ratnam, 1987) a boy from southern Tamil Nadu, having stabbed a policeman who killed his father in an encounter, reaches Bombay and, in the first shot of him in the city, he is outside Victoria Station, walking away. An almost identical entry is accorded the stranger Satya in the film of the same name, except that this time, the explanatory prologue about the protagonist has been replaced by one about the city and its underworld, in the form of a voice-over urban sociology lesson accompanying shots of the city and gangster activities, which sets the scene for Satya's introduction as yet another stranger who will enter into this world. This absence of a glimpse into prehistory makes Satya all the more mysterious as the spectators are free to imagine any of a range of possible flashbacks, available from previous films. In all these films, a central character, usually the hero, joins an underworld gang. What is striking about these characters is their intense pathologization: they are tragic heroes, creatures in thrall to some memory or desire, as if their destiny had been written in one stroke at some decisive moment. *Deewar* and *Nayakan* are alike in their emphasis on the confrontation between community and state, whereas in both *Parinda* and *Satya*, the emphasis is on individual desire and longing for a normal life. *Deewar*, *Nayakan*, and *Parinda* place the characters within a moral framework, accounting for the destinies of the tragic characters to some extent by reference to the morally devious nature of their actions. *Satya*, interestingly, dispenses with this outer frame of morality, thus enhancing the pathological dimension of the character, even as it maintains and successfully communicates to us the relative moral superiority of the hero's gang in opposition to the rival's. Even the fragmentary memory of the village that infused the protagonists with a deep pathos and ultimately served as a lever to upset the other burdensome complex of memories in *Parinda* is gone. What we see, in other words, is an intensification of the pathological element, the irrational dimension, in proportion with technical sophistication: as if an enhanced realism (aided by technological advances) had enabled Varma to dispense with the moral framework. The result is a stark portrayal where, instead of the epic confrontation between the community and the law, which earlier served as the horizon of representation, we are witness to a tragic spiral of events culminating in the extinction, at once gory and banal, of the protagonist's fantasies, as he collapses and dies in front of his terrorstricken middle-class girlfriend. Here pathology has triumphed over the *reason* that the memories of the village represent: a fateful destiny is signalled by the receding memory of the village, but at the same time, our sympathies are solicited with the aid of this testimony to a painful dislocation. For Satya, on the other hand, the memory fragment as a locus of subjectivity is replaced by romantic love in the present. In other words, what Varma has done is to create a domain of fantasy where what is desired is not the restoration of a lost pastoral bliss (standing in for the bliss of the maternal embrace, no doubt), but the achievement of an impossible 'normality', the fantasy of a romantic union which the objective image-series contradicts at every step. It is through this disjunction between reality and fantasy, which is beyond Satya's immediate grasp, that his character recovers the pathos that, in other films, was generated by the memory fragment.

In spite of these variations, however, the narratives of these films continue to be overdetermined by the theme of epic confrontation between the community and the law. In *Satya*, this confrontation simply recedes into a different plane of viewer experience and determines our reading vertically, from outside the frame of representation. The law or the state is figured here as an unsympathetic alien entity and in some films (*Deewar*), the law is seen as turning against the poor after establishing itself through a primitive accumulation at the expense of the poor. The reformist possibilities that provided an overarching framework for an earlier genre of city films has become a vast illusion by the 70s, and the politician and the police are seen to be in cahoots with the developers who are intent on razing slums to raise five star hotels. By contrast, the gangsters, whose personal lives are character-ized by an earthy simplicity, a vulnerability to cheap fantasies, the charms of illiteracy and folk wisdom, seem to be on the right side of a higher justice, whose time is yet to come. It is as if the gangster alone retains an original humanity, acting ruthlessly in his own interest, but also instinctively loyal to his comrades and kind to strangers.

From the reformist state's field of vision as the site of representa-tion, the films of the 70s and after throw us without warning into a world where the state/law survives only as a minimal outer edge of legality, and a radical disenchantment with the promises of a passive revolution has taken deep root. This was the season of the 'view from below', of life in the metropolis seen through the eyes of the under-class: beggars, vagrants, thieves, alcoholics. While the real estate developers see the city from above, in the Holmesian mode (typically from the giant glass windows of an apartment on top of a skyscraper), and imagine slums as vacant plots for construction, these outcasts have another view of the city, which gives them no power but enables them to survive for a while. This trend, which can be seen in *Zanjeer* (dir. Prakash Mehra, 1973) already, culminates in the figure of the leg-less Abdul of *Shaan* (dir. Ramesh Sippy, 1980), who speeds around town on his wheeled seat, pushing forward with his hands. Abdul sings a song, *'Aate jaate hue main sabpe nazar rakhta hun, naam Abdul hai mera sab ki khabar rakhta hun'* (I keep a watch on everyone as I move about, my name is Abdul and I keep track of everybody). Characters like these, apart from bringing a new visual perspective to the city in cinema, with their low-angle views of familiar locations, also indicate the extent to which the formal shift in the 70s was premised on the centrality of a subaltern perspective, which necessarily includes a strong sense of community solidarity. This does not mean that the elite's leadership has been replaced by a more representative one, only that the old reformist leadership had ceased by this time to be effective as a narrative device. Besides, this was the time when the urban proletariat was drawn into the theatres in larger numbers than ever before, edging out the middle class audiences, according to some accounts. In particular, it would seem that the Muslim subaltern was positioned in these films as the mobilized constituency of the populist hero. The devices of dis-identification with the norm, with the state, which gave the figure of Amitabh Bachchan its peculiar power, were an attempt to respond to an audience that was seen as bound together by bonds of community solidarity.

In *Deewar* and other films, we see the cityscape invested with new affect, the tables turned on an ideology that had naturalized the differences between the poor and the rich. Henceforth, the skyscraper reminds the spectator of the labour that went into its construction. The publicity for the film generated the widely circulated rumour that the real-life smuggler Haji Mastan was the model for Amitabh Bachchan's character. This rumour, for which the film provides very little confirmation, is interesting in itself as an indication of the mood of the times and the new horizon of representation or grid of intelligibility that was in formation at the time. Here was a cinema that, either through the publicity strategies of the filmmakers or through the desires and wilful distortions of the expanding viewership, was being made to accommodate its form to the streetside aesthetics of rumour, populist hero-worship of social deviants, etc. A mythical Bombay kept alive by popular lore and memory is here inscribed onto a film that belongs to the mainstream Bombay genre. Here we must note that although in terms of fidelity to a cityscape these popular films seem deficient, these references to real-life personages provide the associations with the city that make up for the lack. Mani Ratnam's *Nayakan* is also of interest in this respect: again a film centred around a gangster figure, *Nayakan* inevitably generated rumours that it rendered the life of notorious real-life don Varadaraja Mudaliar. For all its visual novelty when it first appeared, however, *Nayakan*'s narrative proceeds along a familiar melodramatic route, and there is as much narrative similarity to *Deewar* as there is visual or characterological tribute to *The Godfather. Nayakan* is nevertheless something of a turning point in the history of urban representation in popular cinema for several reasons. Its studied evocation of an ethnic look for the Tamil migrant community in Bombay slums, the underworld don's own home and family, and other features expanded cinema's access to the city beneath the metaphorical *shahar* of allegorical tales. Added to this was the evocation of a social geography that is part of contemporary Indian reality: the ethnic enclaves within Bombay slums, each with its own crop of representative gangsters (seen in *Dharavi* as well) plus a characteristic Mani Ratnam touch which involves tracking the destiny of the Tamil in other regions of the nation.

The city slum as site of epic confrontations has flourished as a genre for some time and one of its recent examples, in Malayalam, *Vietnam Colony* (dir. Siddique-Lal, 1992), though not set in Bombay, is notable for its allegorical-realist narration of a slum community's struggle to save their homes (with Vietnam serving as a metaphor for the internal divisions within the slum which prevent them from fighting off the real estate mafia which is plotting to evict them.) We may note here how the opposition between the Concept City and the city of experience serves many popular films as the axis along which class conflict can be represented. The squalor of the slums contrasts sharply with the clean, well laid out plans for hotels, residential complexes and other facilities with which the villains launch their assault on the dwellings of the poor. Other films like *Piya ka Ghar* (dir. Basu Chatterji, 1971) oppose the reality of the present to the dreams of a more utopian cityscape. Most strikingly, in *Rajnigandha* (dir. Basu Chatterji, 1974), the stable love relations and the comfortable coincidence of urban geography and middle-class society that characterizes Delhi (the Concept City), is contrasted to the disorienting, unsettling, treacherous world of Bombay.

The middle cinema examples cited above share the intensification of the pathological that marked the popular films of the 70s. More and more, the city figures in both kinds of films, in its experiential aspect, and the transparent Concept City recedes into the distance, almost disappearing from view or functioning as the primary weapon of the exploiters. Some, like *Gaman*, bring to the cinema a literary evocation of urban alienation, assisted by the haunting lyrics of songs like '*Seene me jalan*'. The helplessness, the daily struggle, the desperate holding on to minimal dreams of normality, the expected as well as systematic threats to these dreams, the dejection and despondency on the faces of the city's working population, are combined here with the inevitable memory of elsewhere, where the protagonist's wife awaits his return. One important difference that marks the middle cinema films is that here (but also in *Satya*), the realist imperative leads to a loss of certainty about the identity of the exploiters: the sordid lives of slum-dwellers in *Chakra* or *Dharavi* for instance, seem to have their own inbuilt tendency toward disaster and tragedy. There are the politicians, who come and make promises, the developers who survey the land with a hungry eye, but there are no heroes to protect the victims, nor a single villain or group of them to be got rid of. In *Chakra*, the four principal protagonists are Amma (Smita Patil), her son Benwa (Ranjit Chowdhury), Lukka the petty criminal (Naseeruddin Shah) and Amma's occasionally visiting lorry-driver lover (Kulbhushan Kharbanda) with whom she hopes to settle into a better life. They live in a slum, surrounded by others who are in a similar plight, on the brink of existence, surviving by any means, including prostitution, bootlegging and other activities. Death is a constant visitor but life goes on. The film takes us from Amma's little hut to those of the neighbours, to the land along the water pipes and railway tracks where the young loiter, to the brothel, the restaurant and other spaces that constitute the neighbourhood. Lukka's melodramatic speeches about freedom underscore the irony of his steady descent into syphilis and crime, Amma's dreams of a better life with the lorry driver seem to flower for a while before being smashed to bits by his employer. The film leaves us with the neighbourhood with a few souls less but otherwise unchanged, as if every event were only a repetition of another, to be repeated again in the future. This view of the slum as a permanent sore with occasional itches, betrays, behind the representation, the activity of a reformist agency. In the more complex *Dharavi* the reformist vision is less apparent. Repetition here takes the form of the protagonist's (Om Puri) indefatigable optimism. The hero, a taxi driver, along with three others, decide to invest their savings and some borrowed money in a little factory, which gets him involved with a gangster from his native place, leading to inevitable ruin. At the end of the film when, having lost his taxi and been forced to start life anew, he makes new plans for a rapid route to prosperity, we know, through what we have seen of his previous ventures, that this is going to be one more failure. He has daydreams, in which the film star Madhuri Dixit patiently listens to his schemes and boosts his ego with approving responses and gestures of love. Here the realist documentary effect of *Chakra* is supplemented, if not replaced, by a style that emphasizes the constitutive role of fantasy in the schemes and struggles of the poor. The sordid drama of his decline and his wife's attempts to find a new life with her ex-husband are watched over by his mother, who comes visiting from their home town in north India. Again, we have, within the film, the embodiment of a gaze that belongs to an elsewhere, occasionally mediating our experience of the world shown. While it leaves us in no doubt as to the fate of the hero's schemes for prosperity, *Dharavi* is one of the few films in the middle-cinema category which place a strong emphasis on the characters' undying optimism and constant readiness for struggle as the qualities that redeem them from the realist-sociological prison in which fictional representations tend to place them.

In these instances of representation of the underside of metropolitan life in contemporary India, we see, over time, and across different genres, the slow birth of the city as the unsymbolizable remainder from the womb of the symbolic geography, in which the encounter between city and country is the fulcrum of representation. From the pure symbolism of a *Neecha Nagar* to the city that exceeds all attempts at symbolization that we see in a *Dharavi* or a *Satya*, Hindi cinema either makes peace with a sociological realism, as in *Chakra,* or tries to go beyond it to represent the subjectivities of the dispossessed, stranded in a space that they cannot ever inhabit with equipoise but where they nevertheless wage a ceaseless struggle to escape into utopias lurking in cleaner neighbourhoods or in movie halls.

Consequently, the pathological subject occupies centrestage within this evolving de-symbolized space of representation, caught up in the cycles of desire, the city serving as the site of movement of this desire but also serving as a relentlessly ironicizing, demystifying backdrop. The city's changing reality is reflected as much in the characters' disposition to/in it as in the *images* of it, which may often be shot elsewhere. Changing representations of urban subjectivity are as crucial to tracking the evolving cinematic city as the realism of the image. The realist achievements of the representation of city life contribute to a distancing of the ideal subjects of an earlier genre of films into a space where their ideals reveal themselves to be fantasies. The changing look of the city in Bombay cinema, its increasingly intense realist evocations of urban spaces, has been aided by an assimilation of new techniques and technologies, as well as the dispersal of the representational burdens of the 'new cinema.' The great achievement of this genre, which thrives on gangsters and slumdwellers, is to have retained a stark sense of alienation, of an un-domesticatable (historical) compulsion: nothing less than the *resistance of the real*, a resistance which is felt in the contemporary cinematic image of the city—threatening, seductive, disgusting, fascinating, elusive, engulfing—more starkly than anywhere else.

Let us briefly return to the two grand themes that predominate in discussions of the city, to wit, the Concept City versus the living city and the city–country opposition. In the Indian cinema, the latter serves at once to privilege the values of the countryside as well as assert the precedence of national identity and unity over thematics of class conflict and urban disillusion. In *Naya Daur* not only is a confrontation staged between the city and the village, but this contest is witnessed by an urban representative, playing the 'anonymous citizen', who endorses the village's assertion of its supremacy over the city's capitalist incursions. After the 50s, the popular cinema by and large maintained a loyalty to this consensual valuation in its narratives, until the 70s when, with the rupturing of the national consensus, the city suddenly re-entered the screen as a self-sufficient space for the staging of epic conflicts and allegorical narratives, with the village figuring increasingly as no more than a memory fragment, a psychic residue, or as an outside element that threw the otherwise overpowering presence of urban life into some sort of perspective.

Notes

1 The typical Holmesian fantasy is that of looking down from the sky at the houses of the city, with the roofs removed to reveal everything that goes on inside.

2 Of course, there is no such thing as a social space without social relations which account for everyone in the population. But the inhabitants of a city do not bear the marks of these relations as openly and readably as they might in the countryside. The city is also structured to provide for spaces where these relations are suspended.

3 In 1890, a nationalist reformer gave expression to such views about Bombay, concluding with these words: 'Just as all solid objects possess one centre of gravity, Bombay city has become the ultimate point to which the wealth of this Presidency, or even the country, gravitates ... If a major misfortune should befall Bombay tomorrow, other cities are going to be affected in the same way that the limbs of a person are affected when his head receives a severe blow' (G. G. Agarkar, cited in Kosambi, 1995).

4 Since most of the films discussed here were made before the city's name changed to Mumbai, I have retained the old name. For a discussion of the ideology of city name changes, see Prasad, 2000.

5 See Gangar, 1995, for a comprehensive discussion of Bombay as the 'city of dreams'.

6 Anand Patwardhan's *Hamara Shahar* (1985) and Mira Nair's fictional *Salaam Bombay* (1988) contributed to the elaboration of the city's life on film.

7 Although I will not discuss it here, we should also mention a third group of films, including Basu Chatterjee's *Piya ka Ghar* (1971), *Guddi* (dir. Hrishikesh Mukherjee, 1971), *Dastak* (dir. Rajinder Singh Bedi, 1970), which are preoccupied with the problem of domesticity and privacy in the midst of crowded urban spaces. Some of these films are discussed in Prasad, 1998.

References

Donald, James (1995), 'The City, the Cinema: Modern Spaces' in Chris Jenks (ed.), *Visual Culture*, Routledge, London.

Gangar, Amrit (1995), 'Films from the City of Dreams' in S. Patel and A. Thorner (eds.), *Bombay: Mosaic of Modern Culture*, Oxford University Press, Bombay.

Kaviraj, Sudipta (1998), 'The Culture of Representative Democracy', in P. Chatterjee (ed.), *Wages of Freedom: Fifty Years of the Indian Nation-State*, Oxford University Press, New Delhi.

Kosambi, Meera (1995), 'British Bombay and Marathi Mumbai: Some Nineteenth Century Perceptions' in Patel and Thorner (eds.), *Bombay: Mosaic of Modern Culture*, Oxford University Press, Bombay.

Lefebvre, Henri (1996), *Writings on Cities*, Blackwell, Oxford.

Prasad, M. Madhava (1998), *Ideology of the Hindi Film: A Historical Construction*, Oxford University Press, New Delhi.

— (2000), 'What the Other Calls Me', *The Telegraph*, 24 February.

A CLOSE-UP ON SALMAN RUSHDIE'S *MIDNIGHT'S CHILDREN*

MARTIN ZERLANG

'Nobody from Bombay should be without a basic film vocabulary', the narrator declares in Salman Rushdie's *Midnight's Children* (Rushdie, 1982:33), and throughout this novel, references to this vocabulary abound: trailer, close-up, flashback, point of view, fade-out, etc. Obviously, Salman Rushdie has made his novel into a kind of verbal Bombay film, and the aim of this article is to explore why this is so. In other words, what is the significance of cinema in this novel? Why does cinema have such a prominent position as theme? How are verbal characters and actions made visual and even cinematic? What is cinematic form? To open the discussion, let us begin with some general remarks on the relationship between the novel and cinema.

Modernity and Visuality in the Novel

'Novelists have sought almost from the first to become a camera', Leon Edel observes in his essay 'Novel and Camera' (Edel in Harrison, 1992:177). Since long before the invention of the film camera, novelists have cultivated the camera-eye and the camera's movements: panning, jump cutting, moving into close-ups. In fact, the camera and the novel 'have come down to us like a pair of siblings, each intent on asserting itself and capturing the attention of the world' (Edel in Harrison, 1992:178).

At the birth of cinema, Henry James wrote extensively on point of view in the novel, and he and his contemporaries prepared the way for what Arnold Hauser in his *The Social History of Art* calls 'the film age'. According to Hauser, this new medium became the key to experiments within the other arts; new ways of representing reality arose from the spirit of cinematic form: 'the abandonment of the plot, the elimination of the hero, the relinquishing of psychology, the "automatic method of writing", and above all, the montage technique and the intermingling of temporal and spatial forms of the film' (Hauser, 1968: 226). The new concept of time was characterized by simultaneity, and the new concept of space was characterized by dynamism: 'it comes into being as it were before our eyes. It is fluid, unlimited, unfinished, an element with its own history, its own scheme and process of development' (Hauser, 1968:227). He mentions techniques such as close-ups, flashbacks, cross-cuts, slow motion, fast motion, double exposure, and he shows how all these techniques spill over from film to literature. Among writers giving cinematic devices a prominent place in their work, he mentions Marcel Proust, James Joyce, John Dos Passos and Virginia Woolf.

Of course it is not only technique that explains the influence of film. Hauser also mentions 'the awareness of the moment in which we find ourselves' (Hauser, 1968:231) and the 'universalism' of this moment: 'the discovery that, on the one hand, the same man experiences so many different, unconnected and irreconcilable things in one and the same moment, and that, on the other, different men in different places often experience the same things, that the same things are happening at the same time in places completely isolated from each other' (Hauser, 1968:231). Much easier and much more directly than literature, film transcends national and linguistic borders, and if the early film was a contemporary of the age of imperialism, modern film is a facet of the age of globalism.

Underlying all aspects of the development towards a dynamic, ever-changing modern culture, one finds a new stress on the visual aspects of things, and here it is obvious that already in the 19th century, a 'visual turn' took place in literature—which explains why a film pioneer such as David Griffith has praised Charles Dickens as his great teacher. But what made visuality so important? Why did writers turn from 'telling' to 'showing'?

In *Fiction and the Camera Eye*, Alan Spiegel suggests that the development from a traditional society to a modern society may explain the growing importance of the visual world. Taking Cervantes' *Don Quixote* as his example, he says that the writer of a traditional society displays a remarkable indifference to the sensuous surface details of the physical appearance and that the reason for this is that 'a stable society cultivates the habitual, the quintessential, and the general' (Spiegel, 1976:13). Here reality is not found 'through the five sense modalities' (Spiegel, 1976:14), but rather through the mind and what the mind knows and understands.

In a modern, dynamic society this conceptual reality must yield to a much more perceptual understanding of reality. Taking Gustave Flaubert as his counter-example, Spiegel points to the new importance of visual representation and visual precision. 'Flaubert strives to be "pitiless" and "exact" because he lives in an unstable society where there appears increasingly less to be "pitiless" and "exact" about. He must visualise every element of his narrative precisely because it is the visual that can no longer be taken for granted' (Spiegel, 1976:18).

In his *Notes on the Novel*, José Ortega y Gasset points to the difference between the pre-modern belief that actions follow and derive from being and the modern belief that 'the being of a thing is nothing else than the sum total of its actions and functions' (quoted in Spiegel, 1976:20). Writing from a pre-modern point of view, Cervantes is able to offer general statements on his characters, whereas Flaubert 'as the member of a sceptical, unstable, man-oriented society' has to build up his characters from moment to moment, focusing on particular and visual details, knowing that the qualities that reveal character are not the typical and habitual forms, but 'forms that are unique, circumstantial, and transitory'. This again is what makes Flaubert a cinematic writer avant la lettre—'showing', not 'telling', his world to his readers.

Character or Crack-pot

In *Midnight's Children*, the narrative takes off with a presentation of the protagonist, Saleem Sinai. The takeoff is at the same time verbal and visual, literary and cinematic. It updates the 'I was born' of

Dickens' *David Copperfield* into 'I was born in the city of Bombay'—then tries the tone of a fairy tale—'once upon a time'—but finally gives up all efforts to generalize: 'No, that won't do, there's no getting away from the date: I was born in Doctor Narlikar's Nursing Home on August 15th, 1947.' The birth of a person is equated with the birth of a nation, since this is 'the precise instant of India's arrival at independence', and the situation is described in a way that reminds the reader of slapstick comedy, when this mythical moment is followed by the ridiculous accident of Saleem's father breaking his toe. The account of the birth is recounted through Saleem, and this of course would take away the immediacy of action in a film, but may be compared to voice-over technique. Anyway, the introduction ends up in a direct and highly concrete reference to the importance of visuality: 'guided only by the memory of a large white bedsheet with a roughly circular hole some seven inches in diameter cut into the centre, clutching at the dream of that holey, mutilated square of linen, which is my talisman, my open-sesame, I must commence the business of remaking my life . . .' (Rushdie, 1982:9f).

In spite of Hauser's claims, plot is not abandoned, nor is character eliminated in this cinematic novel; the plot dissolves into episodes, and as a character, Saleem, who grows up in a society experiencing a process of modernization, is built up from moment to moment through these episodes. His life is narrated by focusing on particular visual details; the 'remake' of his life shows how circumstantial, transitory and fragile individuality is. Only step by step or look by look through the circular hole in the sheet, does Doctor Aziz succeed in making 'a badly-fitting collage' (Rushdie, 1982:25) of Saleem's grandmother-to-be; in the same way Saleem is a collage rather than a whole person. The fragmentation of his body is rendered very visually:

> I am not speaking metaphorically; nor is this the opening gambit of some melodramatic, riddling, grubby appeal for pity. I mean quite simply that I have begun to crack all over like an old jug—that my poor body, singular, unlovely, buffeted by too much history, subjected to drainage above and drainage below, mutilated by doors, brained by spittoons, has started coming apart at the seams (Rushdie, 1982:37).

Grotesque Realism

The most important fragment of this fragmented body is Saleem's nose, and at the very beginning of the novel his grandfather, who is also equipped with an enormous nose, learns that the nose is 'the place where the outside world meets the world inside you' (Rushdie, 1982:17). Thus, Rushdie's use of grotesque images may be interpreted as: i) an indication of the vulnerability of characters who are not able to separate themselves from their surroundings; ii) as a cinematic way of representing inner and invisible phenomena—such as remembrance, which is likened to 'chutnification', or panic, which is likened to 'a bubbling sea-beast com[ing] up for air' (Rushdie, 1982:37) or disbelief, which is described as a muscle that 'began to nictate' in Padma's calves (Rushdie, 1982:443).

Saleem himself explains the grotesque in this way: '. . . perhaps, if one wishes to remain an individual in the midst of the teeming multitudes, one must make oneself grotesque' (Rushdie, 1982:109). Normally the surface of the body sets up a clear borderline between inside and outside, but the grotesque features of Saleem's body make his inner tension visible:

> O eternal opposition of inside and outside! Because a human being, inside himself, is anything but a whole, anything but homogeneous; all kinds of everywhichthing are jumbled up inside him, and he is one person one minute and another the next. The body, on the other hand, is homogeneous as anything. Indivisible, a one-piece suit, a sacred temple, if you will. It is important to preserve this wholeness. But the loss of my finger (. . .), not to mention the removal of certain hairs from my head, has undone all that (Rushdie, 1982:236f).

Another example of this visualization of internal or abstract things is the Rani of Cooch Naheen 'who was going white in blotches, a disease which leaked into history and erupted on enormous scale shortly after Independence.' As the Rani herself puts it: 'My skin is the outward expression of the internationalism of my spirit' (Rushdie, 1982:45).

Saleem is 'public property' (Rushdie, 1982:77), and the consequence of the grotesque analogue between his small, private world and the extra-large public world of India is a constant lack of control over his life. He tries to hide away in a washing-chest as Nadir Khan tries to evade public light under the carpet, but it turns out that it is impossible to secure a private space, especially in the modern India where 'such places have been expropriated by the State' (Rushdie, 1982:433). Nevertheless, approaching the end of his story and his life Saleem makes a solemn declaration—secretly whispering the following to the walls of his prison:

> Politics, children: at the best of times a bad dirty business. We should have avoided it, I should never have dreamed of purpose, I am coming to the conclusion that privacy, the small individual lives of men, are preferable to all this inflated macrocosmic activity (Rushdie, 1982:435).

Inflation is the trademark of the grotesque, and simultaneously inflation is a matter of visuality. At the beginning of the chapter on Saleem's metamorphosis into an All-India radio, he states that 'reality is a question of perspective', and that distance makes things look plausible which in close-up appear to be incredible—or, one might add, grotesque. Following on this statement, he asks his listeners/readers to imagine themselves 'in a large cinema, sitting at first in the back row, and gradually moving up, until your nose is almost pressed against the screen. Gradually the stars' faces dissolve into dancing grain; tiny details assume grotesque proportions' (Rushdie, 1982:165f). This comparison is taken up in connection with his statement on politics as a dirty business, but this time he votes for the close-up, subjective and grotesque as it is:

> No, as to the question of guilt, I refuse absolutely to take the larger view; we are too close to what is happening, perspective is impossible, later perhaps analysts will say why and wherefore, will adduce underlying economic trends and political developments, but right now we're too close to the cinema-screen, the picture is breaking up into dots, only subjective judgments are possible (Rushdie, 1982:435).

Action and Media

New media take older media as their contents, Marshall McLuhan once claimed, pointing to the novel's dependence on oral culture as its content. In the final chapter, Saleem compares his role 'as that of any redundant oldster: the traditional function, perhaps, of reminiscer, of teller-of-tales . . .' (Rushdie, 1982:448), and the whole narrative of

Midnight's Children is presented as good old-fashioned story-telling, as an oral exchange between Saleem, a modern and sophisticated narrator, and Padma, a working woman who cannot read or write and whose name among village folk is 'The One Who Possesses Dung.' Accordingly, Saleem's style is informal, colloquial, adequate for this face-to-face-contact—and if he leaves this direct style, Padma bullies him 'back into the world of linear narrative, the universe of what happened next' (Rushdie, 1982:38).

The concept of 'linear narrative', however, belongs to the medium of writing, and to the reader Saleem's story is manifested as writing, and intertextual references to novels such as *Tristram Shandy, A Passage to India, The Tin Drum* and *One Hundred Years of Solitude* emphasize the importance of the literary medium. This is also a novel discussing the relationship between nation and narration, and according to Benedict Anderson, 'the birth of the imagined community of the nation can best be seen if we consider the basic structure of two forms of imagining [. . .] the novel and the newspaper' (Anderson, 1983:30). What Rushdie calls 'what-happened nextism' (Rushdie, 1982:39) is a manifestation of the novelistic concept of time as a '"homogeneous, empty time", in which simultaneity is, as it were, transverse, cross-time, marked not by prefiguring and fulfilment, but by temporal coincidence, and measured by clock and calendar' (Anderson, 1983:30). In a paradoxical way, Padma and Saleem have changed the roles of traditional story-telling and modern, novelistic writing. Padma wants a linear narrative, Saleem embodies the traditional world of prefiguring and fulfilment—or unfulfilment.

However, as already mentioned, Rushdie also transforms his novel into a film, and his narrator constructs his narrative with a lot of cinematic devices. At one point Padma exclaims, '. . . you've learned how to tell things really fast' (Rushdie, 1982:109), and there is no doubt that he has learned a lot about motion from the motion pictures. Thus, at the beginning of the third part of the novel, he once again makes an explicit comparison between his story-telling and a fast moving Bombay melodrama:

> (While Padma, to calm herself, holds her breath, I permit myself to insert a Bombay-talkie-style close up—a calendar ruffled by a breeze,

its pages flying off in rapid succession to denote the passing of the years; I superimpose turbulent long-shots of street riots, medium shots of burning buses and blazing English language libraries . . .) (Rushdie, 1982:346).

Saleem also praises the Bombay films for their movie-trailers, telling how he 'smack[ed] his lips of the title NEXT ATTRACTION, superimposed on undulating blue velvet!' and tries to raise the great narrative expectations of Padma, saying 'Padma, there is still plenty worth telling (. . .) there are still next-attractions and coming-soons galore' (Rushdie, 1982:346).

In her book on Salman Rushdie, Nancy E. Barry suggests that in fact the dynamic construction of the novel may be compared to the construction of an episodic film or a serial with 'synopses of previous events provid[ing] a rhythmic counter-point to the tantalizing teasers which anticipate events to come' (Barry in Harrison, 1992:63). These synopses are instruments that enable Saleem to speed up the tempo in anticipation of 'next-attractions' and slow down the tempo in reca-pitulations of what-happened-before, and joining forces, these devices bind the narrative together in spite of all breaks and discon-tinuities.

At one point Saleem defines himself as 'the sort of person *to whom things have been done*' (Rushdie, 1982:237), and therefore he of course fits in perfectly with the reigning genre within the Bombay film industry: the melodrama. A melodrama combines the high level of action in an adventure film with the passivity of the hero/victim in a horror film, and Saleem would be the perfect melodramatic hero if comic distance did not accompany his sufferings. Again and again he is forced into episodes in which the plot culminates in a highly sym-bolic picture—as in the episode where he loses control of his bicycle and runs into a political demonstration: 'In this way I became direct-ly responsible for triggering off the violence which ended with the partition of the state of Bombay, as a result of which the city became the capital of Maharashtra—so at least I was on the winning side' (Rushdie, 1982:192).

Saleem's uncle Hanif and aunt Pia Aziz both work within the film industry, Hanif as a director and Pia as an actor, and to live with them is 'to exist in the hot sticky heart of a Bombay talkie', especially since Pia, deprived of film roles, turns her own life 'into a feature picture, in which I was cast in an increasing number of bit-parts' (Rushdie, 1982:241). Hanif, however, wants to reform the Hindi cinema by replacing melodrama, with its villainous villains and heroic men and exotic locations, with documentary realism writing 'about ordinary people and social problems, for instance a film titled "the Ordinary Life of a Pickle Factory"' (Rushdie, 1982:242).

The irony of it is that Saleem succeeds where his uncle Hanif fails. The narrative of Saleem is based on this ordinary life of people in a pickle factory, since Padma is working in one of these—and since Saleem's 'chutnification of history' (Rushdie, 1982:459) is obviously based on this very ordinary work. The ironic point is that only by magic or melodramatic exaggeration is it possible to give an adequate picture of life in India. Already his father—or rather the man whom he believes to be his father—recognizes the melodramatic exaggeration as an aspect of reality: 'The swollen events of the night of the crescent knives reminded Nadir Khan of his room-mate, because life had once again, perversely, refused to remain lifesized. It had turned melodramatic: and that embarrassed him' (Rushdie, 1982:48f). And Saleem himself implores his listeners and readers to accept the fact that only by melodramatic exaggeration does this reality become visible: 'Yes, you must have all of it: however overblown, however Bombay-talkie-melodramatic, you must let it sink in, you must *see*!' (Rushdie, 1982:440).

Approaching the end of the novel, Saleem declares that reality is nagging him, and that love does not conquer all, 'except in the Bombay talkies' (Rushdie, 1982:444). But in spite of this recognition, the last pages of the novel have all the effects and excess of a melodrama—love, marriage and child included—and when Saleem impatiently states that 'it's time to get things moving' (Rushdie, 1982:448), he makes them move by moving pictures: 'a taunt, a last railway-train heading south south south, a final battle . . .' (Rushdie, 1982:448).

Encompasser of the Earth

In an interview on *Midnight's Children* and *Shame,* Rushdie makes a distinction between two kinds of novels. One is the inclusive novel, a loose baggy monster of fiction that tries to incorporate everything. Another is the exclusive novel, which proceeds on the basis of excluding most of the world in order to concentrate on one strand plucked out of the universe. Rushdie's own work of course belongs in the first category, and all along through his narrative Saleem comments on 'this urge to encapsulate the whole of reality' (Rushdie, 1982:75).

In the first chapter the boatman Tai is introduced. He is characterized by his 'chatter', which must remind every reader of Saleem's own chattering style: It was 'fantastic, grandiloquent and ceaseless' (Rushdie, 1982:14). Listening to Tai's chatter, Saleem's grandfather learns about an emperor who was called 'Encompasser of the Earth' (Rushdie, 1982:17). This megalomaniac ambition is later transferred to the sphere of arts, and Saleem tells about Nadir Khan's friend the painter, who suffered from this 'Indian disease' (Rushdie, 1982:75) to want to encompass the earth:

> As a young man he had shared a room with a painter whose paintings had grown larger and larger as he tried to get the whole of life into his art. 'Look at me,' he said before he killed himself, 'I wanted to be a miniaturist and I've got elephantiasis instead!' (Rushdie, 1982:48).

A little later, Lifafa Das enters the novel with his peepshow, which he advertizes by the words: '"Dunya dekho", see the whole world. [. . .] See the whole world, come see everything!' (Rushdie, 1982:75).

Saleem himself is an artist who tries to put the history of modern India, from Independence to the Emergency, into thirty chapters that are visualized as thirty jars of chutney. But the attempt to contain a whole nation is impossible, at least without cracks in the personality, cracks in the jar and cracks in the work of art. 'I have been a swallower of lives', Saleem says on the first page, and he reveals that '[c]onsumed multitudes are jostling and shoving inside me' (Rushdie, 1982:9). On the last page he admits to having become 'a broken creature spilling pieces of itself into the street, because I have been so-many, too-many persons' (Rushdie, 1982:463).

He ends up 'in the street', and this is where his life and death belongs. His real father was a street-musician, and early in the novel he recognizes that '[e]ntertainers would orchestrate my life' (Rushdie, 1982:101). Therefore his real world is the ghetto of street magicians—which is bulldozed towards the end of the novel in a 'Civic Beautification programme' during the Emergency (Rushdie, 1982:429)—and his ceaseless, grandiloquent chatter is a clear example of what Mikhail Bakhtin calls 'the language in the marketplace.' It is a loud and public voice, without intimacy, making a show of itself. It is a manifestation of the way people speak in the market-place and in the streets, where barkers and hawkers and peddlers want to catch the attention of customers by a highly performative language, nourished on an atmosphere of freedom, frankness and familiarity (Bakhtin, 1968:153). Here they toy with the objects they announce, they transform everything into playthings, they toy with their own oratory, and in doing this they create an open and free game in contrast to the rigid borders of religious and political life.

The final chapter contains the final battle between Picture Singh and the Maharaja of Cooch Naheen to find out who is 'the Most Charming Man In The World'. Saleem is the one who performs 'the function of barker' (Rushdie, 1982:449) in loud words which inevitably remind the reader of Lifafa Das and his peep-show—'Roll up, roll up—once in a lifetime an opportunity such as this—ladees, ladahs, come see come see come see! Who is here? [. . .] this, citizens, ladies, gents, is the Most Charming Man In The World!' (Rushdie, 1982:449).

Entertainment is key to the understanding of *Midnight's Children*. Entertainment—the verbal entertainment of tall stories, the visual entertainment of larger-than-life melodrama, the plastic entertainment of grotesques—lends the whole novel a remarkable unity of tone, in spite of all its centrifugal forces, and the same unity of tone, this all-pervasive gay and grandiloquent, festive and triumphant tone, makes the impossible possible—to include the history of modern India with all its differences within one novel. Modern entertainment is mass-entertainment, and 'spittoon-hittery' (Rushdie, 1982:448), 'chutnification of history' (Rushdie, 1982:459), the

Bombay film industry and Saleem's high-pitched story-telling all have this in common, that they are not addressed to a solitary reader or viewer, just as 'spittoon-hittery' permits intellectuals 'to practise the art-forms of the masses' (Rushdie, 1982:448). Saleem's 'chutnification' is an example of mass-production for the 'All-India' market:

> . . . at Braganza Pickles, I supervise the production of Mary's legendary recipes; but there are also my special blends, in which, thanks to the powers of my drained nasal passages, I am able to include memories, dreams, ideas, so that once they enter mass-production all who consume them will know what pepperpots achieved in Pakistan, or how it felt to be in the Sundarbans . . . believe don't believe but it's true. Thirty jars stand upon a shelf, waiting to be unleashed upon the amnesiac nation (Rushdie, 1982:460).

Entertainment is play put on display and in the same way as Lifafa Das announces the universal capacities of his little peepshow, every sentence of Saleem's is an invitation to take a look and find a perspective on what became of the 1001 possibilities of India after Independence. The message may be one of resignation, but the medium of representation tells quite a different story.

References

Anderson, Benedict (1983), *Imagined Communities. Reflections on the Origin and Spread of Nationalism*, Verso, London.

Bakhtin, Mikhail (1968), *Rabelais and His World*, M. I. T. Press, Cambridge, Mass. and London

Harrison, James (ed.) (1992), *Salman Rushdie*, Twayne Publishers, New York.

Hauser, Arnold (1968), *The Social History of Art*, vol. 4, Routledge and Kegan Paul, London.

Rushdie, Salman (1982), *Midnight's Children*, Picador, London.

— (1991), *Imaginary Homelands: Essays and Criticism, 1981-91*, Granta Books, London.

Spiegel, Alan (1976), *Fiction and the Camera Eye: Visual Consciousness in Film and the Modern Novel*, University Press of Virginia, Charlottesville.

THE 'BOLLYWOODIZATION' OF THE INDIAN CINEMA: CULTURAL NATIONALISM IN A GLOBAL ARENA

ASHISH RAJADHYAKSHA

Rajnikant in Japan

The West may have the biggest stalls in the world's media bazaar, but it's not the only player. Globalization isn't merely another word for Americanization—and the recent expansion of the Indian entertainment industry proves it. For hundreds of millions of fans around the world, it is Bollywood, India's film industry, not Hollywood, that spins their screen fantasies. Bollywood, based in Mumbai, has become a global industry. India's entertainment moguls don't merely target the billion South Asians, or desis, at home: they make slick movies, songs and TV shows for export. Attracted by a growing middle class and a more welcoming investment environment, foreign companies are flocking to Bollywood, funding films and musicians. The foreign money is already helping India's pop culture to reach even greater audiences. And it may have a benign side-effect in cleaning up an Indian movie industry business long haunted by links to the underworld ('Bollywood Goes International', *Newsweek International*, 28 February 2000).

Let us keep aside for a moment the gross misrepresentations in *Newsweek*—the Indian film industry is not solely based in Mumbai, 'foreign money' is still hardly available for film *productions* even though it would like to cream off non-local *distribution* profits; such money is not necessarily distinguishable from the 'underworld' and is, therefore, not exactly what you would describe as 'benign'. *Newsweek*'s assumptions about good and bad money are unsustainable and pernicious.

Let us concentrate instead on just what this literature claims is happening. For something like the past decade, leading up to *Newsweek*'s final consecration, a range of print and television media have been claiming some rather dramatic developments in the Indian cinema. Practically every newspaper has commented, usually in the same breathless prose as *Newsweek*, on the phenomenon: there is a craze for 'Bollywood' *masala* that quite exceeds anything we have ever seen before; from Tokyo to Timbuctoo people are dancing to Indipop, names like Shah Rukh Khan are circulating in places where people may never have heard of Indira Gandhi, and there is apparently money to be made. Everyone, it seems, is scrambling—new Bollywood websites continue to emerge, new distributors and intermediaries rise with new ideas of how to exploit this development, new television channels are seen, satellite technology is projected with unprecedented ability to overcome distribution inefficiencies—every one of these powered by entrepreneurs and their venture-capitalist backers, and their unique idea about what will earn money.

On what is this hype based? Interestingly, in the past year, the box office of an Indian cinema made indigenously was itself less central to the phenomenon than a range of ancillary industries, mostly based in London, including theatre (the much-hyped London stage musical *Bombay Dreams*, a collaboration between Indian composer A. R. Rahman and Andrew Lloyd Webber), the music industry, advertising[1] and even fashion (the extraordinary month-long 'Bollywood' festival of food, furniture and fashion marketing in Selfridges, London), all of which culminated in the extraordinary marketing exercise known as *Indian Summer* in July 2002 (see BBCI, 2002).

All of this began, it is usually said, with the four films which *Newsweek* too mentions as having made distribution history, three of them directly or indirectly Yash Chopra productions: *Dilwale Dulhaniya Le Jayenge* (*DDLJ*, 1995), the film which in some ways started it all, *Dil To Pagal Hai* (*DTPH*, 1997), Karan Johar's *Kuch Kuch Hota Hai* (*KKHH*, 1998), and Subhash Ghai's *Taal* (1998). Before all these, there is of course the original box-office hit *Hum Aapke Hain Kaun?*

(1994). Of *Taal*, for example, producer and noted 'showman' of Hindi cinema Ghai said,

> There'll be 125 prints of *Taal* only for the foreign market. This is almost a three-fold increase since *Pardes*, for which I'd made 45 prints, and five times that of *Khalnayak*. Hindi films now have a significant market in the US, Canada, UK and the Middle East. It is making inroads into South Africa and Australia. And it is also popular in Japan, Hong Kong, South East Asia and, of course, Mauritius. In most if not all these countries, Hindi films are no longer weekend events, they are showing three shows everyday wherever they're released. Now, beginning with *Taal*, there will be vinyl banner hoardings advertising the films on the roads of the Western cities. Everybody, including the Westerners, will now see what films are on! The whole world will take note, because we will also be on the net (Sengupta, 1999).

How much did these films collectively earn? That is difficult to say, but *The Economic Times* reported that

> The first big success of the new Bollywood is *Who Am I to You?* (*Hum Aapke Hain Kaun?* dubbed), a musical that focuses on two weddings. Thanks to its untraditional (sic) plot and effective marketing, it's India's biggest hit ever. Playing for nearly a year, the film grossed more than $30 million, a phenomenal amount in a country where the average moviegoer pays 65 % admission and the average movie makes about $3 million—barely what an art-house film makes in the U.S.' (Moshavi, 1995).

Of *Taal*, the same paper reports that it was

> released around the world on August 13 (and) grossed the highest average collection per cinema hall (per screen average) for movies released in north America on the August 13-15 weekend. According to Weekend Box-Office figures, the first three-day collections were $591,280. Released simultaneously in 44 theatres in North America, *Taal* has set a record for Bollywood releases abroad by notching the highest first three-day collections with $13,438 per screen. Though there is no independent verification, a press release by Eros Entertainment Inc, the distributor of the film abroad, claimed that *Taal*'s initial collections have even surpassed that of Hollywood blockbusters like *Haunting*, *The Blair Witch Project* and *Eyes Wide Shut* (*The Economic Times*, 21 August 1999).

All these are undoubted marketing successes, and the releases in particular of *Kuch Kuch* in South Africa, *Dil to Pagal Hai* in Israel and the brief weekend when *Taal* made it to the top 10 in the US domestic market are now the stuff of marketing legend. On the other hand, here is a salutary fact: *Newsweek* claims that 'India's movie exports jumped from $10 million a decade ago to $100 million last year, and may top $250 million in 2000.'

Contrast these figures with the brief dot.com boom when every Indian Internet portal such as satyam online, rediff-on-the-net and planetasia marketed itself with Bollywood paraphernalia. Following the unprecedented sale of just one portal, indiainfo.com, for Rs 500 crore (or over $100 million), it would have been a safe argument that just 10 of the top websites of the time (as computed by a *Businessworld* issue, 'Hot New Dot.coms', 24 January 2000) were in that period collectively worth more than the total box-office earnings of the Indian film industry.

There was and continues to be a real discrepancy involved. Contrary to *Newsweek*'s statement that Bollywood is 'India's film industry . . . based in Mumbai', perhaps we could argue instead precisely that at least in one sense this is not so: that Bollywood is *not* the Indian film industry, or at least not the film industry alone. Bollywood admittedly occupies a space analogous to the film industry, but might best be seen as a more diffuse cultural conglomeration involving a range of distribution and consumption activities from websites to music cassettes, from cable to radio. If so, the film industry itself—determined here solely in terms of its box office turnover and sales of print and music rights, all that actually comes back to the producer—can by definition constitute only a part, and perhaps even an *alarmingly small part*, of the overall culture industry that is currently being created and marketed.

If *this* is so, then behind it all is a real difficulty, one that for all its being unprecedented has a disarmingly familiar tone. The fact is that nobody responsible for the production of the film narrative, if we include in this the producers, directors and stars responsible for the nuts-and-bolts assembly of the cinematic product that goes into these markets, actually knows what's going on. How do they make sense of these developments? Why is *Dil To Pagal Hai* popular in Tel Aviv, why now? How would they convert all this hoopla into a stable market that would guarantee their next product an audience? Nobody quite knows the overall picture, and it's worth exploring some of the literature that's emerged on these developments to speculate on just why that is so.

Amitabh Bachchan, for example, was one of the iconic stars of the 1970s and early 80s, before his career nose-dived following the 'first-ever' effort to corporatize the film industry with the lame-duck ABCL which most critics say was 'an idea before its time'. Despite not having had a substantial hit for over a decade, Bachchan is India's most famous 'film personality' mainly through a Bollywoodized makeover that owes itself to television (he hosted the Hindi version of *Who Wants to be a Millionaire* for Star TV), and he has this to say:

> Evidently, our film personalities have begun to matter in world fora. Hindi cinema is gaining worldwide recognition and I don't mean only those films which make it to Berlin or Cannes. Once, I was walking down London's Piccadilly Circus and I saw this group of Kurds running towards me. (*Laughs*) I thought they wanted to assassinate me. But they stopped right there and started singing songs from *Amar Akbar Anthony* and *Muqaddar Ka Sikandar*. Rajnikant is tremendously popular in Japan. And I'm told that our stars are known even in Fiji, Bali and Chile. Amazing! But we're not marketing ourselves properly. Someone out there is making pots of money at our expense' (interview, 'Netvamsham!', *The Times of India*, 18 July, 1999).

Who is this mysterious 'someone' making money and how come Bachchan does not know? Let us explore this further with the instance that Bachchan himself provides, perhaps the most bizarre instance in this whole new development: the sudden, inexplicable, popularity of Rajnikant in Japan.

Rajnikant is, of course, well known as perhaps the biggest Tamil film star ever, after the legendary M. G. Ramachandran, but it is also important to say that his career has largely been restricted to that language, despite several efforts to get into Hindi film where he has often played subsidiary parts in Bachchan films (*Andha Kanoon*, 1983; *Giraftaar*, 1985; *Hum*, 1991) and one marginal effort in a Hollywood production (*Bloodstone*, 1989). Within Tamil Nadu where he reigns supreme, on the other hand, he has demonstrated all the hallmarks of a major star who knows his audience and his market: he has carefully constructed his screen persona, built a team around him that understands how to work it, has even tested out his popularity politically when he campaigned on behalf of the DMK and was at least partially responsible for its victory in the 1996 elections.

And then came his Japanese success. Here is the *New Indian Express* on this phenomenon:

> An entire generation of recession-hit Japanese have discovered a new hero: Rajnikant. Jayalalitha's bete noire and the man with that unflagging swagger and oh-so-cool wrist flicks has emerged there as the hippest craze after Leonardo Di Caprio and *Muthu*, his 150th film, is the biggest grosser in Japan after *Titanic*. So far the film has been seen by over 1,27,000 Japanese in a 23-week run at Tokyo's Cinema Rise alone, netting as much as $ 1.7 million and premieres on satellite television in June ('Rajnikant Bowls over Japanese Youth', *The New Indian Express*, 10 June, 1999).

So how does one explain this success? B. Kandaswamy Bharathan, executive producer at Kavithalaya, credited with having masterminded the Japanese marketing of this film, offers a typically 'Bollywoodist-culturalist' explanation:

> The movie carries an important message—that money is not everything in life. Instead, it propagates human values, highlighted in the first song itself—and this philosophy appealed to the Japanese audience. This is especially significant for a youth that's been talked down about for not being as hardworking as the post-war generation (ibid).

Indeed. Keeping aside the distortions by which the producer of *Muthu* represents his own production, in fact a violent feudal drama addressing caste differences, I am reasonably sure that if one were to ask Bharathan why this film proved a hit and no other, and how he suggests that Rajnikant capitalize on this sudden popularity to stabilize a Japanese market for his next film and his future career, we may perhaps get an honest answer, that he has no idea why *Muthu* did well in Tokyo.

Cinema Versus the Bollywood Culture Industry

> 'Says Ft. Lauderdale housewife Sameera Biswas, "We go to the movies to keep our culture alive"' (*Newsweek International* 28 February, 2000).

> 'Kids in Bombay go to night clubs to become Western. Here (i.e. in Brisbane) we go to assert our Eastern identity. The basic difference lies there' (Fiji Indian enthusiast of Indipop, quoted in Ray, 2000).

The main contention of this paper seeks to separate out the Bollywood industry from the Indian cinema. It suggests that while the cinema has been in existence as a national industry of sorts for the past fifty years (the Indian cinema of course has celebrated its centenary, but the industry, in the current sense of the term, might be most usefully traced to the post-World War II boom in production), *Bollywood* has been around for only about a decade now. The term today refers to a reasonably specific narrative and a mode of presentation—the *Newsweek* essay, for example, quotes Plus Channel's Amit Khanna as saying that 'Indian movies are feel-good, all-happy-in-the-end, tender love stories with lots of songs and dances . . . That's what attracts non-Indian audiences across the world' and to this we could add 'family values' and their palpable, if not entirely self-evident, investment in 'our culture'. To such content we would need to also add a distinctive mode of presentation, couched in the post-Information Technology claims that Indian enterprise has been making in the past few years of global competitiveness, and by language such as:

> Spurred by competition from dubbed versions of such flashy Western hits such as *Jurassic Park* and *Speed*, Bollywood is rushing to enter the era of high tech films. Producers are founding new companies, boosting their marketing, and seeking new sources of financing . . . [C]ameras are rolling for the first Bollywood high-tech films. CMM Ltd., an 18-month-old special-effects company backed by such stalwarts as State Bank of India, has bought more than $1 million worth of software and hardware from Silicon Graphics Inc., the Mountain View (California) computer company whose special-effects equipment is used by nearly every Hollywood studio. The technology is key to a still untitled film featuring Indian megastar Shah Rukh Khan in a double role, allowing him to appear with himself in the same scene. Silicon Graphics is lining up other clients in India as well (Moshavi, 1995).

There are further distinctions to be made: while Bollywood exists for, and prominently caters to, a diasporic audience of Indians, and sometimes (as with Bhangra-rap) exports *into* India, the Indian cinema—much as it would wish to tap this 'non-resident' audience—is only occasionally successful in doing so, and in almost every instance is able to do so only when it, so to say *Bollywoodizes* itself, a transition that very few films in Hindi, and hardly any in other languages, are actually able to do.

Speaking historically, ever since the film industry in India assumed something like its current form—the period roughly between 1946 and 1975—the export market of films has been a relatively minor, disorganized and chaotic, but at the same time familiar, field. Few films were made with a non-Indian audience in mind, and the 'foreign market' (usually a single territory) remained small, and entirely controlled by the government of India's Indian Motion Picture Export Corporation, which in its initial years was accountable to the Reserve Bank of India and later merged with the National Film Development Corporation. Film was dominated by State policy on export and remained, until 1992 when the area was de-controlled and opened out to private enterprise, subsidiary to the policy of exporting 'art' films within the film festival circuit. It was generally assumed in this time that Indian mainstream films, to the extent to which they had an off-shore audience at all, addressed émigré Indians or their descendants. In 1975-77, for example, statistics show that Indian films were exported to Africa, the Arab states, Trinidad, Guyana and Barbados, Burma, Hong Kong, Indonesia, Iran, Malaysia, Singapore, Sri Lanka and Thailand (UNESCO, 1981). Perhaps the most visible form of export in this time was the 'gulf boom', of workers—domestic, industrial, white-collar—exported to the Middle East becoming an audience for Malayalam films through the 1970s. Apart from this kind of market, the only other that existed was the one related to bilateral trade arrangements with the Socialist bloc as part of what came to be called Nehruvian internationalism, but which nevertheless did yield some spectacular marketing successes, such as Raj Kapoor's films, and later Mithun Chakraborty's, in the former USSR.

Such audiences, and such modes of marketing could hardly resemble what we are trying here to identify as the Bollywood culture industry of the 1990s. The term itself, Bollywood, has been around notably in film trade journals—it was probably invented in a slightly jokey self-deprecating way by the journal *Screen* in Bombay and by its page 'Bollywood Beat', with the companion words Tollywood for the Calcutta film industry based in Tollygunge and even for a while

Mollywood for the Madras industry, which is not used these days. It is probable that its current usage is a British one, associated with Channel 4's ethnic programming (see Channel 4's publication *Bollywood: The Indian Cinema Story* by Nasreen Munni Kabir, 2001) and came into circulation via literary speculations on film as mass culture by writers like Shashi Tharoor or Farrukh Dhondy, coming to mean what it does today: an expression of the outsider's fascination with a slightly surreal practice that nevertheless appears to possess the claim to be a genuine popular art form. So Tharoor, for example, says:

> The way in which different communities have come together for sim-
> ply secular ends whether in ecological movements like the Himalayan
> agitations against deforestation, or in the social work of Baba Amte, or
> in the cinema industry of Bollywood—points to the potential for co-
> operative rather than divisive mobilisation. It is when groups have
> stayed apart, and failed to interact in secular activities, that their com-
> munal identities prevail; the lack of brotherhood guarantees their
> 'other' hood. And then conflict, hatred and violence can erupt.
>
> Not surprisingly, this idea of India is one that is sustained by our
> popular culture. Some readers might think my reference to Bollywood
> out of place. One of my novels deals with the trashy world of commer-
> cial cinema—because to me, Indian films, with all their limitations and
> outright idiocies, represent part of the hope for India's future. In a
> country that is still 50 % illiterate, films represent the prime vehicle for
> the transmission of popular culture and values ('Make Bollywood's
> India a Reality', *The Indian Express*, 19 April 1998).

Today, as Tharoor shows (or rather unwittingly demonstrates), the term comes with its own narrative, one that we could perhaps call techno-nostalgia, and is clearly not restricted any more to solely the cinema but informs a range of products and practices. It would cer-tainly have informed the displays around the Swaminarayan Sanstha's Cultural Festival of India in Edison, New Jersey, in 1991, when you apparently entered through large gates signifying traditional temple entrances and named Mayur Dwar (Peacock Gate) and Gaja Dwar (Elephant Gate), and saw traditional artisans sharing their space with entrepreneurs from Jackson Heights selling electronic products, with sponsorship from AT&T. Of this form, most directly demonstrated in recent cinematic memory by the foreign-returned Rani Mukherjee in

KKHH suddenly bursting into the bhajan *Om jai jagdish hare*, Sandhya Shukla has this to say:

> Emerging as it did out of a constellation of interests—Indian, Indian-American and otherwise American—the Cultural Festival generated questions about common ground: where was it and how did it function? [T]he Cultural Festival deliberately intertwined culture, nation and identity in its production of metaphors and myths. *With the synchronous developments of international capital and diasporic nationalism, we see infinitely complex realms of cultural production* (*Cultural Studies*, 11:2, emphasis added).

The 'our culture' argument, of which Bollywood forms an admittedly prime exemplar, clearly then also informs a range of productions, all combining the insatiable taste for nostalgia with the felt need to keep 'our (national) culture alive': from websites to chat shows, from Ismail Merchant and Madhur Jaffrey cookery programmes to advertising, soap operas to music video, niche marketing of various products, satellite channels, journalism, the Indipop 'remix' audio cassette and CD industry.

If, then, we see Bollywood as a culture industry and see the Indian cinema as only a part of it, even if a culturally significant part, then it is also likely that we are speaking of an industry whose financial turnover could be many times larger than what the cinema itself can claim. This would be true of the export market, but, if we include the extraordinary 'dotcom' boom being witnessed in India right now, it may even be already true within India itself.

The transition, or crossover in marketing terms, from a domestic film product which has comparatively few options for merchandising its products to one that more successfully gears itself for exploiting the new marketing opportunities that Bollywood now presents, are today palpably evident, certainly to any clued-in filmgoer. The difference between the 'Bollywood' movie and the rest of the Hindi and other language films being made would be, say, the difference between Karan Johar and David Dhawan, between Shah Rukh Khan and Govinda, between *Phir Bhi Dil Hai Hindustani* and *Anari Number 1*.[2] While *Hum Aapke Hain Kaun?* was perhaps the first Indian film to recognize and then systematically exploit a marketing opportunity here, it has since been most visibly Shah Rukh Khan who has been committed to the Bollywood mode, earlier mainly as an actor (*DDLJ, Pardes, DTPH, KKHH*) but this year with *Phir Bhi Dil Hai Hindustani,* having personally taken charge of its global marketing.

I want to drive a further wedge into the difference, by pointing to two crucial consequences of making this a distinction between the cinema and the more generalized Bollywood culture industry. In one obvious sense, Bollywood is of course identical to the Hindi (if not Indian) cinema: film continues to remain the most prominent presence, the figurehead of the global 'Indian' culture industry. However, in ironic contrast, whereas practically every other ancillary industry seems to have by now defined an audience, a market, and a means of sustained production for that market, the cinema continues to suffer from its old difficulties of defining a generic production line and thus of defining a stable channel of capital inflow.

Let us see the problem as one of *defining culture economically*. If one were to extrapolate a larger theoretical question from all this, it would be: what are the circumstances under which cultural self-definitions *resist* economic or (we could now add) political resolution? And why does the cinema suffer from this problem in India, when other forms from television to radio to the music industry and, of course these days, the Internet, seem to have no problem here?

To ask the question in these terms is, I suggest, to get to the very basis of why the Indian cinema exists at all. It is the further contention of this paper that since the second World War, when the Indian cinema first defined itself as a mass-culture industry, the very reason for why it occupied so crucial and prominent a space in the emerging post-war and—more crucially post-partition—public sphere has actively forced it to resist capitalist organization. The globalization of this duality in the past decade under the aegis of Bollywood, I finally suggest, leads us to important insights into the phenomenon that I shall argue is also, and among other things, the globalization of a crucial set of conflicts bred into Indian *nationalism*.

The Resistance to Industrialization

On 10 May 1998, the former Information and Broadcasting Minister Sushma Swaraj declared at a national conference on 'Challenges before Indian Cinema' that she would shortly pass a government order declaring 'industry status' to the film industry in India. This was a direct response to perhaps the most intense lobbying the film industry had yet done to achieve what Hollywood, for instance, achieved in the 1930s and what the Indian cinema has been denied since its inception. K. D. Shorey, General Secretary of the Film Federation of India had already, in 1996, sought to include this declaration into the Ninth Five Year Economic Plan, saying that

> the situation in the film industry is very alarming. While the cost of production is on the increase, the revenue at the box-office is dwindling because of the rampant piracy of feature films on the cable and satellite networks. India should have more than a lakh of theatres, considering its population and according to an UNESCO report. But unfortunately, there is a declining trend in cinema houses from 13,000 and odd to 12,000 ... What is worrying us, producers, is that the entertainment tax, which was started by the Britishers as a war-time measure, has been increased to such large proportions by various state governments that it is eating into the revenue of films. Nowhere in the world is entertainment tax levied, barring in countries like India, Pakistan and Sri Lanka ... What is Rs 800 crore to the Government? The Planning Commission can ask state governments to abolish the entertainment tax and the Central Government can easily allocate that much of reimbursement. As far as the other central duties are concerned, they hardly work out to Rs 35 crore ... If only financial institutions lend money for the construction of theatres and institutional finance for film production (is made available) as it is prevalent in western countries ... the film industry can survive in a healthy atmosphere' (*The Indian Express*, 3 October 1996).

Shorey was of course not talking about Bollywood here: the problems to which *he* refers are the old ones, the ones that the film industry still continues to face on the ground, problems we have heard since at least the 1960s. However, for independent and more contemporary reasons, this seemed an appropriate time for the government to make the move of declaring film as an industry capable of attracting institutional finance.

By the early 1990s, the growing economic power of the non-resident Indian or NRI, people of Indian origin who were domiciled abroad—whom the Indian government was actively wooing with attractive investment schemes which already formed a substantial part of the Reserve Bank of India's foreign exchange reserves—had already announced the arrival of a new culture industry that we have here named Bollywood. The failure of the Broadcast Bill by the previous government had placed growing pressure upon the Bharatiya Janata Party (BJP)-led coalition to come up with some kind of consolidated media bill that would address in an integrated fashion the merger of satellite communications with cable, television and the internet, all of which featured film prominently in their output, and all of which stood at the threshold of attracting serious financial investment from a range of international investors. Already Rupert Murdoch's entry into the satellite television market with his STAR-TV had transformed the field, and it appeared as though film production would be the next target as Murdoch's Twentieth Century-Fox acquired a majority stake in the Bombay-based UTI-TV production house.

This was then not merely a matter of abolishing entertainment tax or making local institutional finance available for production alone, as K. D. Shorey seemed to think. The reform of the film industry through corporatization, signalled most directly by the formation of the Amitabh Bachchan Corporation and indirectly by a range of films from Shekhar Kapur's *Mr India* (1987), Mani Ratnam's *Roja* (1992) or Vinod Chopra's *1942 A Love Story* (1994), all addressing the theme of techno-nationalism that was on its way to being incarnated as *the* Bollywood thematic, had made it a prime candidate for international, including NRI, investor support.[3]

Behind it all, there was also the more complex political issue involved, of the Indian state itself negotiating a transition from an earlier era of decolonization and 'high nationalism' into the newer times of globalization and finance capital. The BJP's own investment into the concept of a 'cultural nationalism'—a rather freer form of civilizational belonging explicitly delinked from the political rights of citizenship, indeed delinked even from the State itself, replaced by the rampant proliferation of phrases like 'Phir Bhi Dil Hai Hindustani' and 'Yeh mera India/I love my India'—have clearly taken the lead in resuscitating the concept of nation from the very real threats that the State faces as an institution of legitimation, particularly following its policy of widespread disinvestment in a range of functions. The significance of the cultural turn has been well documented, as has the unexpected support that such a brand of cultural definition—and the ensuing industry that, to quote the Fort Lauderdale housewife mentioned earlier, functions to keep 'our culture alive'—extended to the form of 90s Hindutva governance in which Sushma Swaraj has been of course a prominent presence.

It was for both economic as well as political reasons that the cinema had to feature prominently in all this, if for no other reason than simply by virtue of its presence as *the* most prominent culture industry in modern India. There are however deeper issues involved, as well as a few problems, which involve an investigation into just why the cinema occupies such a prominent location in India in the first place. We may need to digress here slightly, to revisit a situation in the late 1940s, which I want to suggest bears both direct relevance to and helps illuminate the 'Indian cinema versus Bollywood' divide that I am trying to map.

The period to which I refer is between 1945 and 1951, when film production in India suddenly more than doubled (from 99 films in 1945 to 221 in 1951). This is usually seen as a low moment in Indian film history, when a whole range of independent financiers and producers jumped into the fray, effectively ending the more stable studio systems of the pre-war period, whom the Film Enquiry Committee Report of 1951—the most elaborate and authentic record of this crucial time—castigates in no uncertain language as 'leading stars, exacting financiers and calculating distributors' who 'forged ahead' at the 'cost of the industry and the taste of the public' (Patil, 1951).

It was nevertheless an extraordinary achievement, perhaps unparalleled in the history of world cinema, that in this period the film industry set itself up as a national industry in the sense of assembling a national market, even devising a narrative mode that has since been extensively analysed as nationalist melodrama in ways that actually *precede* and even anticipate institutionalized State functioning in this field (see Prasad, 1998, and Chakravarty, 1993). Film theory has demonstrated the crucial role nationalist–political constructions play in determining narrative and spectatorial practices. Even in the instance of American film, it has been demonstrated that it was only around 1939 when the notion of 'American unity', informed by the pre-War situation that 'both necessitated and enabled national cohesion', that saw the 'unified, national subject—the paradigmatic American viewer' being put in place, that Hollywood actually deployed several of the technical and narrative conventions for which it is today renowned (Cormack, 1994: 140-142), and for which *Gone With The Wind* (1939) remains so crucial an event in American film history.

This departure from the more usual condition of a decolonizing nation-state was a source of some embarrassment to the Nehru government, as the Film Enquiry Committee report consistently shows. Unlike any other comparable instance—where, much more conventionally, newly formed 'third-world' nations established national film industries from scratch, usually by reducing or eliminating their financial and infrastructural dependence on the erstwhile colonial power, and where, from North Africa to Latin America to large parts of East Asia, the founding of a local film industry has almost always been a culturally prominent part of national reconstruction—India inherited an already established, even if chaotic, production and exhibition infrastructure for a cinema industry that was poised, even then, to become the largest in the world.

The Enquiry Committee Report's main thrust is in startling contrast to the stand taken by film organizations in other countries with whom India in fact had exchange links, like FEPACI (the Federation of Pan-African Cineastes, affiliated to the Organisation of African Unity, OAU), who believed their 'prophetic mission was to unite and to use film as a tool for the liberation of the colonized countries' (Diawara, 1992: 39). The Indian government wanted to keep the film industry in check, to regulate it in some way, to reform its dubious credentials as a national form and to also thereby address cultural nationalism's discomfort at having to depend on such inauthentic resources; eventually to replace it with something better, something that more authentically represented the modernist aspirations of India's newly enfranchised civil society (Rajadhyaksha, 1993).

Some of these perceptions of the industry would seem quaint today, and were even then controversial. Critic Chidananda Das Gupta, India's leading theorist of precisely the kind of cinema that the government of India tried to launch after the 1950s with the direct involvement of State agencies, for instance, tried to re-integrate the difficulties posed by the typically modernist divide between 'good' and 'bad' culture. He attributed to the mainstream cinema a specifically, even consciously, nationalist function. Coining the term 'All India film', he suggested that India had evolved an idiom, and industry, that appropriated aspects both from indigenous popular film and theatre genres and from Hollywood, subordinating them to an all-encompassing entertainment formula designed to overcome regional and linguistic boundaries, providing in the process 'cultural leadership [that reinforces] some of the unifying tendencies in our social and economic changes [a]nd provides an inferior alternative [to a leadership that] has not emerged because of the hiatus between the intelligentsia, to which the leaders belong, and the masses' (Das Gupta, 1968). The contention that the All-India film performed by default an integrating nationalist function similar to the consciously stated aim of say All India Radio (which name Das Gupta clearly evokes in his term All India Film) and more recently Doordarshan, went on to have an important influence on India's national film industry policies after the Enquiry Committee Report. The industry's inability to be financially self-sustaining thereafter often came to be counterbalanced by its alleged ability to foster a unified contemporary 'indigenous' culture.

The claims of the mainstream cinema as a repository of national-cultural values in one sense have their origin in these times. The claim by itself does not, however, explain how the cinema industry pulled together a national market or national audience even before national independence, and consequently without state support. How, to return to our earlier question, did the cinema pull this off and how did it come to occupy its crucial presence as a 'cultural unifier' and a keeper of the flame in the sense in which that Fort Lauderdale housewife sees the ritual of cultural bonding involved in going to the movies?

I suggest that the answer would need to be sought in the very categories of national culture that India invoked in the 1940s and early 50s, and identify something of a zone, a domain of some sort, a blind spot, in the role that this *national culture* had to play *politically*, a zone into which the cinema came to ensconce itself. Partha Chatterjee offers here a larger argument around the 'hiatus' that contextualizes Das Gupta's move, for what was going on at the time.

> [W]hereas the legal-bureaucratic apparatus of the state had been able, by the late colonial and certainly in the post-colonial period, to reach as the target of many of its activities virtually all of the population that inhabits its territory, the domain of civil social institutions as conceived above is still restricted to a fairly small section of 'citizens'. The hiatus is extremely significant because it is the mark of non-Western modernity as an always-incomplete project of modernisation (Chatterjee, 1997a).

Given a corresponding analytical problem posed by the usual ways of working through this hiatus—that we either 'regard the domain of the civil as a depoliticised domain in contrast with the political domain of the state' or blur all distinctions by claiming that everything is political, neither of which helps us get very far—Chatterjee posits the existence of an intermediary domain of some kind: a 'domain of *mediating institutions between civil society and the state*' (emphasis added). He names this 'political society'.

It is not the purpose of this essay to go into the complex nature of political manoeuvres that ensued within State functioning and within the domain of private capital at this time, the late 1940s-50s, in India. Suffice it to say that if part of Indian nationalism defined itself in terms of a modern 'national' culture, and instituted a whole paraphernalia of activities defining the identity of the 'modern citizen', then there was another part of the national State functioning at another level altogether, the level for example of population control, welfarism, democracy, and finally, there was a 'domain' of something in between, something that enabled the protagonists of national culture, its civil society, to talk to, negotiate with, the State, something that we more commonly refer to as the sphere of 'politics'.

It is mainly the concept of 'mediating institutions' that I shall briefly explore here, and their relevance to the cinema of this time. Let me trace back into this era yet another familiar characteristic of the 90s Bollywood movie, one incarnated by its first big manfestation *Hum Aapke Hai Kaun?*, that this cinema addresses a 'family' audience and deals with 'family values', as against another kind of film, the non-Bollywood variety, that didn't and maybe still doesn't know how to do this. In this time, says Chatterjee, there was a move by the dominant State to name its people as 'citizens' of some kind, and this move was a displacement away 'from the idea of society as constituted by the elementary units of homogeneous families to that of a population, differentiated but classifiable, describable and enumerable'.

It is possible to see the cinema as the suturing agency par excellence of such displacement and mediation. The cultural role of the neighbourhood movie theatre as a prominent institution of the new public sphere in this time is crucially accounted for by the fact that a ticket-buying spectator automatically assumed certain rights that were symbolically vital to the emerging State of the 1940s-50s. (In some ways the contentious aspect of 'entertainment tax'—effectively equating the spectator with the price of his ticket, extended into equating the film solely with its box office income, all the problems to which K. D. Shorey refers above—is a legacy of these times). These rights—the right to enter a movie theatre, to act as its privileged addressee, to further assert that right through, for example, various kinds of fan activity both inside and outside the movie theatre (Srinivas, 1996) went alongside a host of political rights that defined the 'describable and enumerable' aspects of the population, like for example the right to vote, the right to receive welfare, the right to have a postal address and a bank account. Film historians through this period repeatedly assert how, for example, in many parts of India the cinema was perhaps the first instance in Indian civilization where the 'national public could gather in one place that was not divided along caste difference' (Sivathamby, 1981).

It is not important that these rights were not necessarily enforced on the ground. It is important instead to recognize that spectators were, and continue to be, *symbolically* and *narratively* aware of these rights, aware of their political underpinnings, and of their ability to do various things—things that constitute the famous 'active' and vocal Indian film spectator—that we must understand as a further assertion of these rights in the movie theatre. I am suggesting here that, firstly, the many characteristics of film viewing in India—as well known as its 'masala' and songs—of vocal audiences, throwing money at the screen, going into trances during devotional films and so forth, were in turn characteristic of *spectators identifying themselves* through identifying the film's address. And secondly, that this entire process of identification and counter-identification narratively spans precisely the divide that Chatterjee's 'domain of mediating institutions' would play in the world outside the movie theatre. It now appears that the aspect of 'identification' that film theorist Christian Metz, for instance, once defined when he answered the question, who does the film spectator 'identify' with?, by suggesting that the spectator identifies with '*himself* . . . as a pure act of perception' (Metz, 1982)—that this reasonably well-known aspect of film theory developed a distinctly political meaning in the India of the 40s and early 50s.

There now developed a serious contradiction, from which the Indian cinema never really recovered, as glaring today in the Bollywood versus film industry divide as it has ever been. In one sense, the film industry was able to manoeuvre itself into a position that made it indispensable to the State. As in many ways the most prominent independent cultural exemplar of the national market and the provider of leisure activity to the 'people' in the larger populational sense to which Chatterjee gestures in his more encompassing definition of the citizen, the cinema demanded the right to exist and receive some kind of industrial sustenance. It did, for example, win certain regulatory concessions in the form of the various State Film Chambers of Commerce, a certain limited amount of infrastructural support such as subsidy for imported film stock (via the public sector Hindustan Photo Film); and in turn it also chose to view disciplinary institutions such as the Censor Board as not merely capable of punitive action, but also, and more positively, as agencies underscoring and validating the objects of its spectatorial address.

On the other hand, the very space that the film industry came to occupy disqualified it by definition from the range of *new* concessions and supports that the Film Enquiry Committee recommended, including most crucially institutional finance. Indeed, all these concessions, then and since, were meant for precisely a kind of cinema that the film industry was *not*. They were meant for a different cinema which the State hoped to encourage, one that would fit better into what Chatterjee calls the 'pedagogical mission' of civil society and its agendas of modernization: a 'different' cinema that we could today see as the direct ancestor of the Bollywood mode.

Indeed, in the barely concealed claims to some sort of reformism that Bollywood so often presents these days in its biggest successes—the claims of commitment to family values, to the 'feel-good-happy-ending' romance that carries the tag of 'our culture'—one can see the ghosts of past trends going quite far back into time. The problem of the cinema's legitimacy has, since the pre-War years, consistently produced version after version of what was claimed as culturally authentic cinema—authentic because authenticated by the national culture. One distant ancestor to, say *HAHK*, would be the pre-War 'Swadeshi' movie—the devotionals and socials emphasizing *indigenism* of story and production. Post-War and in the early years of Independence, there was the first descendant of this indigenism—the cinema that the State repeatedly anointed as 'authentically national'. The process of authentication in this time was more palpable than the films that benefited by various declarations of recommended viewing—and continues to be so, if we see, for example, the extraordinary premium that the film industry continues to place upon the government's national film awards and its tax exemption criteria. One could safely say, however, that among the candidates vying for this kind of accreditation were included Devika Rani and Ashok Kumar socials from the Bombay Talkies studios, reformist musicals such as some of Raj Kapoor's work or some from Dev Anand's Navketan production house (both of which often hired ex-practitioners from the IPTA movements of the 1940s) and realist-internationalist films by directors from Satyajit Ray to Bimal Roy to the early Merchant-Ivory (Rajadhyaksha, 1993).

This then was the situation. The film industry had won for itself a distinct, even unique, space of spectatorial address and spectatorial attention that is even today not shared by any of its other ancillary industries—not, for example, by television, despite the programmes seeking to evoke the excitement of the filmgoing experience with its coverage of the industry, its 'behind the scenes' programmes and its efforts to get stars to endorse televized versions of the Indian cinema. It has extended this spectatorial space into some kind of peripheral, perennially unstable and yet functioning economy with a rough-and-ready system of funding for its productions. It has also weathered a divide within its production processes, between those who control infra-structure (licensed stockists of film stock, owners of laboratories, dub-bing theatres, editing suites, sound studios and other post-production facilities, all of whom routinely get banking and corporate institutional support) and those who invest in *production*, bear the entrepreneurial risks of a film doing well or badly, and *never* receive institutionalized funding support. They do not receive support because they cannot, for to do so would be to certainly threaten the very *raison d'etre* of why the cinema is so popular, the space the industry occupies.

This is the situation—an evidently backdated, relentlessly mod-ernist, even Statist, situation, wedded to governmental support while at the same time aware of its peculiar illegitimacy—to which K. D. Shorey refers, when he enumerates the problems that film producers continue to face. This is self-evidently not the situation that Bollywood faces. The old movie spectator, the member of Chatterjee's political society, would—and does—feel distinctly uncomfortable in plush new foyers with Pepsi soda fountains. And Bollywood, in its turn, quite explicitly qualifies for a range of corporate funding support systems.

Bollywood does however manage something else in its turn, it seems, something that none of its cinematic predecessors could quite achieve. It succeeds, on the whole, in mediating the transition into the new category of citizen-as-family-member while maintaining intact the cultural insiderism of film spectatorship. Few films being locally made in Bombay, Chennai or Calcutta can aspire to such a transition. Few films, ergo, can claim international venture capital support.

Exporting the Spectator: New Sites for Modernism

There is a near unanimity that the right kind of recognition would eventually lower the cost of an industry, where expenses and price of funds are mindboggling. Thanks to the well accepted practice of tapping undisclosed money, particularly the mega-budget ones, the string of financiers (mostly operating through fronts) extract a rate of return which is three to four times the interest a commercial bank would possibly charge . . . This unpredictability has become inseparable from films. Immediately, I can't think of an evaluation procedure by which I can call a production viable,' said a senior PSU bank official. Bringing the activity within the banking parlance of 'productive purpose' appears to be the crux of the matter. 'Is it an income generating asset? This is neither manufacturing nor trading nor agriculture nor self-employment,' said a private bank official . . . 'We may consider the track record of a producer, personal investments and net worth and ability to repay if the production flops and then take a short-term loan backed by sound collaterals. But will this attract the filmwallas? They might get a better deal from sources they have been tapping so far,' said an official of one of the older private banks (Ghosh, 1998).

Sushma Swaraj, then, offering 'industry status' to the cinema, was clearly making an intervention more complex than what the Film Federation of India necessarily saw as the issues. The problem was old, even tediously familiar; the circumstances however were brand new.

There is one crucially important sense, perhaps, in which the new international market opening up for Indian film could be continuing its old symbolic-political adherences. It is possible that the Indian cinema's modes of address have opened up a new category for spectatorial address that appears not to be accounted for by, say, the American cinema after it discovered the story-telling mode for itself and after numerous critics and theorists went on to assume that this mode was globally relevant, that 'we all internalize at an early age as a *reading competence* thanks to an exposure of films . . . which is universal among the young in industrial societies' (Burch, 1990). If this is so, then in several places, like Nigeria, whose distinctive reception of Indian cinema has been analysed so remarkably by Brian Larkin (1997) or among the Fijian Indians in Australia who even make their own Hindi films on video, as examined by Manas Ray (2000), or for that matter among audiences who still flock to Indian films in Trinidad and South Africa, there could be people still going to these films precisely for what Hollywood cannot be seen to offer. It is possible that the cinema's addressees are entering complex realms of identification in these places which would definitely further argument around the nature of the cultural-political mediation that the Indian, or possibly the Hong Kong, cinemas continue to allow.

Evidently, *this* was not the market that was pressuring Swaraj to define a law offering industrial status to film. Nor was this the market that has film distributors and producers in Bombay in a tizzy, wondering how they can rake in their megabucks or go corporate. In fact, a recent news item about Burma and how popular Hindi films are there, speaks of print rights of *Taal* being sold for $10,000, a 'relatively high amount by Burmese standards (Jha, 2000).

In the Bollywood sense of the export of the Indian spectator to distant lands, I want to suggest another kind of export: the export of Indian nationalism itself, now commodified and globalized into a 'feel good' version of 'our culture'. If so, then what we are also seeing is a globalization of the conflict, the divide, central to nationalism itself: the divide of *democracy* versus *modernity*, now playing itself out on a wider, more surreal, canvas than ever before.[4]

We don't know too much about this right now, but in conclusion, I would like to state the following issues that could be of relevance.

First, the question of *modernism*. If the civil and political society divide means anything at all, it shows how prevalent, foundational, and indeed how virtually unbridgeable the divides in India have been across the chasm of modernity. It is true that *something* has happened recently which seemingly wipes them away as though they have never existed, and different people have tried to explain this erasure differently. Arjun Appadurai's famous formulation of 'modernity at large', modernity cleansed of the mechanics of geographical belonging by the diaspora and the cyber-neighbourhood, certainly offers the *terrain* on which this insiderism is acted out (Appadurai, 1997). There do nevertheless seem to be larger, and still unanswered questions, which might be asked of the theorist but even more directly of the practitioner of Bollywood culture. For example, why now? The transition of cultural insiderism away from its heartland, away then from its historic political function of creating a certain category of citizen, and into something that informs the feelings of the visitor to the Brisbane night club, quoted earlier, who wants to go there to 'assert her Eastern identity'—this transition would clearly have something basic to offer in its rewriting of the *very trajectories of modernism* that have historically linked places such as India to the 'West'. Why does it seem so simple to pull off today when the Indian cinema has sought this transition to national legitimacy since at least the 1960s, without success?

A second question deals with the area of cultures resisting economic and political resolution. Bollywood clearly is reconfiguring the field of the cinema in important ways. What does it pick as translatable into the new corporate economy, what is it that this economy leaves behind? This would be as important a cultural question as an economic one.

For example, I believe it is demonstrable that practically all the new money flowing into the cinema right now is concentrating on the ancillary sector of film production. On one side, software giants such as Pentafour and Silicon Graphics use film in order to demonstrate their products, so that it is unclear as to whether, say Shankar's *Jeans* (1998), noted for all its digitalized camerawork and produced by Hollywood's Ashok Amritraj was more an independent feature film surviving on a pay-per-view basis or a three-hour demo take for Pentafour's special effects. On the other, the range of consumables increasingly visible on film screens—Stroh's beer in *DDLJ*, Coca Cola in *Taal*, Swatch watches in *Phir Bhi Dil Hai Hindustani*—are symptomatic of the nature of funding that the cinema increasingly depends on.

If so, it would be the final irony of the Bollywoodization of the Indian cinema that the very demand that the industry has sought from the government for so many decades could be the reason for its demise. The arrival of corporate–industrial–finance capital could reasonably lead to the final triumph of Bollywood, even as the cinema itself gets reduced only to a memory, a part of the nostalgia industry.

Notes

All references in this essay have been drawn from the Media and Culture Archive of the Centre for the Study of Culture and Society, Bangalore. I am grateful to Tejaswini Niranjana and to S. V. Srinivas for their comments, as well as to the participants in the 'Bollywood Unlimited' conference at the University of Iowa 1998, and to Philip Lutgendorf, Corey Creekmur and Rick Altman, for their responses to an earlier version of this paper.

1 So *The New Indian Express* (29 October 1999) reports that 'The opening titles of Sooraj Barjatya's forthcoming film *Hum Saath Saath Hain*, billed as the most cracking release this Diwali, will feature an important new player in Bollywood: Coca-Cola. The cola giant, in its bid to scramble to the very top of the Rs 3500 crore soft drinks market, has spent a comparatively smaller amount, Rs 1.5 crore, on branding Barjatya's family film and ensuring its release as *Coca-Cola Hum Saath Saath Hain*'.

2 While difficult to define precisely, the difference is roughly that between a low-end local production with little ambition to new global markets, and a glossy internationalized production.

3 Tejaswini Niranjana defines this newly forged relationship, in *Roja*, of a 'techno-aesthetic' with a new category of the 'national' subject—see Niranjana, 1994.

4 Chatterjee elaborates his 'civil' versus 'political' society argument by suggesting that while modernity was the main agenda for the former, democracy could be seen as the main issue addressing the latter. So, in effect, the entire debate around modernism, around high and low art, around areligious secularism versus theories of caste and religion could be mapped around this often unbridgeable divide between modernity and democracy (Chatterjee, 1997a).

References

Appadurai, Arjun (1997), *Modernity At Large: Cultural Dimensions of Globalization*, Oxford University Press, New Delhi.

BBCI (2002), www.bbc.co.uk/asianlife/film/indiansummer/index/shtml

Banker, Ashok (2001), *Bollywood*, Penguin Books, Harmondsworth.

Burch, Noel (1990), *Life to those Shadows*, University of California Press, Berkeley.

Chakravarty, Sumita (1993), *National Identity in Indian Popular Cinema 1947-87*, University of Texas Press, Austin.

Chatterjee, Partha (1997a), 'Beyond the Nation? Or Within?', *Economic & Political Weekly*, 23:1-2, 4 and 11 January.

Cormack, Mike (1994), *Ideology and Cinematography in Hollywood, 1930-39*, St. Martin's Press, New York.

Das Gupta, Chidananda (1968), 'The Cultural Basis of Indian Cinema', in C. Das Gupta, *Talking About Films*, Orient Longman, New Delhi.

Diawara, Manthia (1992), *African Cinema: Politics & Culture*, Indiana University Press, Bloomington.

Ghosh, Sugata (1998), 'Industry status: Cinema may find itself going round trees', *The Economic Times*, 12 May.

Jha, Lalit K. (2000), 'Mania for Hindi movies sweeps Myanmar', *The Hindu*, 29 February.

Kabir, Nasreen Munni (2001), *Bollywood: The Indian Cinema Story*, Channel 4 Books, London.

Larkin, Brian (1997), 'Indian Films, Nigerian Lovers: Media and the Creation of Parallel Modernities', *Africa*, 67:3.

Metz, Christian (1982), *The Imaginary Signifier: Psychoanalysis and the Cinema*, Indiana University Press, Bloomington.

Moshavi, Sharon (1995), 'Bollywood breaks into the big time', *The Economic Times*, 3 October.

Niranjana, Tejaswini (1994), 'Interrogating Whose Nation? Tourists and Terrorists in *Roja*', *Economic & Political Weekly*, 29:3, 15 January.

Patil, S. K. (ed.) (1951), *Report of the Film Enquiry Committee*, Government of India Press, New Delhi.

Prasad, M. Madhava (1998), *Ideology of the Hindi Film: A Historical Construction*, Oxford University Press, New Delhi.

Rajadhyaksha, Ashish (1993), 'The Epic Melodrama: Themes of Nationality in Indian Cinema', *Journal of Arts & Ideas*, 25-26.

Ray, Manas (2000), 'Bollywood Down Under: Fiji Indian Cultural History and Popular Assertion', in Stuart Cunningham and John Sinclair (eds.), *Floating Lives: The Media and Asian Diaspora*, University of Queensland Press, St. Lucia.

Sengupta, Ratnottama (1999), 'Taalis for the Showman', *The Times of India*, 8 July

Sivathamby, K. (1981), *The Tamil Film as a Medium of Political Communication*, New Century Book House, Madras.

Srinivas, S. V. (1996), 'Devotion and Defiance in Fan Activity', *Journal of Arts & Ideas*, 29.

UNESCO (1981), *Statistics on Film and Cinema 1975-77*, Office of Statistics, Paris.

CHALO JAHAJI: BOLLYWOOD IN THE TRACKS OF INDENTURE TO GLOBALIZATION[1]

MANAS RAY

John Davies, a Canadian commentator on Fiji's coup of 2000, describes it as a tragedy of 'separate solitudes'. Nothing could be more apt. He holds the Fiji Indians squarely responsible for this absence of cultural dialogue: their condescending attitude towards Fijians, their consumerist ways, economic domination and media power. The culture of indigenous people needs to be safeguarded from the globally massive Indian culture, he warns. Towards this he advocates a series of positive discriminations, including the abolition of Hindi from the list of Fiji's official languages (Davies, 2000).

Off-track in crucial ways, since the latest crisis is a fallout of a disintegrating native Fijian social order and the rise of its middle class leadership (Lal, 2001) among other causes, Davies' prescription is both old and new, and typically western. It is new because it is in tune with a certain turn of current western cultural politics that yearns to define the nation in terms of its ethnic roots, once the project of 'nationalizing the ethnic' proved difficult with the different non-western communities living in the western metropolis. It is old, because it is part of the same vagaries of colonial pragmatics that once kept the native Fijians away from the plantations. The back-breaking toil of the Indian 'coolies', the Plantation Raj had calculated, would make the new colony of Fiji pay, while the Fijians could continue with their pristine lives in indolent villages unexposed to the corrupting effects of a capitalist economy.

Utilizing the discipline of the 'lines', the Indians in Fiji in course of time have contributed much to what today's Fiji is—economically speaking—with their labour and management. This is a huge achievement given the way they began their journey. The culture that evolved, the fashioning of 'little India' as it is called, was not so much an expression of the desire to return, an idle nostalgia, nor a docile willingness to replay on a minor scale a 'mammoth' original. Rather it was an active attempt to yoke an identity in the face of little or no recognition as cultural or political beings. Much later, once Bollywood entered the scene as the principal provider of motherland culture, the reconstructed home would attain a new dynamics in keeping with the dynamics of this quasi-globalizing media.

This paper examines the process of the imagining into existence of a sense of nationhood by a specific diaspora of Indian origin—the Fiji Indians—in Australia and the role that Bollywood, in its different manifestations, plays in this. This paper seeks to understand how mass images of India can be made to speak and/or represent history far outside the geographical limits of India and the place of viewers in that history. For this we bring together two separate but related journeys: the cultural trajectory of these 'splintered' people—from indenture to subsistence farming to their participation in the urbanization of Fiji and finally the coup of 1987 that resulted in a big exodus to western cities and the struggle for cultural identity in a new vortex of power and cultural ecology. We try to lace this journey with another journey, that of the images of Bollywood over the decades and how it impacted lives far beyond the shores of India.

Bollywood in its contemporary manifestation offers Indian diasporic youth a platform for organizing their cultural life which is 'acceptable' to the West and at the same time retains a measure of difference. The widely held notion that for Indians, *no matter where they live*, India largely derives from its movies (Rajadhyaksha and Willeman, 1994: 10) holds a special significance for Fiji Indians for whom India is largely an imagined entity ('mother' but not 'home', as a number of our respondents have pointed out). For the Fiji Indian youth in Australia, the relation between Bollywood and India is even more an imaginary one. This might suggest that reception takes place in a historical vacuum, but young Fiji Indians, more than any other Indian group in Australia, are keen on appropriating Hindi popular films to fashion a cultural identity that is their own.

Be it in the special meaning that Bollywood has for the Fiji Indian community or the re-invigoration of folk traditions inherited from India, be it in their friction with mainland Indians or their bid to re-imagine an entity called 'India' (from which they were once 'extracted' and to which they do not harbour any illusion of return but to which they nonetheless continually seek recourse as an imagined nodal point of identity), be it in their relatively westernized values or in the emphasis placed on tradition, the cultural life of Fiji Indians in their current western locations is inalienably linked to their genealogy of the last 130 years—the history of the Plantation Raj and after. We will not so much embrace celebration of the ontological condition of the diasporic imagination as focus on the contingent course of the historical subjectivity of this twice-displaced community, a course that has vital links to the changing political economy of Bollywood, its images and image-making over the years.

Indian Diaspora and Diasporic Media Discourse

Kay Rasool's film, *Temple on the Hill* (1997), is a short documentary on the banana-growing Punjabi community of Woolgoolga in northern New South Wales. The film is about continuity in the face of change: while the older generation harp on the former, the younger people perform the difficult negotiation between the demands of a traditional, rigid order and the attractions of the liberal, individualized West ('We stick to our culture but the mind travels'). Encased in the performance of Sikh religious rituals, the film stacks up the evident values of Punjabi life for no one to miss: deep attachment to the preachings of the holy saint, Guru Govind Singh ('who forms our identity'); allegiance to the family profession (boys return to work in the plantation after completing their university degrees); abiding respect and care for elders; photomarriage ('the parents have to say yes first'); the imported *desi* bride quietly performing the domestic chores ('we wanted a girl who will do all the housework'); assertion of strong familial ties ('my brothers will do anything for me, I will do anything for them'); and so on. Men play billiards or maybe display the new video camera which is 'so light', as women milk the cows or look after the children. Breaking this seamless pattern is the girl who felt 'more and more uncomfortable with being an Indian' and 'just wished I could be an Australian'. Glimpses of her preferred Australian life leads to a wholesale change in the visual milieu: swimming in the house pool with her daughter and white husband, the Australian lunch of salad, sausage and roasted meat (in place of *pooris* and hot *bhajis*), her sleek performance as a sales girl in a department store. The other figure to rupture the settled patriarchal order is the son who takes to Christianity and becomes a passionate evangelist, drawn by the attraction of Christian universalism which he contrasts to the hypocrisy of Sikh religious practice. A Hindi movie of song and dance provides solace to the lonely mother. What is remarkable about the documentary is that in about twenty-five minutes, it manages to encapsulate a whole portfolio of accepted Orientalist 'knowledge'.

Marie Gillespie's influential *Television, Ethnicity and Cultural Change* (1995) is a comprehensive study of the Punjabi community of west London. A media sociology of Punjabis living in one particular suburb, Southall, and sharing more or less the same history, cultural profile, media habits and class location, the work has been praised widely for its meticulous ethnology and has been influential in the rise of academic interest in the media of diasporic Indian communities (as only befits one of the largest diasporas in the world).

The differences of Gillespie's book with Rasool's film are apparent. The working class suburb of west London where more than 65,000 migrants (Gillespie, 1995: 33) jostle for space is a far cry from the sprawling green of a remote Australian plantation settlement. In economic terms too, they are studies in contrast: while the Punjabis of Woolgoolga have it good, the Southall Punjabis continue to struggle. However, in spite of the manifest differences, the picture that emerges of the cultural life in the struggling Punjabi ghetto in London bears real similarities to the time-warped, banana cultivating Punjabis in obscure Woolgoolga. Both constructions draw on an essentialized understanding of an *oriental* community. John Hutnyk points to this in his review of Gillespie:

> (t)here is not, in this book, any disruption of an ethnographic project that requires particular, not global, essentialized, although hybrid, traditional, although translated, ethnic categories to proceed . . . (S)he never leaves go of a notion of culture, which though it changes, is still an unexamined hold-all category doing work for time-honoured anthropological simplicities (Hutnyk, 1996: 420-21).

Gillespie's ethnography produces reasonably predictable results—the parental regime of social control, suspicion and adherance to a homeland culture of unquestioned obedience and religious devotion; the vicious networks of rumour and gossip aimed at constant surveillance of girls' chastity (25-27; 153-57); young people's preoccupation with style and fashion endorsing western images; the gendered pattern of viewing (boys prefer science fiction, science programmes, documentaries, news and crime series; girls prefer watching pop and quiz programmes, cartoons and children's TV and of course soaps); girls who (along with the older generation) mostly love Hindi movies while a majority of boys find them not to their taste (77). What is so specifically Punjabi or for that matter Indian about these findings? Gillespie will often throw up more questions than she answers. For instance, if boys are generally condescending about Indian traditions and Hindi films' unrealistic modes, how could the whole family group (boys as well as girls) so intently watch B. R. Chopra's televisual melodrama, *Mahabharata*?

Gillespie asserts that identity is 'not an essence but a positioning,' but she rarely makes use of Appadurai's insight that she quotes programmatically:

> [T]he Hindu diaspora has been exploited by various interests both within and outside India to create a complicated network of finances and religious identifications, in which the problem of cultural reproduction for Hindus abroad has become tied to the politics of Hindu fundamentalism at home (Appadurai, 1990: 302, quoted in Gillespie, 1995: 20).

Instead, what we have is a replay of classic ethnographic persuasion in a new form: she respectfully watches the Dhanis watch the teleserial, *Mahabharata* as an *authentic* moment of Indian devotion.

Gillespie's book is professedly about the 'cultural routes of diaspora' (6). But what is privileged is her attention to the values 'rooted in the subcontinent' (46) to which the youth are attached even as they try to 'maximise their chance of acceptance' (5) in British society. Gillespie's stress on both the irreducible difference of migrant cultures and the evolving trajectories of assimilation is in a way the crux of contemporary western multiculturalism: 'it "respects" the Other's identity, conceiving the Other as a self-enclosed "authentic" community towards which he, the multiculturalist, maintains a distance rendered possible by his privileged universal position' (Zizek, 1997: 44). The extent of the similarities between a painstaking work of academic ethnography and a film (*Temple on the Hill*) made by a young graduate point to the well-established order of knowledge about migrants from which both draw.

For all of her meticulous research into the kinds of audiovisual media watched by the Punjabis in London, Gillespie makes little or no attempt to link diasporic media use with the life of media back in India. We consider this significant, given the intimate relation Indian film and television have had with the politics of Indian nationhood. As a result, Gillespie's readings of film/video as a means of recreating cultural traditions suffer from a degree of aestheticization. The account that she provides of Hindi films (78) would be applicable to Bollywood of any decade after the emergence of the 'social' as a super-genre (see below). So she misses the potential of post-liberalization Bollywood from the late 1980s to frame a new diasporic cultural identity for Indian youth. Gillespie draws on the Habermasian notion of 'an enlightened public sphere of communications' (15) which in her scheme of things fits well with the notion of 'postcolonial space' defined as 'pluralistic conception of nationality and perhaps beyond that to its transcendence' (8). The burden of racism is placed on the nation-state which constructs its internal ethnic 'others', its 'racial minorities' (14). This gives her a reason to ignore the realities of the imbrication of nation-states with the contemporary movements of global capital (both economic and cultural); instead, she places hope on the traffic between 'the local and the global that nevertheless transcends the national' (6). As part of her distrust of the category nation-state, she refuses any consideration of the political background from which Hindi movies emanate and the fact that this cinema is inalienably attached to the politics of the Indian nation-state. Such depoliticized understanding of Indian films inevitably gives them the look of self-enclosed, exotic cultural artifacts whose consumption in the western world by the Indian diaspora Gillespie makes the centrepiece of her careful ethnography.

Different Diasporic Indias

The paper addresses two theoretical issues central to understanding diasporic media. First, we argue that the different postcolonial diasporas are not 'splinters' in a transnational world, ready to re-articulate their identity on the lines of extra-territoriality or nomadism; on the contrary, it is the *historical* subjectivity of a diaspora which holds the key to its cultural life. At one level, there is a need to club the different (postcolonial) diasporas together as those not party to what Partha Chatterjee calls the 'original historical contract' (Chatterjee, 1995: 11) that gave birth to the western nation-states. At another level, it is also important to recognize the different historical trajectories of these diasporas. Hence, the alienation that postcolonial people face in the multicultural west is multilayered; citings of the more visible signs of racism do not register its historical depth. The case of the Fiji Indians will amply demonstrate this. Second, diasporic media needs to be seen in the context of the politics of its production and dissemination. This is particularly so with Bollywood, which from its inception has situated itself in the locus of contending definitions of 'Indianness' (Rajadhyaksha and Willeman, 1994: 10).

By no means does this paper seek to analyse the media use of *the* 'Indian' diaspora seen as one monolithic whole. In fact, it is the globality of such a concept that needs be contested and read as a sign of the ahistoricity and ethnocentrism that so often underwrites the perception of postcolonial societies. This is not to deny that the different Indian diasporas do deploy their notions of 'India' as the broad symbolic horizon for constructing their respective identities. Neither is it to underestimate the crucial role that such pan-'Indianness' (largely derived from Orientalist discourse about India) played in imagining a nation into existence during the course of struggle against colonial rule or continues to play so long after the Raj. It is however to highlight the fact that for Indians (both inside India and outside) such 'Indianness'—like any other identity concept—is always already fissured. As a matter of *positioning* and not essence, this 'Indianness' varies with different communities, is used at times for contradictory purposes and quite often gives rise to unintended consequences. It may be argued that different empirical factors like language, region or religion do not by themselves hold the key to cultural difference. It is the positioning of communities in postcolonial space that underpins the cultural lives of different Indian diasporas and sets the course for possible futures.

The different ways in which different Indian diasporas frame their identities and cultural lives is remarkable. If the Fiji Indian community is the highest consumer of Hindi films, for the Indian Bengalis Indian-sourced film and video is not only a private affair—in many cases, it is of little interest and even active disparagement. At one level it may seem that this is a function of class, since the Indian Bengali diaspora in Australia, as elsewhere, is composed of professionals. But class cannot be a major cause, because South Asian diasporas in Australia are more or less of the same class composition, given the history of Australian immigration laws and the entry system it uses to select its migrants.

It is again a case of historicizing the question by addressing Bengal's specific encounter with the British regime and the systems of knowledge of post-enlightenment Europe. In its bid to imagine otherwise than the modular western (Chatterjee, 1993), cultural nationalism in Bengal had made the *self* the locus of a complex and difficult elaboration from the middle of last century onwards, that led to an enormous growth in every department of the Bengali cultural sphere. The basis of the *bhadralok* (the educated, Hindu Bengali gentry) was neither trade nor industry but land. Very early on, Bengal's commerce and industry was dominated by either the colonialists or the traders and capitalists from western India. As a result, the *bhadralok* concentrated on education, hoping to achieve through education what was denied through the economy (Chatterjee, 1997: 11). The process was accentuated with the introduction in 1885 of legislation limiting zamindari powers. This made the collection of dues more difficult, and rentier incomes began the long process of decline, both in real and absolute terms (Chatterji, 1994, among others).

The project of modernity that the Bengali *bhadralok* had framed for itself faced its real challenge after independence with the civic disarray caused by Bengal's stagnant economy and the change in the constellation of political forces. Subaltern classes, empowered by electoral democracy, now staked their claims to enter the political institutions of modernity, originally framed to keep them out. It is from this Bengal that the *bhadralok* flees, either to the relatively prosperous parts of India or, if possible, abroad, to the affluent West, taking with them the dream of a nation that they were once so passionate about and the cultural baggage which had expressed that dream.

The Indian Bengali community's relation to their home country is marked by a past which is lost and a present which is a lack. It justifies its rupture from motherland by attempting to become 'better' Bengalis: to evoke a past when Bengal's 'today' was India's 'tomorrow' is what frames Indian Bengali diasporic cultural life. This has meant framing their cultural lives around the high culture of the past, which has become a fossilized 'taste culture'. There is a surprising similarity between the menu of Bengali cultural programmes in Brisbane or Sydney and that of such places like New York, Toronto or London, where their number is vastly more. Ironically, the cultural products once deeply rooted in the soil with organic links to the independence movement and to early post-independence hardship and hope have now come to form an imaginative global geography, lacing together Bengalis in such diverse places as Philadelphia, Boston, London, Dusseldorf, Dubai and Sydney. In a diasporic context, the project of Bengali modernity has been emptied of all political significance, save its impossibility.

If the Indian Bengali community is locked in the past, the twice-displaced Fiji Indian community looks outside, to India, for its cultural sustenance. For the Fiji Indians in Australia, Hindi films mean a whole way of life. Movie theatres that regularly run Hindi films, film music nights, a number of bands that specialize in Hindi film music, nightclubs, design shops offering the latest of Bollywood, film maga-zines—Bollywood for Fiji Indians is by no means restricted to con-suming videos in the seclusion of the home. In this sense, the Fiji Indians of Australia bear a degree of resemblance to Gillespie's Punjabis of Southall. However, the differences between these two com-munities are crucial. India properly speaking is for the Fiji Indians a wholly imagined entity about which they know very little and have experienced even less. The fact that they were drawn mainly from the lower castes also helped them to largely free themselves as a social group from the shackles of the caste mentality or religious sectarian-ism over the last hundred years in Fiji. This is in sharp contrast to the mainland Indians and also to the Southall Punjabis.

Migration to Australia from mainland India has mostly been of the professional category. The social composition of India being what it is, this also means that the Indian representation in Australia is largely from the upper castes, many of whom are unwilling to give up their historical memory of unquestioned superiority vis-à-vis the lower castes. (There is also the phenomenon of large-scale Anglo-Indian emigration, but that is a separate issue, since the identity conflict we are referring to here would have little bearing on this community.) 'Going out' at times also means going back in time. As far as the Fiji Indians are concerned, the romantic construction of India (and Indians)—derived most significantly from the movies—faced in Australia for the first time the rude shock of caste discrimination through their interactions with 'compatriot' Indians. This has resulted in a change of focus of cultural antagonism—from the native Fijians, the mainland Indians now constitute the community's 'other'.

The pervasive dominance of Hindi film culture amongst diasporic Fiji Indians is complicated by the continued presence of folk traditions like *Ramayan katha* (i.e., the recitation and enactment from the Hindu epic, Ramayan), or *bhajan* (devotional songs) that they had carried with them from the villages of India a century or more ago. The Ramayan, in its simplified version of *Ramcharitmanas* by Tulsi Das, functioned as a binding force in the fissiparous environment of indenture. It provided a nostalgic identification with the motherland and also acted as a vehicle to relativize worldly realities by means of transcendental promises. This paper will show that, while the rural traditions in their present manifestations are thoroughly imbricated with Hindi filmdom, historically they have provided—in terms of narrative, iconography, and emotional and moral ambience—the ideal ground for the overwhelming popularity of Hindi cinema amongst Fiji Indians.

The size of diasporic Indian groupings found in a country like Australia rarely reaches 'critical mass'. Our research shows that the cultural implications of the numerical strength of a particular grouping depend on the specificity of its diasporic postcolonial subjectivity. The identity politics of the Fiji Indian community in Australia is more a *post*-colonial practice, while that of the Indian Bengali community, their higher professional profile notwithstanding, is distinctly post-*colonial*. Being *post*-colonial means being beyond the operative hold of memory, 'nostalgia without memory' as Appadurai phrases it (1990), while a post-*colonial* cultural politics is essentially an act of re-routing one's identity through the past.[2] For the former, the size of the community plays a vital role. Fiji Indians living in Sydney (upper estimates put the figure at about 50,000) have been able to form in the course of the last ten years a whole cultural ecology around Hindi popular filmdom. This has then been transmitted to other cities—for instance, Brisbane, where their presence is much thinner (around 7000). The crucial importance of this process lies in the fact that second generation Fiji Indians now have a cultural platform that, though not counter-hegemonic, is markedly different from the host culture. This paper examines the role 'post-Zee' Bollywood (the era since television was substantially de-regulated) and the current trend of re-mixes of earlier songs to new beats play in this form of identity construction. As a contrast to this, the emphasis of the first generation (post-*colonial*) Indian Bengali diaspora on aestheticized cultural forms of the past offers the second generation very little in terms of a home country popular youth culture with which they can identify.

In an era of the global spread of corporate capital and great demographic shifts, one of the key projects of political modernity is faced with serious crisis: instead of the 'nationalization of the ethnic' that western nation-states banked their hopes on, we now face the opposite scenario, 'the ethnicization of the nation'. The yearning for 'roots', as it is called, has become a common phenomenon for both the majority white community and the different diasporas, in different ways. As a result, the notion of shared public space is increasingly challenged by a different ordering of space—namely, a criss-cross of different primordias tied together by the universal function of the market. (Stuart Cunningham and John Sinclair characterize this phenomena as 'public sphericules') (Cunningham and Sinclair, 2001). For the Fiji Indians, if it was legislated racial discrimination that compelled them to leave Fiji, in Australia they find themselves in the middle of a new entanglement of different, contesting imaginings of 'roots'. One of the results of this process is that Bollywood is taking on a new significance in their lives. Historically, the bond between them and India has been one of imagination. With time, as memory of 'roots'—the *real* India—was fading away, films took over the responsibility of constructing an empty, many-coloured space through its never-ending web of images, songs, 'dialogues' and stars. In the new political context of Australia, this empty space would be shorn of even the pretence of a referent—it is space unto itself, a *pure* space so to say. Bollywood reciprocates this gesture by placing the diasporic *imaginaire* at the very heart of its new aesthetics.

Indenture and Beyond

The Fiji Islands was declared a British colony in 1874 when a group of indigenous 'chiefs' signed a Deed of Cession with the British. Five years later the first Indian indentured labourers arrived in the coolie ships from India, the labour for the sugar plantations and other enterprises that would make the new colony pay without exposing the indigenous population to the harmful consequences of an industrial economy (Kelly, 1991; Jayawardena, 1980). By the end of indenture in 1919, 60,965 Indians came to Fiji as indentured labourers (see Mishra, 1979 and Lal 1983). They called themselves *girmitiyas* (from the English word 'agreement', a reference to the labour contract). The British called them 'coolies', as did the indigenous Fijians (the word has an interesting twist, since the word for dog in Fijian language is similar: *kuli*). Once indenture ended—five years per contract, but mostly extended for another five years—many of them did actually return to India, but mostly they stayed back as subsistence farmers.[3]

By 1986, the Indian population was in the majority in Fiji (348,704 as against 329,305 ethnic Fijians) (Lal, 1992: 337) and the country's economy was based on Indian management and labour.

By the time extraction for Fiji began (in the 1870s), Madhya Pradesh and Bihar had started drying up and the eastern parts of Uttar Pradesh became the main source, constituting about 75% of those who left for Fiji from northern India. North Indian representation in Fiji constituted around 300 castes (mostly agrarian, with brahmin cultivators constituting around 10%) from 200 villages. The Muslim presence was 13% (Lal, 1983). Though as North Indians they all spoke Hindi, the dialects varied widely from one region to another. The difference in dialect is particularly important in this case, since the overwhelming majority of those who went to Fiji as indentured labourers were unlettered people. The *lingua franca* that developed among Fiji Indians (known as Fiji Hindi or Fiji Buli) reflects many different dialects, with occasional European and Fijian words. From the standpoint of ethnic identity, the important point is that the Fiji Indian population retained Hindi, which is not always the case with other indentured diasporas (see Jayawardena, 1980).

South India came into the picture only after 1903. However, even as latecomers, the total number of South Indians going to Fiji between 1904 and 1917 was 14,536, constituting 23.8% of the Indian population when the indenture period was over. The reason for such bulk migration is the different system under which they went—the *Kangani* system—where the village head corralled his village people and took them to the colony. In their new destination, the South Indians were moved around and scattered in different plantations and as such they had to adjust to the lingua franca. This was a matter of great effort on their part, since the languages of the South, emanating from the Dravidian family of languages, are so different from Hindi (which is part of the Indo-European group of languages).

In the post-indenture period, Indians worked mostly as independent farmers on leased land for different sugar companies owned in Australia and Britain. Their economic condition gradually improved and the hardship of back-breaking routine work also eased. News of the exploitation of Indian labourers, particularly the sexual harassment of Indian women by European males, caused major flare-ups in India and provided inspiration to India's independence movement (Kelly 1991). It has been argued that it was the movement against indenture in Fiji (with the active support of the Indian National Congress) that brought an end to the system world-wide in 1917 (Lal, 1985; 1992).

The Gujaratis first came in large numbers in the 1920s and 1930s as shopkeepers, moneylenders, artisans, *sonars* (goldsmiths) and in numerous other trades and services. There were occupational as well as residential differentiations. Mostly they lived in urban areas with little social interaction with the rest of the Indian community.

Unlike mainland India, Fiji was governed by British Common Law with no room for separate laws for different religious communities. However, this did not mean that for Fiji Indians the social system of Indian villages (which reinforces compliance with accepted rituals) gave way to the impersonality of a secular order. This could not have happened, given the built-in conditions of inequality of a plantation regime. For the indentured population, re-creating 'mother-land' in its social, cultural and religious manifestations became part of their wider political struggle.

Jayawardena observes that the complete proletarianization of Indians in Guyana meant near total loss of home traditions, while the Fiji Indians could maintain cultural traditions because of isolated post-indenture subsistence farming (1980: 436). With time, the population become more scattered and professions diversified. This re-emphasized the need to preserve their culture and religion in order to boost support and solidarity amongst themselves. Culturally speaking, the passage from indenture to post-indenture can be seen as one from 'amnesiac recollection' to an active bid to construct a 'national memory' (Kelly, 1998: 880). And what initially had provided fodder to the construction of national memory (in spite of its many divides like north Indians vs those who came from the south, Hindus vs Muslims, Gujaratis vis-à-vis the rest) were the folk traditions of North India and particularly, the ancient epic Ramayan (or better, the popular version composed by Tulsi Das in the 16th century, *Ramcharitmanas*). This epic—along with other cultural expressions of the *bhakti* movement—

not only provided cultural and moral sustenance to the community; in the very process of doing so, it also paved the way for the overwhelming popularity of Hindi popular cinema amongst Fiji Indians.

From the Ramayan to Bollywood

The cultural diet of Indians in Fiji right from the beginning of indenture was profusely imbued with elements of the *bhakti* movement, the popular religious, social and aesthetic movement that spread across India from the 12th century onwards (Embree, 1988). It is through the prism of *bhakti* that they imagined their 'motherland' and embraced the popularity of Hindi commercial cinema.

Bhakti, beyond the narrow sense as a form of worship, set the paradigm for popular creative expression almost singularly from the 12th to the 18th centuries, and later in combination with other currents of thought. Mostly a gesture against authoritarian rule, it was spearheaded by the subaltern classes. The movement was a confluence of many traditions and was not a particularly radical movement, at times showing an uncanny ability to suppress other emergent trends. While the transcendent is to be read in the everyday, it is figured in such a way that it has a levelling influence on all social and cultural divides of mundane existence. *Bhakti* songs were composed in the vernacular, using quotidian metaphors. They advocated struggle against Brahminism and upheld the sacrosanct nature of every human relationship. Tulsi Das' *Ramcharitmanas*, written in the 16th century, formed the centrepiece of *bhakti* tradition and became the unchallenged cultural meta-text of Hinduism. In the course of time, Gandhi was to privilege *Ramcharitmanas* to frame a semiotics of cultural politics against colonial rule, as for different and opposed ends was the Rastriya Sawangsevak Sangha (RSS—the martial arm of the currently ruling Bharatiya Janata Party). Throughout the nationalist movement, the Ramayan would function as one of the primary sites of investment for various kinds of re-writings for different cultural and political ends (see Lutgendorf, 1995; Bharucha, 1994).

Unlike India, in indenture Fiji there was no class of gentry to put through a nationalist sieve the various cultural forms that emerged in the encounter with colonial modernity and selectively adopt and combine the reconstituted elements of the supposedly indigenous tradition.[4] In the absence of any philosophical tradition, what prevailed at the beginning was the memory of numerous local cultural traditions of the villages of India. The north Indian village cultural expressions are compact, complex and part of a living tradition. The *girmitiyas* simplified those traditions they remembered—the dances, the songs, the religious rituals, sports, the games, the riddles. But most of them disappeared with time, since there was no institutional support for those traditions (Lal, 1992).

The traditions of village India that survived were basically derived from *bhakti*—the devotional songs (*bhajans*) of composers like Kabir, Mira and Sur Das. But over and above anything else what inspired their imagination was the Tulsi Das *Ramcharitmanas*. Very early on, reciting, singing and enacting the Ramayan was revived amongst the Indians of Fiji. This bound together a *cultural* community to survive the chains of bondage in the fissiparous environment of plantation capitalism, where everyone was an individual unit of production and daily existence was measured by work hours.

The Fiji Indians never accepted the status of a racially and culturally doomed proletariat and went to great lengths to fashion new hybrid diasporic realities. During the indenture period and the early days of post-indenture, both Hindus and Muslims participated in the major ritual festivals like Holi, the riotous Hindu ritual of reversals, and the Tazia, the Shi'a Islamic Moharram re-enactment of the martyrdom of Husain and Hassan. Both also participated in Ramlilas, the dramatic re-enactments of the Ramayan narrative, which in indenture days was told as a tale of Ram's exile, climaxing with the burning of the giant effigy of Ravan symbolizing destruction of evil in the world.[5] In these rituals (which were also to be dynamically appropriated into the Bollywood universe), the Indians found their social identity in relation to gods outside of, and in tension with, their colonial racist and economic definitions as 'coolies'.

The Ramayan was shorn of deeper philosophical meanings. Its primary function was emotional satisfaction and not individual spiritual enlightenment. As mentioned before, the majority of North Indians in Fiji came from the Ayodhya region of India, the homeland of the

Ramayan. The reasons for an overwhelming emotional identification with the epic is directly related to the predicament of an indentured diaspora. The central god character, Ram, was banished for fourteen years. For Fiji Indians, it was for at least five years. Ram's banishment was no fault of his; similarly, it was not the fault of the Indians that they were extracted from their homeland and subjected to inhuman physical labour on this remote island (Lal, 1998). The triumphant ending of all ordeals provided a kind of moral strength to withstand the brutalities of indenture. If Ram could survive for fourteen years, surely the Fiji Indians could do so for five years. The Ramayan thus was used to heal the wounds of indenture and provide a cultural and moral texture in the new settlement. There is another reason for this strong identification and this involves the question of woman and sexual virtue. Throughout the phase of indenture and even later, the paucity of women vis-à-vis men was one of the primary social concerns among the *girmitiyas*. In a situation where many men lived without wives of their own, women were expected to serve two contradictory functions: they were at times forced by circumstances and even by violence to leave one man for another, while the pressure was on them to comply with the standards of a good, chaste woman (Kelly, 1991). Hence, one central moral thematic of Hindi cinema—the image of the devoted wife, the heroine struggling to be chaste—had a special appeal for the Fiji Indians, given the peculiar existential circumstances of indenture. A strong emotional identification with the Ramayan and other expressions of *bhakti* movement, a constrained cultural environment, continued degradation at the hands of the racist white regime, a disdain for the culture of the ethnic Fijians, a less hard-pressed post-indenture life and finally, a deep-rooted need for a dynamic, discursive site for the imaginative re-construction of the motherland: all of these factors together ensured the popularity of Hindi films once they start reaching the shores of Fiji. This was because Hindi film deployed the Ramayan extensively, providing the right pragmatics for 'continual mythification' of home.

The two epics, the Ramayan and the Mahabharat, have been a cardinal influence on Hindi cinema right from its inception. Apart from providing moral succour, they were also magnificent sources for narrative tropes and cinematic spectacle. Films based on them initiated from the earliest days of cinema a different mode of spectatorship—devout villagers coming to the cities in their bullock carts to have a *darshan* (devotional sighting) of Lord Ram on the screen (Chakravarty 1993: 35-36). Madhava Prasad explains the *darshanic* gaze in the following way:

> Contrary to the voyeuristic relation, in the darsanic relation the object gives itself to be seen and in so doing, confers a privilege upon the spectator. The object of the darsanic gaze is a superior, a divine figure or a king who presents himself as a spectacle of dazzling splendour to his subjects (Prasad, 1998: 75-76. See also Rajadhyaksha, 1987; Vasudevan, 1993)

Thus a thoroughly western technology of representation was deployed to generate an altogether different gaze—one that will not be found in the visual codes of Hollywood melodramas but is deeply ingrained in Indian religious modes. With time Bollywood increased its repertoire of different modes of address but the *darshanic* gaze remained one of the most important moments in its relations with spectators.

Most of the films made during the silent period were mythological and devotional. In the course of time, the predominance of the mythological receded as other genres like the social, historical, comic or fantasy began increasing in popularity (Derné notes the decline in the number of mythologicals statistically: in 1923, 70% of the films made belonged to this genre, in 1935, 22% and in 1970, 5% (Derné, 1995: 195)). But with the decline of studio production and the rise of independent producers, all these genres gave way to a super-genre called the 'social'. By the end of the 1960s, this transition was complete. However, it did not mean that all these genres (including the mythological) simply disappeared; rather, they were subsumed within the 'social'. The genealogy of 'the all-inclusive Hindi film', which comes to have a 'variety show' look, is contemporaneously called the masala film (Prasad, 1998: 48).

Even during the days of the mythologicals, religion was never an offensive presence. Producers were cautious not to annoy the sensibilities of other religions, due to strict censorship regulations. Partly due to the prevailing censorship norms and partly because Hindi films cater to a multi-religious market, religious motifs are present but subtle (Derné, 1995). A Hindu way of life constitutes the broad environment for moral elaboration while narrative strategies draw very often, even if allusively, from the two epics. Prasad (1998) has shown that at its most stable, the social genre included a version of the romance narrative, a comedy track, an average of six songs, as well as a range of familiar character types; the masala aesthetic served as a handy catchall, an emotional and cultural 'map' of the diversity of Indian spectators.

The epics helped Bollywood to fuse the history of the nation and the history of the family. In the Indian narrative tradition, family history is not strictly demarcated from social history. The most obvious examples are these two epics, which are popularly believed to have a historical basis. In the Mahabharat, the battle between the Kauravas and the Pandavas, two branches of the same family, engages vast social, political, and cosmic forces, all of which are then sought to be compressed within a single philosophical framework; in the Ramayan, Ram's relationship with Sita is largely determined by his obligation to his family and, more importantly, his social *dharma*. Of the two epics, the Ramayan is again privileged because of its elaborations of the familial self and the focus on the duties and sufferings of *sati*, the chaste wife. Also to be taken into account is the fact that in North India, Ramayan's popularity far exceeds that of Mahabharat. The usual character stereotypes of Hindi films—the suffering but faithful wife (Sita) who is also a loving and somewhat indulgent sister-in-law; the courageous, dutiful and detached husband (Ram); the faithful brother (Lakshman) and the vengeful, evil villain (Ravan)—are mostly drawn from the Ramayan. Bollywood would experiment with these role models, bringing in other stereotypes (like that of the frolicsome Krishna of the Radha-Krishna *bhakti* motif popular in eastern India; or that of *dosti*—the friendship between two adult males which will be posited against heterosexual love for creating emotionally charged moments in the narrative). But never would Bollywood transgress the moral limits of the Ramayan.

What this effectively means is an inscription of the epics into the discourse of the nation through Hindi cinema. Partha Chatterjee (1984) has argued that Gandhian ideology led to the political appropriation of the subaltern classes by a bourgeoisie aspiring for hegemony in the new nation-state. Hindi cinema situated itself in this hegemony and aided the historical possibility of the appropriation of the masses into the evolving political structures of the Indian state. This explains its popularity across class lines and ability to reconcile within its narrative scope the contradictory aspects of social order.

Vijay Mishra (1985; 1992) points to the various underlying drives structuring the epics, invoking mythic figures from the epics as the substratum from which the various Bollywood character-types emerge. The traffic between the epics and Bollywood is, however, complicated by the role of music and romance. Music functions to transform the epic narratives by foregrounding a romantic repertoire. Romance is absolutely crucial for Bollywood; it is defined by romance. Here Bollywood draws more from the Radha-Krishna trope (of love, desire and erotica) of *bhakti* than it does from the epics. Bollywood, operating within the moral and social limits of the epics, extends its narrative scope by negotiating with other folk and emerging popular traditions.

Hindi cinema established its traffic to Fiji in the late 1930s (mentioned at the beginning of the essay). By then the period of indenture was over, the Indian community as independent cultivators had lost the solidarity that characterized life on 'the lines' of indenture, and linguistic and religious identities were being differentiated. Hindi cinema's primary impact in Fiji was to bond through meta-narratives with which all the different groups of Fiji Indians could identify. In this cinema, the Fiji Indians found the most lively expression of their yearning for roots and bid to re-construct an imagined homeland culture in an alien surrounding—at once simplified, quotidian and concrete but with a long tradition. And since in Hindi films *nation* is imagined in familial terms, the physical distance between mainland India and Fiji did not interrupt this 'work of imagination'. Evidently the folk traditions borrowed from the villages of India did not come in the way of Hindi cinema's popularity; on the contrary, by simplifying these traditions on a remote island with very little scope for other kinds of cultural traffic, the folk culture actually prepared the way for the unprecedented popularity of this quasi-globalizing mass culture.

As Fiji started urbanizing, the local Indian village cultures began to recede in influence, at least in the public cultural spaces of the cities. Once in place, Bollywood created its own public and psychic platform for people's interaction. (My numerous respondents have narrated how as boys or girls they used to gather around the movie halls long before show-time.) The gossip columns, the 24 hour Hindi service, the occasional visits of singers and stars from the then Bombay, all this went into constituting the culture of a community which harboured no illusion of return but for reasons of identity and cultural make-up yearned for a romanticized version of India that Bollywood amply provided. The genealogy of the unprecedented popularity of the mass cultural tradition of Bollywood in Fiji thus lies in the diasporic re-discovery of 'little' traditions that the *girmitiyas* brought with them and preserved over a century.

> The platform that Bollywood provides has much to do with its particular mode of enunciation:
>
> > Repeat viewing is . . . a common part of the everyday parlance of film appreciation in Bombay, where people will often tell each other that they have seen a film 10 to 15 times. While it is not always clear that these numerical claims are exactly accurate, they indicate an aesthetic in which repeat viewing is a sign of the committed connoisseur (Appadurai, 1998).

The typical Bollywood film is not a psychologically integrated unit but a loose compound of various elements like action, love, song and dance, dialogue, crime, devotion, special effects, and so on. What keeps these disparate elements together is the star system, with its retinue of reviews, magazines, interviews, blow-ups, television shows, advertisements, publicity materials, gossip columns, auto/biographies, fan club hagiographies and enormous billboards, displaying the stars in larger than life proportions, dotting the urban landscape. Rajadhyaksha and Willeman (1994: 10) call this 'the distinctive "insiderism" of a buddy culture of speech and body-language'.

Satellite television, with its plethora of programmes on Bollywood (mostly but not exclusively of song and dance sequences), has made this 'insiderism' very much a part of daily living. With the availability of cheap audio cassettes and recorders, the cult of music has spread rapidly, even to the remotest corners of India. Appadurai describes how these songs form a big part of the acoustic ecology of everyday life in cities and small towns. They are a crucial part of the repertoire of street singers who take the place of the 'star' duets in the films. All these feed into the social space of the auditorium:

> Anyone who has been to a popular Hindi film knows that a large amount of the leadership in any given audience signals its authority by indicating its command of both songs and script, largely by cheering when a certain 'hit' song or song-and-dance sequence is about to begin, by singing along on occasion, and by expressing various bodily signs of pleasure when key songs arrive. This anticipatory pleasure and mnemonic command, which is part of the folk aesthetics of cinema, is closely tied to the collective and interactive nature of film going and cannot be separated from two other elements of popular reception, dialogue and stars. (Appadurai, 1998; see also Srinivas, 1996)

While the very different historical trajectory of indenture and post-indenture paved the way for Bollywood, once in place in Fiji Bollywood did not need 'the particular conditions of the experiment', i.e., similarity to the cultural, economic and political conditions of India. The cult of Bollywood that the Fiji Indians *re-produced* in Fiji is not a case of mimicry, since *repetition* is inscribed in the very mode of being of Bollywood. If Bollywood is made the mainstay of cultural life (which to a very large extent is the case with Fiji Indians), it will of necessity repeat its entire cultural ecology—its 'insiderism'. This insiderism constructs a sense of mythological nationhood with very tenuous links with the *actual* geography of a nation. Hence, living in the realities of Fiji and participating in the life of Bollywood is not a case of split existence, since such a split is postulated on a divide between the real and the imagined, something that Bollywood disavows.

Fiji Indian Cultural Ecology in Australia

Despite their recent arrival in Australia and the structural deficits they face in employment, the Fiji Indians have re-established themselves with a cultural dynamism that is out of all proportion to their numbers and which can be sourced to their embrace of the cultural repertoire proffered by Bollywood.

In Sydney, the professional Fiji Indians are scattered all over the city while those in blue collar jobs tend to concentrate in one or two regions. In the immediate years after the coup, they concentrated in the Campsie region of Sydney. Latterly, Liverpool and to some extent Bankstown are the two suburbs into which a majority of the working-class Fiji Indians have moved. All these suburbs, with a number of big Indo-Fijian grocery stores, garment houses, movie halls, auditoriums and night clubs, have emerged as the different nodes of Indo-Fijian cultural life, complete with beauty contests (where participants come from all over Australia, New Zealand and Fiji), bands specializing in Hindi film music, music schools for filmy songs, DJs, karaoke singers, film magazines and community radio programmes. A number of Fiji Indian singers of Sydney have bought out CDs in India. These are mostly popular Hindi movie songs and a couple of *ghazals* (light classical North Indian music that had its roots in the Mughal courts). It is not unknown for well-known artists to have appeared on the popular commercial television network in India, Zee TV. One of the DJs, DJ Akash, has several CDs of Bollywood re-mixes to his credit. He works in close consultation with DJ Bally Sagoo, a second generation Indo-Britisher, who initiated the trend of re-mixes of old Bollywood music scores with his album, *Bollywood Flashbacks*, in 1994.

Brisbane's Bollywood cultural life, very much like in Sydney, is mostly a Fijian Indian affair. It has one regular band, Sargam, but relies on Sydney bands for major occasions. There are neither night clubs nor an established tradition of karaoke. Public performances, far less in number compared to Sydney, are hosted in rented auditoria. Like other Indian communities, for the Fiji Indians of Brisbane the relation to Bollywood is mostly restricted to renting Hindi videos, though as a community they are undoubtedly the highest consumers.

The reason for Brisbane's lack of a public face for Bollywood culture is partly due to the composition of the Indian community, with a preponderance of the professional class. But primarily it is a factor of size. With a population of less than ten thousand, the Fiji Indian community does not have the resources to support an on-going Bollywood cultural economy and, with migration having dwindled to barely a few hundred every year, there is no sign that the Fiji Indian presence in

Brisbane will increase substantially. The absence of a public culture of Bollywood impacts on the identity politics of second generation Fiji Indians. In general, the young Fiji Indians of Brisbane prefer to portray themselves as much less 'out-going' vis-à-vis their Sydney counterparts, less experimental about Bollywood ('interested in the professional part of singing and not merely re-mixes'), less hyped and much more rooted in the *values* of Indian culture. As a young woman active in Brisbane's Fiji Indian cultural world puts it: 'We are more Indian. In the way we mix with people, our morals and culture, the way we dress—in every way, we are truer to our Indian ways. For Sydney, India is a commodity to be bought and sold; for us, India is a way of life.'

One of the expressions of the overwhelming influence of Bollywood in Sydney is the community's attempts to make video films in Hindi. The process started in 1994 and, till 1998, four such films have been produced and two were in the process of being produced. *Starblitz* calls it 'Bollywood Down Under' and has a regular column devoted to it. These are locally financed, low budget, somewhat experimental Hindi films (on one occasion, the director has tried Fiji Hindi). These films are sold through Indian video shops and on public occasions shown by overhead video projector. Interestingly, these films are usually closer to Hollywood than Bollywood in narrative and moral scheme. One film, *Achanak* (meaning, sudden), is loosely based on *Basic Instinct* while another, *Biswas* (faith), is based on the *Rocky* films. These films are less convoluted in their narrative strategies than the average Bollywood product, with very few songs. The appeal of such films is restricted so far to the younger generation only, who have no illusion that the films will travel beyond Australia or in any way infringe on Bollywood's market. Rather, these films are more an expression of the deep involvement with the culture of cinema amongst young Fiji Indians and a desire to capture the new diasporic locale and the specificities of migrant experience. Another example, *Kayalat* (about the desire to be somebody else), narrates the story of a Fiji Indian girl who is trapped in her marriage with a Fiji Indian man. The husband does not try to appreciate the changes in self-perception that a diasporic situation has brought to her life. Interestingly enough, she does not solve her dilemma by embracing western culture but tries to find an identity which is her own. Towards the end of the film, she is found involved with a Fiji Indian man of working-class background. At a deeper level, these films reflect both the attachment to Bollywood culture and the measure of unease felt by Fiji Indian youth regarding Bollywood's continued reliance on 'traditional Indian mores and morals', notwithstanding the vast changes it has undergone in recent years.

Intercommunal Discord and Cultural Assertion

The ethnic, caste and class differences between mainland Indians and Fiji Indians has given rise to intracommunal tensions and rivalries which are neither new nor restricted only to Australia (see Buchignani, 1980). Many mainland Indians exhibit deeply entrenched casteist attitudes and view the indentured past of the Fiji Indians as a non-negotiable barrier.[6] On the other side, Fiji Indians often assign to mainland Indians the same kind of negative attributes that they were wont to use for ethnic Fijians. Both realize the need for a united front to deal with Australian racism but view each other as an obstacle to better acceptance by the 'white nation'. Mainland Indians now constitute an *other* for this community, just as the ethnic Fijians did back in Fiji.

Such rivalry between the two communities has seen the re-assertion of culture and ethnicity by Fiji Indians. This involves a positive mobilization of indenture history and an emphasis on a Hindu way of life in a western context that bears similarities to Gillespie's account of self-construction of identity through the positive assertion of ethnicity (Gillespie, 1995: 8-11). The dominant racism of white Australia, the ostracization by mainland Indians, the need of the older generation for a platform to socialize and to reflect (which will also function as a moral regime for younger people) have together fed in to a resurgence of religion and revival of folk traditions, neglected in today's urban Fiji.

Jayawardena notes that in urban Fiji, European culture is the medium in which members of different ethnic sections interact with one another (1980: 441-42). The impact of western institutions has been more profound than in India since, unlike mainland Indians, Fiji Indians have been subject to a uniform civil code. However, this uniform civil code in Fiji operates in a power matrix where Fiji Indians were in a distinctly disadvantageous position, initially with regard to the white indenture regime and then vis-à-vis ethnic Fijians. The result of a process of 'uniformity in the context of inequality' has been that as a community Fiji Indians retain their own cultural identity while their public life moves freely in and out of the European, Fijian and Indian cultural spheres. This heritage has contributed to Fiji Indians adapting rapidly to an advanced western lifestyle in their diasporic contexts.

One of the most creative methods of adaptation is the assertive construction of a cultural community around *Ramayan Katha* and *bhajan mandalis* (small gatherings for devotional songs) which paved the way for Bollywood's popularity. For the last couple of decades, these traditions were mostly on the decline in urban Fiji. Once in Australia, they have regained their popularity as a platform to unite the community and act as a moral regime for young people.

Significantly enough, in the Hindu religious tradition devotion and erotica are rarely separate departments of life and one very often evokes the other. This is particularly so with the *bhakti* tradition from which Tulsi Das's *Ramcharitmanas* emanates. In the *bhakti* taxonomy, *shringar* is the highest form of devotion—the erotic bond between the devotee (a woman) and the deity (a man). In one of the forms of *shringar*, the female denies herself, her family, all bonds and social constrictions, and pursues the love of Krishna. Radha is the epitome of this love and devotion. The trope of Radha and Krishna puts together social transgression, erotica and devotion. As the supreme expression of desire and pathos, it has for centuries provided inspiration for *bhajans*. It has also served Bollywood as a source of much of its music, narrative and allegory. This means that cultural and religious assertion of tradition has not been in opposition to Bollywood; in fact, in a western diasporic context, it provides young Fiji Indians with the cultural capital to really appreciate Bollywood.[7]

Fiji Indian Youth Culture and post-Zee Bollywood

The most dynamic aspect of Fiji Indian youth culture centres on the use of Bollywood to negotiate a kind of parallel cultural platform to the dominant western pop culture. This can be understood through grasping the enormous changes that Bollywood itself has undergone in recent years, especially since the advent of Zee TV. Zee programming has branded itself as a half-way house between Star TV and traditional Hindi film, creating a hybrid genre that refers strongly to western style music and dance. Such types of dance and music are now also the mainstay of Bollywood, especially of the new genre of 'teen-age romance' that has come into being in the liberalizing India of the 1990s. The Bollywood of tear-jerker melodramatic plots and folksy music with the male and female protagonists dancing in the luxuriant Himalayan foothills or the vast, empty stretches of a beach has not disappeared, but contemporary Bollywood is increasingly driven by contemporary music culture, and in large part by hugely extravagant song-music sequences with ever more tenuous links to the plot. DJ Akash of Sydney explains the implication of what he calls the 'MTV-ization' of Bollywood music for young diasporic Indians in the following terms:

> Ten years back a young Indian would listen to his music in a very low volume. He would consider his music to be very 'tacky' and would have felt awkward to play it publicly in a western context. The contemporary Bollywood music, by blending Indian melody with western beats, has changed all this. Nowadays if you go down the streets of Sydney very often you will hear Indian music blasting. Young people no longer consider the Bollywood songs as curry music. It no longer sounds strange to the average westerner (1998, interview with author).

Arguably because of this hybridization of Bollywood music, it manages to signify something special to the diasporic young Indian. Asked about the continued influence of Bollywood music, a young Fiji Indian woman, Sharon Pratap, performed this analysis:

> Bollywood has got the potential. It has got feeling. When you are happy you have something to sing, in love you sing, when you are sad you sing. You can relate to it. Consider the recent hit, 'Dil To Pagal Hai' ('my heart has gone wild'). It is about love and affection with which a young person can immediately identify. All those who are in love would buy the CD for their girl friends; they would send requests to the radio channel for the song to be played. We relate to it in two ways: i) visual part—i.e., what the main guy and main girl did in the movie, and ii) the meaning of the lyric. Compared to this, Hollywood music hardly

has any message that we can relate to. Take *Men in Black* for instance. We could barely identify with the hit score. The messages of Bollywood with which we are brought up hardly gets conveyed to us there. There is nothing of our own in such music (1998, interview with author).

Fiji Indian young people use a wholly hybridized genre like the re-mixes to fashion a discourse of authenticity. On the one hand, they will deploy the re-mixes as part of syncretic metropolitan culture and thus break out of the cartography that views their culture as *ethnic*. On the other hand, they perceive these re-mixes (for them, an essentially diasporic phenomenon) as part of their attempt to promote Indian popular music by making it contemporary; this they will compare to the Indian nightclub crowd which according to them is hooked on unadulterated western hard rock and heavy metal. Aiyasha, a young Fiji Indian enthusiast of 'Indi-pop' describes her experience in terms that combine being 'western' and being 'Indian': as a westerner, she prefers Indi-pop to traditional Indian popular music (which for her is 'a bit too romantic and at times unacceptably melodramatic'); she is also 'far more of an eastern person' vis-à-vis her Mumbai counterpart:

When I went to India, I found that kids are not thrilled with re-mixes. To be honest, I got the impression that they are quite wary of this kind of experiment; they think that it is corrupting the original music scores. On the other hand, I found nightclubs in Bombay (sic) are more influenced by Hollywood than Bollywood. I was shocked to find many Indian girls dancing to heavy metal and hard rock. This is pretty aggressive by Indian standards. I haven't seen any girl of Indian origin doing that sort of dance in Sydney . . . Kids in Bombay go to night clubs to become western. Here we go to assert our eastern identity. The basic difference lies there (1998, interview with author).

Diasporizing Bollywood

Contemporary Bollywood is unabashedly urban and increasingly global in its settings. Less than 5% of films now have rural stories as opposed to 15-20% ten years back (Chopra 1997, 54-55). Western locales are being juxtaposed with rural and urban India: for example, in *Pardes* (1992), a north Indian village seamlessly gives way to Los Angeles in the middle of the plot; or, in a reverse pattern, the diasporic protagonists of the highly successful *Dilwale Dulhaniya Le Jayenge*

(1995) travel through the continent to reach the bountiful Punjab villages of their ancestors where the main action will take place. The urban market now accounts for more than 60% of a film's earnings compared to 45% ten years ago; the overseas market too, now a substantial 20–25%, is increasing with every passing year. Many Bollywood films both promote and reflect the diasporic *imaginaire* that has squarely set in for the post-liberalization new urban middle class. For Thomas Hansen (1996: 603), the cultural significance of globalization for a postcolonial nation like India lies in the crucial ambivalence between its promises of recognition of nations and cultures, and its simultaneous threat of subversion of political sovereignty and cultural particularity. In these days of a global cultural economy where more than half of the world's economy revolves around communication and life-style industries, the distinction between the cultural-spiritual and the technological-economic is difficult to maintain. And if that is so, it is all the more imperative that differences are imagined all over again.

Bollywood has not only coped with the challenges of globalization but taken advantage of the new situation by enlarging its terrain. This it has achieved by creating a spectatorship aware of the specific requirements of the diasporas as well as those living in India. A globalizing world of communication and capital flow, instead of imposing a hegemonic cultural world order, has triggered a politics of space whereby the diasporas of a particular community dispersed world-over are networked to the homeland culture to such an extent that the traditional divide of outside/inside loses much of its analytical purchase. In contemporary Bollywood, it is interesting to see how the inscription of the citizen consumer, its ideal contemporary spectator, has offered spaces for assertion of identity for Bollywood's diasporic clientele vis-à-vis the host culture and in the case of Fiji Indians, with the mainland Indian communities as well.

Perceived as vulgar and prolific, at once strangely irrational and easily masterable, Bollywood till recently generated very little scholarly interest: for western film academia, it was a matter of indifference while for Indian film criticism, it was a target of unequivocal condemnation. The reasons were: a tendency to stasis at the level of narrative and character development; an emphasis on externality, whether of action or character representation; melodramatic sentimentality; crude or naive plot mechanisms such as coincidence; narrative dispersion through arbitrary performance sequences; and unrestrained and over-emotive acting styles (Vasudevan, 1993: 57). What such shock reactions to this cinema's 'lack of realism, restraint and psychological feasibility' conveniently overlook, however, is its enormous innovation in fashioning itself as the most reliable archive of popular hopes and disillusionment, and the ability to locate itself in the locus of influential and contesting definitions of 'Indianness'.

It can be argued that since the emergence of the super-genre of the 'social' in the 1960s, Bollywood underwent its next major change in the late 1980s–early 1990s coping with the tides of globalization. As part of this change, the diasporic Indian (popularly known as the Non-Resident Indian (NRI)) is now very much part of its address. This was necessary not only to embrace Bollywood's diasporic clientele but also to secure its popularity at home since the one self has to see its reflection in the other for its globalizing ideal self-definition. In the new troping of the home and the world, those who are brought up outside India have *India* inside them very much as the *West* is inscribed in the heart of India. This enmeshing of identities has enabled Bollywood to address the moral and cultural alienation that diasporic youth feel with Hindi films made on 'standard formula', while it also offers them the difference they want vis-à-vis Hollywood.

Earlier Bollywood was not governed by consideration of community 'out there'; community was securely at home. Hence representations of abroad could only take the form of the travelogue. For instance, towards the later part of the super-hit *Sangam* (1964), the couple go on an exotic tourist-album honeymoon trip to the West. The exotic locales of such narratives provided not only visual pleasure but constructed a site for marking self's absolute difference from the *other* (one that lies outside the imagined boundaries of home). The mass scale use of colour on Indian screen in the 1960s and other technological innovations demanded a prismatic view of the world. The demands of the technology, however, intersected with the demands of social history to produce such 'picture postcard' films.

In the 90s, with the rising tides of both regionalism and globalization, Bollywood has incorporated a diasporic *imaginaire* to cater to its
all-India market as well as the market outside India. In this new incarnation Bollywood not only very often physically locates itself in the
West, the central roles in the narrative too are reserved increasingly
for the figure of diasporic youth. Blockbusters such as *Dilwale
Dulhaniya Le Jayenge* and *Pardes* are only two examples of a host of
such films that include *Lamhe, Virasat,* and *Aur Pyar Ho Gaya*. With consumption acquiring a different inscription, recent Bollywood has
offered for its diasporic youth clientele a trajectory of 'western-style'
glamour, wealth and liberty, but on its own terms. Bollywood manages
the ensuing alienation with the mass audience of India by the sheer
strength of its vast repertoire, which even now has a large space for
films of earlier eras. For the new Bollywood too, it is not as if it merely mimics Hollywood. Rather, the semiotics of exchange with
Hollywood has in recent years taken an interesting turn. The biggest
hit in recent years, *Kuch Kuch Hota Hai* (1998), for instance, completes
this India/West circuit by not venturing to go abroad at all; instead, it
creates a virtual 'West' within the bounds of India.[8] In fact, in terms of
mise-en-scene, the film has internalized the West into India to the
extent that it does not even have to announce that it is the West.
Thematically, once the tomboy character of the heroine (played by the
mega-star, Kajol) is established, the rest of the narrative concentrates
on bringing to the fore her femininity. The framing of the woman as
powerless, and above all a wife and a mother, and at the same time
allowing her a certain space, a freedom for the pleasure of her subsequent disciplining, has been the general narrative-ethical guideline
since the early days of the 'social' in the 1950s. *Kuch Kuch Hota Hai*
does not alter the terms of what we might call this 'Sita' trope, but
pushes it to accommodate a decisively urbanized, globalized (basket-
ball playing, baseball cap wearing) female prototype; neither is her
subsequent realization of a more feminized, 'Indian' self jarring to her
earlier posturing. In fact, such realization will only act to make her a
more holistic woman. In a similar vein, the other female protagonist
of the film, the Oxford returned, guitar strumming girl (played by
Rani Mukherjee), who can also quickly switch to singing Hindu reli-

gious hymns and to whom the hero gets married but who dies in child-birth—is not a 'vamp from the West' (as earlier films with a similar narrative would almost certainly portray her to be) but a nice, pleasant woman who happens to wear westernized clothes in a sexualized sense. This then would be internalized in the Indian imaginary as not someone who *represents* the West (since 'West' is very much in India) but simply as someone who has lived in the West.

Bollywood representation establishes the 'Indian' community as a national but global community. To ritually assert, as Bollywood characters often do, that one is part of such an ideal community, it is important that one knows what one is part of. This involves returning to India and seeking sanctions from the original patriarchal order. *Dilwale Dulhaniya Le Jayenge* is a remarkable instance of such a re-working of the traditional patriarchal moral scheme. The film begins with the memorable montage of the heroine's father (acted by Amrish Puri): as a Punjabi farmer, he is striding past the mustard fields of Punjab; then through dissolve, he is seen journeying past Big Ben and Westminister (wearing his Punjabi *ajkan*), and finally feeding grain to the pigeons in London and remembering ancestral Punjab in a voice deeply laden with nostalgia. In the film, Puri is the epitome of a *darshanic* figure, bestowing sanction within the orbit of his *darshan*. The narrative then moves from the domestic space of the heroine in London to the continent with the couple and finally reaches rural Punjab, where the heroine (acted by Kajol) is supposed to undergo an arranged marriage with a local boy. Once the couple reach rural Punjab, the film changes gear and becomes unusually slow. The gaze is fixed on the nitty gritty of the marriage rituals, staged in a static, ornate fashion. The point of view is that of the hero, who witnesses the preparations but from a remove. It is important that the occasion is not contested, since the pleasure lies in its staging. The spectatorship at this point is clearly diasporic.

The action takes place at the very end of the film, when the heroine's father throws the hero out of his house and the proposed son-in-law starts beating the hero in a typical vendetta fashion. The hero does nothing to defend himself but significantly once his father is hit by one of the heroine's father's men, he plunges into action and aggression to defend his father. It is at this point that the heroine's father gives sanction to the hero: defending the father means, by the logic of mirroring, defending the future father-in-law, or in a broader sense, the father principle, the originating source of authority. It is interesting for the elaborate carnival of identity, that there is a kind of secret strategy to hold it at bay until one can actualize it on one's own terms, in terms of that freedom that the West has given but which needs to be ratified in the ancestral home. As a form, it has been clearly invented by contemporary Bollywood and has of late been repeatedly deployed as a major device to bring the West and the East to one place. It is also a ploy to re-inscribe the narrative space firmly within the *darshanic* orbit and very much like in the old Bollywood, climax comes in the form of defending the *darshanic* object.

Conclusion

> *London dekha, Paris dekha, aur dekha Japan*
> *Michael dekha, Elvis dekha, Doosara nahin Hindustan*
> *Eh duniya hai dulhan, dulhan ke maathey ki bindia*
> I love my India
>
> (Seen London, seen Paris, and also Japan
> Seen Michael, seen Elvis, no place like Hindustan [India]
> The world is my bride, my bride has *bindia* [dot] on her
>   forehead
> I love my India.)

The 'chirpy' celebration of motherland by a diasporic character on return to India in the film *Pardes* provided the Bollywood superstars, Shah Rukh Khan and Juhi Chawla, a perfect note to conclude their dance and music shows during their tour of Australia and New Zealand in 1998. Such celebration of India is by no means new to Bollywood. In fact, the legendary Raj Kapoor stole the hearts of millions more than four decades back with a similar song (in *Shree 420*, 1955): '*Mera joota hai Japani/Ye patloon Englistani/Sar pe lal topi Roosi/Phir bhi dil hai Hindustani*' (My shoes are 'Japani'/ This pantaloon 'Englistani'/ The red cap on head 'Roosi' [Russian]/ Yet the heart is 'Hindustani').

In spite of their apparent thematic similarity, the two songs register radically different points of view. For Raj Kapoor, the aim is to realize a cosmopolitan Indian self on the very soil of India (in keeping with the reigning Nehruvian ideals of that time). The song in *Pardes* is clearly a song of the Indian diaspora, of re-constructing 'India' outside India. That the song would hit the top charts in India almost instantaneously on its release testifies to the globalization of 'India' across these four decades.

Our previous analysis tries to show how Bollywood in its contemporary manifestation promotes more than ever the category of 'the global and the fully marketized' but manages to stop short of allowing it an over-determining role vis-à-vis what Ashis Nandy calls 'the culturally self-confident but low-brow multi-culturalism' of Indian cinema (Nandy, 1998, quoted in Das, 1998:7). Bollywood's ability to negotiate Hollywood on its own terms has been widely discussed: Rajadhyaksha (1998:173) persuasively demonstrates the error of viewing Bollywood as 'insufficiently Hollywood' and advocates a space for this cinema in its own right within the terrain of film theory. Richard Dyer (1986) has argued that Hollywood associates the factor of glamour with aristocratic privilege and regularly pits it against the 'openness' of western liberal democracy where talent and perseverance are always duly rewarded. As a contrast to this, the world that Bollywood constitutes is one of 'heterotopia' (Foucault, 1986:24) where the *real* world outside the auditorium is simultaneously represented, simplified, inflated, contested, and inverted. Hence very often the basic narrative line is repeated as if the same language game is played time and again and along with it is repeated (as discussed in the section, 'From Ramayan to Bollywood') the whole cultural ecology of Bollywood.

The viewing subject of Bollywood is not so much the individuated spectator of western film theory but primarily a member of a 'narrative community.[9] Indian political theorist Sudipta Kaviraj elaborates the concept of narrative community in the context of postcolonial democracy in the following way:

> The telling of a story brings into immediate play some strong conventions invoking a narrative community . . . To some extent, all such communities, from the stable to the emergent, use narrative as a technique of staying together, redrawing their boundaries or reinforcing them (Kaviraj, 1992:33).

The source of Bollywood's phenomenal success as a commercial medium seems to lie in its ability to bring within its narrative fold the diverse narrative communities not only of South Asian origin but, even more widely, of large parts of the so-called Third World. In other words, inscribed in its address is the postcolonial predicament of an audience which, in the case of the Fiji Indians, has been twice displaced.

I have sought to show how negotiation with the 'culture of the motherland' became for the Fiji Indian community part of a much broader question of negotiation with the (post)indenture definition of the self. Needless to mention, this negotiation could not remain the same from the early days of 'extraction' and the physically arduous schedule of indenture through the post-indenture life of subsistence agriculture, diversification of occupation, and differentiation of the community, to entry into a western context of late modern times with the option of 'multiplicity of forms of life and conscious adoption of lifestyles' (Dean, 1996: 213).

The situation has been made more complex by the recent changes in the western landscape of the 'social'. Here we go by the definition of the 'social' provided by Nicholas Rose: a large abstract terrain of collective experience, the sum of bonds and relations between individuals and events within a more or less bounded territory governed by its own laws. Rose argues that ever since global capital attained prominence, the 'social' in the West has been undergoing a transmutation in favour of the *community*—not one but a series of communities with different aims and constituencies but nonetheless basically constituted of self-monitoring, self-governing subjects (Rose, 1996). However, the norms of such particularized communities of the contemporary West can barely negotiate with the religio-civilizational norms of the 'narrative communities' of a postcolonial formation since the particularized communities allow no inscription of the history of the West as a despotic, colonial power. On the contrary, it can be argued that such framing of community is a renewed attempt to privilege the West's claims to democracy and solidarity. In the vortex of power and positionalities of the multicultural West, every ethnic community *owns* an identity (see Rouse, 1995). As an ethnic community, the Fiji Indians are attracted to the new forms of association and intimacy of the West but written in this attraction also is the sign of resistance. Together they feed a sense of imagined nationhood kept alive by continuously transforming and reconstructing its constitutive myths. Bollywood, as it caters to the changing market patterns of home and abroad, serves this dual purpose extraordinarily well.

Compare the Fiji Indians with Hamid Naficy's Iranians in *The Making of Exile Cultures* (1993). The Fiji Indians who came to Australia just before or after the coup are not an exilic group even though they were dislodged from their country. This is because of their attitude to Fiji ('home but not mother') and the fact that they harbour no hope or determining desire to return, either to Fiji or to India. Hence they made no investment in the kind of exile media that Naficy's Iranians did to form their cultural identity. Rather, they have invested their energies in the *continuation* of cultural practices they were engaged with in Fiji which, as we have shown, contain within them dynamic hybridizing tendencies easily sufficient to withstand the community's displacement into a western culture. Unlike Naficy's instance where the hermeticism of exilic television is forced to negotiate with American mainstream media after a point of time, Bollywood's own momentum will take this platform ahead. The tension of the young Fiji Indians is the tension between Bollywood's representation of change and real-life experiences. This is reflected, though in a very minor way, in the remarkable films they make, discussed earlier.

This paper has privileged the Ramayan and folk traditions of India as well as Bollywood as some of the most significant discourses that framed the cultural life of Fiji Indians and continue to do so. The attempt has been to investigate the historical formation of a cultural community and not to posit any singular determination. A detailed account of how socialization has been constructed around these cultural artefacts—the historical forms they took, the rationalities they deployed, the various registers, practices and institutions through which they were disseminated—is beyond the scope of this paper but could form part of thorough historical anthropology. The paper is a modest attempt to bring into sharp relief the continuing significance of popular cultural formations in the quickening diasporic life of a small and vibrant community.

The literature of transnationality is not known for its interest in investigating the different histories of postcolonial dynamics 'back home' as they manifest in the 'new imaginings and politics of community'. Rather its main concern is to write diaspora as an enigmatic excess and privilege the aleatory nature of diasporic temporalities: the *true* people are the liminal people. It may be argued that what Bhabha does is to route the experience of the South Asian intellectual-in-exile through the discourse of black counter-hegemonic culture (Bhabha, 1994). This intellectual-in-exile syndrome, however, occupies only a minor part in the South Asian diaspora in general. This is not to say that South Asians escape the problem of 'othering' in the West, nor it is to suggest that they would like to give up their own identities and become 'assimilated' in the dominant cultural order without a trace of difference. Perhaps a change of emphasis is in order here. Rather than celebrating the master narrative of diaspora as a 'slipzone' of indeterminacy and shifting positionalities, one focuses on South Asian diaspora's widely agreed ability to re-create their cultures in diverse locations and locates the element of the liminal within the nitty gritty of this changing history. Scholars have often counterposed the reality of hybridity against the illusion of 'nameable groups' (see, for instance, Kelly, 1998, Geschiere and Meyer, 1998). We would like to revise this understanding somewhat and explain hybridity as the nameable held under the sign of erasure. The shift is one of emphasis.

Notes

1 I have borrowed the caption 'Chalo Jahaji' from Brij Lal's autobiographical history of the Fiji islands (Lal, 2000).

2 Keya Ganguly has used a similar set of terms (*post*colonial and post*colonial*), though the meanings we attribute to them are not the same. For Ganguly, *post*colonial refers to the '"extraction" of ... people from an ex-colonial territory to what might be called a neo-colonial one' while post*colonial* refers to the much broader process of 'the exploitative dynamic central to the production of colonial subjectivity'. (Ganguly, 1992: 28).

3 Quite a few of the respondents narrated the story of grandparents who went back after indenture to their village in North India only to find that their funeral rituals (*sradh kriya*) had already been performed by the village people since to have crossed the *kala pani* (lit. 'black waters') was considered the same as being dead.

4 Partha Chatterjee discusses this process in detail in the context of 19th century Bengal. See, Chatterjee 1993.

5 Kelly notes that as the anxiety to understand the sufferings of indenture got taken over by the bid to establish hegemony in Fiji, so did the narrative vicissitudes of Ramlila also shift site: from the climactic immolation of Ravan to the triumphant return of Ram to Ayodhya (Kelly, 1991)

6 The attempt to reassert such values as part of Hindutva in a diasporic setting is indeed ironic. It has been argued that Hindutva for diasporic Indians is on the increase with the rise of Hindu nationalism in India since the mid-1980s. But there is a significant difference between the diasporic practice of Hindutva and the politics of the currently ruling Hindu nationalist Bharatiya Janata Party (BJP). In its attempt to imagine the nation in terms of Hindutva, BJP has inadvertently put the ideology of the upper castes under the greatest challenge that it has ever experienced from inside, namely, the felt political need to expand its ranks and thus give up its claim to monolithic superiority. This can be called the *epistemic crisis* of the BJP. Diasporic Hindutva suffers from no such *crisis* or obligation. In a way, BJP realizes its idealized self outside its actual political terrain.

7 The Fiji Indians, with a long tradition of attachment to *bhajan* and other devotional songs, have been influenced by the recent boom in the devotional music market in India. For more than a century, Fiji Indians were used to singing the Bhojpuri style of *bhajan* called *tambura bhajan*. Now this is giving way (at least for a section of the community) to the more classically-oriented *bhajan* of Anup Jalota, Hari Om Sharan, Anuradha Paudwal and others through audiocassettes produced in India. The CDs of some of the *bhajan* singers of the Sydney community are clear proof of this trend.

8 I thank Ravi Vasudevan for an insightful discussion of textual strategies of what I call 'diasporic Bollywood'.

9 Ravi Vasudevan, discussing how cinema as an autonomous cultural institution comes to be involved in the shaping of civil society in the West, observes:

In the case of film as a cultural institution, we may observe that this formation of the civil by the cultural (as discussed by Charles Taylor) is achieved at the cost of repression. Through the Production Code an anticipatory and preemptive civil consensus developed about the limits of cinematic representation. Clearly, the rules of individuation and association must lie within definite parameters. (Vasudevan, 1998).

References

Appadurai, Arjun (1990), 'Disjuncture and Difference in the Global Cultural Economy', *Public Culture*, 2: 2, 1-24.

— (1998), 'The Politics of Repetition: Notes on the Reception of Indian Hit Films', Workshop on Media and Mediation in the Politics of Culture, Centre for Studies in Social Sciences, International Globalization Network, Calcutta, March, 4-7.

Bhabha, Homi (1994), 'Frontlines and Borderposts', in Angelika Bammer (ed.), *Displacements: Cultural Identities in Question*, Indiana University Press, Bloomington.

Bharucha, Rustom (1994), *A Question of Faith*, Oxford University Press, New Delhi.

Buchignani, Norman (1980), 'The Social and Self-identities of Fijian Indians in Vancouver', *Urban Anthropology*, 9:1.

Chakravarty, Sumita S. (1993), *National Identity in Indian Popular Cinema: 1947–1987*, University of Texas Press, Austin.

Chatterjee, Partha (1984), 'Gandhi and the Critique of Civil Society', in Ranajit Guha (ed.), *Subaltern Studies III*, Oxford University Press, London.

— (1993), *Nation and its Fragments: Colonial and Postcolonial Histories*, Princeton University Press, Princeton.

— (1995), 'Religious Minorities and the Secular State—Reflections on an Indian Impasse', *Public Culture*, 8:1, 11-39.

— (1997), *The Present History of West Bengal: Essay in Political Criticism*, Oxford University Press, Delhi.

Chatterji, Joya (1994), *Bengal Divided: Hindu Communalism and Partition, 1932–1947*, Cambridge University Press, Cambridge.

Chopra, Anupama (1997), 'Bye-bye Bharat', *India Today*, 1 December, 54-55.

Cunningham, Stuart and John Sinclair (ed.), (2001), *Floating Lives: the Media and Asian Diasporas*, Rowman and Littlefield, USA.

Das, Arvind N. (1998), 'Reels of Indian Reality', *Biblio: A Review of Books*, New Delhi, September–October, 7.

Davies, John (2000), 'On the sources of interethnic conflict in Fiji' *Peace Initiatives*, 4:1-3, .

Dean, Michelle (1996), 'Foucault, Government and the Enfolding of Authority', in Andrew Barry, Thomas Osborne and Nikolas Rose (eds.), *Foucault and Political Reason: Liberalism, Neo-liberalism and Rationalities of Government*, University of Chicago Press, Chicago.

Derne, Steve (1995), 'Market Forces at Work: Religious Themes in Commercial Hindi Films' in Lawrence Babb and Susan Wadley (eds.), *Media and the Transformation of Religion in South Asia*, University of Pennsylvania Press, Pennsylvania.

Dyer, Richard (1986), *Stars*, British Film Institute, London.

Embree, Ainslie (ed.) (1988), *Sources of Indian Tradition*, vol. 1, Penguin, Harmondsworth.

Foucault, Michel (1986), 'Of Other Spaces', *Diacritics*, 16:1, 22-27.

Ganguly, Keya (1992), 'Migrant Identities: Personal Memory and the Construction of Selfhood' *Cultural Studies*, 6:1, 27-50.

Geschiere, Peter and Birgit Meyer (1998), 'Globalization and Identity: Dialectics of Flow and Closure' *Development and Change*, 29, 601-15.

Gillespie, Marie (1995), *Television, Ethnicity and Cultural Change*, Routledge, London and New York.

Hansen, Thomas (1996), 'Globalization and Nationalist Imaginations', *Economic and Political Weekly*, 31, 9 March.

Hutnyk, John (1996), 'Media, Research, Politics, Culture', *Critique of Anthropology*, 16:4, 417-28.

Jayawardena, Chandra (1980), 'Culture and Ethnicity in Guyana and Fiji', *Man*, 26.

Kaviraj, Sudipta (1992), 'The Imaginary Institution of India', in Partha Chatterjee and Gyanandra Pandey (eds.), *Subaltern Studies VII: Writings on South Asian History and Society*, Oxford University Press, New Delhi.

Kelly, John (1991), *A Politics of Virtue: Hinduism, Sexuality, and Countercolonial Discourse in Fiji*, University of Chicago Press, Chicago.

— (1998): 'Time and the Global: against the Homogeneous, Empty Communities in Contemporary Social Theory', *Development and Change*, 29, 839–71.

Lal, Brij (1983), *Girmitiyas: The Origins of the Fiji Indians*, Journal of Pacific History monograph, Canberra: Australian National University.

— (1985), 'Kunti's Cry: Indentured Women on Fiji Plantations', *Indian Economic and Social History Review*, 22

— (1992), *Broken Waves: A History of the Fiji Islands in the Twentieth Century*, Pacific Islands Monograph Series no. 11, Centre for Pacific Islands Studies, School of Hawaiian, Asian and Pacific Studies, University of Hawaii Press, Honolulu.

— (1998), Interviews with Manas Ray, Canberra, May.

— (2000), *Chalo Jahaji: On a Journey through Indenture in Fiji*, Australian National University, Canberra.

— (2001): 'Fiji: A Damaged Democracy' in Brij Lal (ed.), *Coup: Reflections on the Political Crisis in Fiji*, Pandanus Books, Canberra.

Lutgendorf, Philip (1995), 'All in the (Raghu) Family: A Video Epic in Cultural Context', in Lawrence Babb and Susan Wadley (eds.), *Media and the Transformation of Religion in South Asia*, University of Pennsylvania Press, Pennsylvania: .

Mishra, Vijay (ed.) (1979), *Rama's Banishment: A Centenary Tribute to the Fiji Indians 1879-1979*, Heinemann Educational Books, London.

— (1985), 'Towards a Theoretical Critique of Bombay Cinema', *Screen*, vol. 26, nos 3/4, May-August.

— (1992), 'Decentring History: Some Versions of Bombay Cinema', *East-West Film Journal*, 6:1, January.

Nandy, Ashis (ed.) (1998), *The Secret Politics of Our Desires: Innocence, Culpability and Indian Popular Cinema*, Oxford University Press, New Delhi.

Naficy, Hamid (1993), *The Making of Exile Cultures: Iranian Television in Los Angeles*, University of Minnesota Press, Minneapolis.

Prasad, M. Madhava (1998), *Ideology of the Hindi Film: A Historical Construction*, Oxford University Press, New Delhi.

Rajadhyaksha, Ashish (1987), 'The Phalke Era: Conflict of Traditional Form and Modern Technology', *Journal of Arts and Ideas*, 14, 15.

— (1998), 'Who's Looking? Viewership and Democracy in the cinema', *Cultural Dynamics*, 10:2, 73

— and Willeman, Paul (1994), 'Introduction', *Encyclopaedia of Indian Cinema*, British Film Institute, London.

Rose, Nikolas (1996), 'The Death of the Social? Re-figuring the Territory of Government', *Economy and Society*, 25:3, 327-56.

Rouse, Roger (1995), 'Mexican Migration and the Social Space of Postmodernism', *Diaspora* 1:1, 8-23.

Srinivas, S. V. (1996), 'Devotion and Defiance in Fan Activity', *Journal of Arts and Ideas*, 29.

Vasudevan, Ravi (1993), 'Shifting Codes, Dissolving Identities: The Hindi Social Films of the 1950s as Popular Culture', *Journal of Arts and Ideas*, 23, 24, January.

— (1998), 'Cinema and Citizenship in the "Third World"', published lecture delivered at Northwestern University, May 4.

Zizek, Slavoj (1997), 'Multiculturalism, or the Cultural Logic of Multinational Capitalism', *New Left Review*, 225, September-October.

COLONIALISM AND THE BUILT SPACE OF CINEMA IN NIGERIA

BRIAN LARKIN

'Drop me at the Plaza.' 'Meet me at the El Dorado.' These casual directions highlight the role of cinema theatres as built spaces in the urban geography of Kano, northern Nigeria. Large, hulking buildings punctuate Kano topography. There, buses stop, taxis load-up, motorbikes deliver people in a constant circulation from home to work to market and back again. Most of these travellers have little interest in films or the theatre but have internalized the demarcation of public space marked out by cinema theatres, mosques, the post-office, the Emir's palace, and other landmarks of urban infrastructure. Outside the theatres merchants, prostitutes, idlers, mechanics, customers, and film fans depend on the particular social space created by cinema for their livelihood and leisure. Around the back and on the sides boys play football against the large dark walls. Men squat and piss against a wall painted with large letters 'AN HANA FISARA A NAN' ('Don't piss here').

This chapter is an examination of the materiality of cinema theatres. It is about the fantasy space of cinema, but by this I do not mean the magical worlds that cinema transports viewers to. Rather, I view fantasy as the energy stored in the concreteness of objects, especially the commodified elements of everyday life (see Benjamin, 1978). These are not just the products people buy but constitute the total sensory experience of urban living. I examine the architectonics of cinema theatres and the arena for social interaction they create as symbolic and physical emblems of the imposition of colonial urbanization and the experience of modernity for urban Hausa in northern Nigeria.

In Kano, the introduction of cinema theatres inaugurated a series of controversies: over whether the practice of showing films was a diabolical, un-Islamic technology; over where theatres could be located; and over the regulation of who was allowed to attend. As a result of these controversies cinema became a symbolically unruly place. It upset gendered and racial divisions of public space by creating new modes of sociability. It offered new, western derived forms of leisure based on a technological apparatus that was religiously questionable. The controversies it produced can be seen as moments of struggle in the reterritorialization of urban space, the attempt to reassert and redefine Hausa moral space in the face of an encroaching colonial modernity. Cinema is a technology whose place in Hausa social life had to be defined. Its mass, stories and rumours about cinema, and the words used to refer to the technology itself all contain traces of the history of colonialism and urban experience. They tell us about the way that cinema as technology entered into Hausa space and took hold in the Hausa imagination.

In African postcolonies like Nigeria, a trip to the cinema has always been trans-local, a stepping outside of Africa to places elsewhere.[1] To step from the foyer into the dark night of the cinema hall was to be magically transported into a universe where American realities, Indian emotions, and Hong Kong choreography have long occupied Nigerian cinema screens. But cinema theatres are a peculiar kind of social space marked by a duality of presence and absence, rootedness and transport, what Lynne Kirby (1997) refers to as the paradox of travel without movement. Cinema is distinctively modern because of this ability to destabilize and make mobile people, ideas, and commodities. This can be threatening by eroding 'the cultural distinctiveness of place' (Watts, 1996:64) but it can also reaffirm and intensify forms of belonging by providing a cultural foil against which local identities may be hardened.

Elsewhere I have approached the social space of cinema in this way, analysing the fantasy worlds cinema transports one to by examining the ways Hausa viewers engage with Indian films as a third space lying in between the reification of Hausa tradition and western modernity (Larkin, 1997). But while often seen as engines of mobility, cinema theatres are also deeply parochial, an intimate part of urban topography that draw around them congeries of social practices that make cinema-going an event that always exceeds (and sometimes has little to do with) the films that are shown on the screen. My focus here is on the 'materiality of specific domains' that direct attention to the 'sensual and material qualities of the object', through which 'we are able to unpick the more subtle connections with cultural lives and values' (Miller, 1997:9). Though Hollywood and Bollywood and other national cinemas have indeed devoted great energy into regularizing relations of textual address in the attempt to create a homogenous viewing audience, in practice the experience of cinema is still profoundly local. This is because cinema theatres, while commodified, do not offer material objects we can take home with us but an emotional experience based on a sensory environment regulated by specific relations of lighting, vision, movement, and sociality.[2] By analysing the built space of cinema theatres and the struggle over where they were sited on the Kano landscape I wish to shift the study of cinema toward the social practices the theatres create. I examine how specific cinematic environments are produced and use this to explore the nature of colonial urbanism.

Cinema, the Phenomenology of the Surface and Colonial Modernity

Objects that were once new and once symbolized modern life but whose historical moment has passed become inadvertent but dense signifiers of transformations in social structure. Walter Benjamin built a powerful hermeneutics around these sorts of objects, around the interrogation of obsolescence—objects swollen with the force of history, but whose significance had ebbed with transformations in social and economic structure. According to his friend Adorno, Benjamin created a 'petrified . . . or obsolete inventory of cultural fragments' that provided concrete embodiments of historical process or 'manifestations of culture' (cited in Buck-Morss and Benjamin, 1989:58). Benjamin shared this evocative theorizing of material culture with

Siegfried Kracauer who also pioneered the historico-philosophical interrogation of the marginal, the momentary and the concrete. Like Benjamin, Kracauer was interested in surface phenomena and argued that their marginal, mass produced nature was revelatory of the social order. 'The position that an epoch occupies in the historical process can be determined . . . from an analysis of its unconscious surface-level expressions,' he wrote in his essay 'The Mass Ornament' arguing that these 'expressions . . . by virtue of their unconscious nature, provide unmediated access to the fundamental substance of the state of things (Kracauer and Levin, 1995:75).

For Kracauer and Benjamin, the quotidian landscapes of life— posters on the walls, shop signs, dancing girls, bestsellers, panoramas, the shape, style and circulation of city buses—are all surface representations of the fantasy energy by which the collective perceives the social order. This structure creates an interpenetrated analysis of urban culture in modernity, one in which strikingly different phenomena are structurally linked. The stained concrete of Nigerian cinema theatres, the open-air screens, their proximity to markets, reveal knowledge of 'the state of things' which in Kano refers to the imposition of a colonial, capitalist modernity. Cinema theatres were part of a much wider transformation of the restructuring of urban space and leisure practices under colonial urbanism (Martin, 1995; Mitchell, 1991; Thompson, 2000). Like the beer parlours, theatres, railways and buses, public gardens, libraries and commercial streets that preceded them, cinema theatres created new modes of public association. In a strict Muslim area such as Kano, for instance, where female seclusion was, and is, a defining moral characteristic of Muslim Hausa space, the institution of mixed-sex and mixed-race public spaces profoundly challenged existing gender and social hierarchies. Cinema theatres thus created new modes of sociability that had to be regulated, officially by the colonial administration and unofficially within local Hausa norms.

As a new mode of public association in the colonial arena, cinema theatres were unruly and often contentious social spaces but this disruption was not something that was restricted to colonial arenas. Scholars of early cinema have made the convincing argument that the rise of cinema must be seen in relation to the wider transformation in urbanism, employment, consumption and leisure that occurred during the *fin de siècle* (see, for example, Allen, 1983; Bowser, 1990; Chanan, 1996; Friedberg, 1993; Griffiths, 1996; Hansen, 1991; Kirby, 1997; Koszarski, 1990; Kuhn, 1998; Musser, 1990; Tsivian and Taylor, 1994. For interesting work on cinematic space outside of the West see Armbrust, 1998; Himpele, 1996; Hughes, 1999; Thompson, 2000). Miriam Hansen (1991) argues that in the United States the rise of cinema generated considerable anxiety about the increasing presence of women in public practices of work and leisure. Cinema played a role in 'changing the boundaries and possibilities of public life' especially for women whose 'relations to the public sphere were governed by specific patterns of exclusion'.

The introduction of new technologies and new sets of social relations that accompany them is often a fraught and anxiety ridden process as societies come to terms with the new political and social possibilities that technologies bring. Reactions by local Arab, African or Asian populations against the introduction of cinema cannot be glossed over as the anti-modern stance of traditional societies toward modernity but more properly should be interrogated as part of a common transnational anxiety toward modernity. What is necessary is to realize that the sort of social spaces cinemas become is the result of a process, an interaction between particular rules of sociability and local relations of gender, religion and class. And this is particularly true for the distinctive dynamics brought about by the racial and political context of colonial rule.

To give one clear example, the rise of cinema in the United States is famously rooted in the leisure practices of working class immigrants. One of the classic themes in cinema historiography has examined the efforts by early entrepreneurs to transform cinema from a working class to a bourgeois form of entertainment. This transformation was effected by a variety of means: from the construction of cinema 'palaces' that resembled the grandeur of theatres; to the seeking of a female, rather than a male audience; to the use of the bourgeois form of novels as a model for cinematic narrative (see, for example, Hansen, 1991; Sklar, 1975). In the colonial context, however, the trajectory was just the opposite: in most cases cinema was introduced as a specifically foreign, colonial form of entertainment intended for European and native elites. Only after it became common with this class were auditoriums constructed (or opened) for the masses. Instead of being a marked lower class activity, then, it was often identified as an elite, racially coded, leisure practice. Despite this, in most places cinema-going quickly became a local, indigenous activity (and in the case of India most notably, film-making itself become an indigenous phenomenon).

The Built Space of Cinema

In its materiality, its reproducibility over space and time and its ubiquitous presence on metropolitan landscapes, the cinema theatre appears reassuringly familiar, a self-effacing transnational technology that seemingly belongs to no particular country. The ontological security of theatres comes from the formal solidity of an auditorium that places audiences in a familiar spatial configuration: arranged in rows sitting beneath the ethereal spectacle of light and dark unfolding on the screen. In most parts of the world the theatre has become second nature; we no longer query its existence or imagine a time when it could be queried, when its innovation brought with it a powerful transformative capacity. But this second nature is illusory and masks the process by which physical, public space becomes social: the forgetting of history in the creation of myth (Barthes, 1972). The taken-for-grantedness of cinema theatres masks the historical conditions of colonial rule that made the technology possible.

The erection of cinema theatres in colonial cities created new social spaces of sexual, ethnic, religious and racial intermixing, making them ambivalent institutions that often threatened existing hierarchies and boundaries regarding the public use of space. This ambivalence is seen very simply in the diverse ways colonies attempted to regulate the transformative capacity of these new institutions and reconstitute them within existing gender hierarchies. In India, for instance, separate entrances were built so that women could enter and exit without sharing the same social space as male cinema-goers (Arora, 1995). In Damascus the same concern over female mobility and the threat of inter-sexual mixing was limited by reserving afternoon performances for women only (Thompson, 2000). The same threat was contained in Lamu, Kenya, by making one night a week 'ladies night' (Fuglesang, 1994), and in northern Nigeria the immoral connotations of inter-sexual mixing were so intense that cinema theatres never became socially acceptable for women. This variety of structural and social regulations points to the necessity of interrogating the social space of the cinema theatre, neither taking it for granted nor seeing it simply as a colonizing technology. Rather, cinema theatres are produced, and in the struggle over that production, tensions over colonial urbanization are foregrounded.

In October 1937, the British colonial administration received an application from a Lebanese businessman for the construction of the Rex cinema, which was to become the first purpose-built cinema in Kano. The Rex was built as an open air cinema, what was known as a 'garden cinema', and consisted of two rooms as well as a bar which the businessman proposed 'to build quite decently and with stones' (Nigerian National Archives, #171; The West Africa Picture Co., #172). This exhibition format was modified two years later when J. Green Mbadiwe, a hotel owner in Kaduna, the capital of Northern Nigeria, applied for a license to build a more formal and elaborate hotel and cinema complex in Kano. It was to include 'all the latest amenities usually associated with first-class Hotels and Cinemas in the Aristocratic Countries of the world' (Nigerian National Archives). His application was denied but his proposal gives witness to the conceptual construct of what constituted a cinema space in Nigeria at this time. In the proud insistence on the quality of construction material and the boast that Kano cinemas would be like 'first-class' cinemas in the West, the applications signify the elite, European clientele that the owners intended to attract. The emphasis on first class quality found in 'the Aristocratic Countries of the world' promised reassuring familiarity for Europeans and created a spectacle of grandeur for local Hausa filmgoers. And the inclusion of a bar would have offered recreation other than the cinematic event itself intended for Europeans only who could 'come out and enjoy the cool air and evening' (Fuglesang, 1994). The design and social function of these early theatres was intimately associated with another public space of colonial modernity: the hotel. Like the hotel the cinema is a public space of anonymity, a transient coming together of people unconnected by relations of kinship, religion or ethnicity. Making the cinema like a hotel means that the experience was not organized solely around watching a film but was part of a wider complex of leisure activities that emerged for expatriate recreation.

As a product of a colonial ideology of transformation, the architectonics of the cinema theatre expressed the particular historical conditions of colonial rule. Cinema as a social space helped create a new public, 'the imagining of human beings as, in principle, an indefinitely extensible horizon of anonymous and interchangeable members' (Barber, 1997:348). Kracauer referred to this public as a 'mass', arguing that the spatial organization of the audience in patterns of 'tier upon ordered tier subordinated the individuality of the audience member to the totality of the mass' (Kracauer, 1998; Kracauer and Levin, 1995:79). The arrangement of seating in cinemas reflected the new bodily configurations of colonial rule, though of course it could never be contained by them. The attempt at constructing an abstract and equivalent public was often frustrated by colonial and Hausa practices of hierarchy and distinction, for instance the creation of specific seating for whites only that were embedded in the conception of cinematic space.

In the highly stratified colonial world one immediate problem of common public space was the potential of racial mixing. What were the possible consequences of mixed race audiences? In response to people's fears the Lebanese owners of the Rex originally intended their cinema for European use and finally divided the exhibition schedule so that two nights a week were reserved for Europeans and Arabs and two for African audiences. This segregation was intentional but informal and was regulated mainly through the pricing of seats.[3] J. Green Madiwe went further, proposing to divide his auditorium into two discrete compartments, one for Europeans and one for Africans, which would be approached through separate entrances. The only connection was a fire door but this, he assured the authorities, 'will be always locked' (Kracauer, 1998; Kracauer and Levin,

1995:79). This attempt at encoding practices of racial segregation into the architectonics of the theatre space reveals how the solid materiality of the cinema theatre expresses local ideologies of (in this case) racial hierarchy. The Secretary of the Northern provinces who wrote to the Chief Secretary in Lagos with a response to fire safety regulations reveals stunningly how the physical space of cinema can be the outcome of a specifically colonial situation of racial prejudice.

> As regards seating—In view of the natural tendency of some Africans when in a crowd to be seized by panic at the mere rumour of danger it is thought that in Cinema halls in Nigeria much wider spaces should be allowed between fixed seats, wider alleyways and more and wider means of exit than is obligatory in England (Nigerian National Archives and M.I.A., ; Secretary Northern Provinces, 1932).

In Kano, the British imperial presence was reflected in the naming of theatres themselves, as was the wider Islamic world (colonialism and Islam representing the two great world systems with which Hausa were intimately involved). The first cinema in Kano following the Rex was the Palace and later came the Queens Theater. These names encoded imperial splendour into the spectacle promised by the experience of cinema.[4] Other Kano cinemas were given Arabic names such as El Duniya (The World) and, most recently, the Marhaba (Arabic for welcome which differs from the Hausa word: *maraba*), referencing the Arab ownership of cinema theatres and the cultural connections between Hausa and the Arab world. El Dorado (long part of the imperialist imaginary as the lost city of fabulous wealth waiting to be 'discovered'), Plaza and Orion connote travel and movement and are titular embodiments of the promise of transportation, of removal from the local and the mundane which is the hallmark of cinematic escapism. Only one cinema in Kano has an identifiably local connection, Wapa (named after the area where the cinema is located).

The Evolution of Urban Kano

The spatial arrangement of cinema theatres in urban Kano was mapped onto a terrain that was already the site of intense confrontation. This tension began in 1903 when, after conquest, the British began to construct a modern city outside the mud walls of Kano. The British divided Kano into what was administratively and symbolically a dual city divided between the walled *birni* (Old City) and a modern Township. The Old City was dominated by the political rule of the Emir and the economic importance of the trading families based around the Kurmi market, one of the major pre-colonial nodes in the trans-Saharan trade. In the old city pre-British custom remained strong and, under the principles of indirect rule, was actively protected from the transformations of colonialism. Missionization and western education were restricted; families still lived in domestic compounds which were largely passed down through inheritance rather than rented or sold;[5] female seclusion and strict sexual segregation was the norm to be aspired to; prostitution and the sale of alcohol were forbidden and the values of conservative Islam upheld.

Economically, ethnically and culturally the Township provided a strong contrast to this pattern. It was divided into several different areas: a commercial area, 'Asiatic' quarters for Syrians and Lebanese, the Sabon Gari for non-Hausa Nigerians, and a European residential area. As Kano grew under colonial rule it did so slowly in the Old City and exponentially in the Township. It was in this latter area that the new banks, companies and businesses were established that connected Northern Nigeria to the wider capitalist world economy and this area became the motor of the Kano economy. It was here that alongside the factories and businesses, new modes of leisure were created for workers to enjoy. For the Europeans there were gentlemen's clubs and restaurants; for the African workers, beer parlours and dancing clubs.

Erecting this new city entailed hardening a series of infrastructural, architectural and symbolic cleavages in Kano. The red and brown ochres of mud buildings in the Old City contrasted greatly with the lush greenery of the residential European sections of the G.R.A. (the European residential area) and the hastily constructed barracks of Sabon Gari. Where the Old City was full of narrow, winding mud alleys, the GRA was built on Ebeneezer Howard's garden city model with sweeping crescents, star shaped intersections and large, ventilated residences set back from the road by gardens (Frishman, 1977). Sabon Gari differed again, built on a grid system reflecting its utilitarian position in the colonial order and occupied by young, male migrants renting space in multi-occupant buildings. The openness of the European area was opposed to the congestion of the African areas and segregation was sealed by the construction of buffer zones of open land 440 yards wide[6] that separated European from African areas. Fear of physical contagion meant that all Africans were prevented by law from residing in a European area overnight (except for domestic servants).

An Enclave of Disrepute

In 1975, the Hausa scholar Ibrahim Tahir described his opinion of the status of Sabon Gari. It was, he wrote,

> the home of strangers, on their way to assimilation, Nigerian and foreign Christians, the European Christian, *Nasara* or Nazarene, the urban drifter, the wage worker, the prostitute and the pimp. It contains churches, beer houses and dance halls, hotels and brothels. There deviant conduct prevails and custom does not have a stronghold (Tahir, 1975:110).

His opinion did not much differ from the 1926 view of the British Resident of Kano who described Sabon Gari as 'an enclave of disrepute,' that was full of 'dissolute characters.'[7] For Kano Hausa, Sabon Gari has come to stand as the moral inversion of proper social relations, a colonially created spatial 'other' against which Hausa Muslim tradition can take shape and be defined.

Sabon Gari was created in 1912, brought about by the political requirements of Lord Lugard's theory of indirect rule. In return for political allegiance, the British promised to preserve Hausa political, religious and cultural structures and protect them from alien influences, especially Westernization (Lugard, 1922).[8] Southerners were seen as necessary because they 'spoke, read, and wrote the language of the colonizer' (Ubah, 1982:54) but while this made them useful to colonialists, the British were as suspicious as the Hausa of the cultural influence of this modernizing population. Besides speaking English, southerners wore European clothes, placed a high premium on western education and were largely Christian. With no religious injunction against alcohol, and dominated (originally) by male migrants, Sabon Gari became the main area in the city to buy alcohol, and the enclave became known for its dance halls, beer parlours and prostitution.

Segregation *between Africans* was seen as the best way to preserve Hausa religious and cultural values, by creating a separate social and ethnic arena which Hausa were banned from inhabiting. As Allyn sees it: 'Controlled in this way . . . the aliens would provide necessary services for the government and European firms but would have limited opportunity for contaminating the highly-regarded [by the British] culture of their Hausa-speaking neighbors'[9] (Allyn, 1976:87). Administratively Sabon Gari was placed under local British authority and legal jurisdiction and the area was kept culturally, religiously and politically apart from its Hausa neighbour with little chance of mixing. Hausa looked down on southerners as 'black Europeans' alienated from their own culture, while southerners returned the condescension, stereotyping Hausa society as backward and traditional. Their liminal position of southerners in the north is made palpable by the oxymorons of 'native foreigner' and 'alien native' by which Sabon Gari residents were officially categorized.[10]

It was onto this highly politicized grid that cinema theatres were mapped. Cinema theatres were and are located primarily outside of the Old City and in the new western-oriented areas. Interestingly, nearly all Kano cinemas are located on the borderlands of ethnic areas, alongside the markets that often act as a formal border separating one part of Kano from another. The Rex, the first cinema in Kano (now torn down) was built next to Sabon Gari market effectively straddling the border between three areas and peoples: the southern Nigerians of Sabon Gari; the Arabs and non-Hausa northern Nigerians living in Fagge and the Europeans living in Bompai, a European industrial area and commercial district. Similarly, the Orion and Plaza cinemas were built just outside the gates of the Old City, one near Kofar Wambai market, the other near Kantin Kwari market, on the boundary between the Old City and Fagge. The El Dorado, located on the edge of Sabon Gari, marked off that area from Bompai, as did the Queens a mile or so to the north. The El Duniya (now destroyed) was also located close to Sabon Gari market, separating it from Fagge, and Fagge from the Commercial District. Cinema theatres physically occupied liminal, transgressive spaces. They were close to Hausa areas, so that Muslim cinema-goers could have access to them, but they were kept separate; and over time, the illicitness of the cinemas themselves worked to harden and exemplify the religious, racial and cultural segregation of colonial (and post-colonial) Kano.

The Moral Aura of Cinematic Space

From their inception, cinema theatres in Kano were saturated with the moral ambience of the areas in which they were located, mainly Sabon Gari and Fagge. The first film screenings took place in Sabon Gari, in irregular venues like dance halls, such as the Elsiepat, where they were sandwiched in as entertainment between dances and prize-giving.[11] By 1934, however, cinema had become popular enough that the British Resident of Kano could report that films were being shown 'with considerable frequency' (Nigerian National Archives, 1934), and within three years the first purpose-built cinema, the Rex, was opened. The Rex showed four films a week in an open-air theatre adjacent to Sabon Gari market. Initially, performances were informally racially segregated with two nights reserved for non-Africans (Europeans and Syrians) and two for African audiences. A garden bar was established and during the early days, alcohol was served, but the British authorities were unsure how to restrict the sale of alcohol to Africans while permitting European consumption (Nigerian National Archives, 1934). Consequently a formal ban was placed on the sale of alcohol at cinemas which exists up until today.

The Rex cinema was situated on the edge of Sabon Gari, placing it in an area that for Hausa was culturally out of bounds. Despite this, or perhaps because of it, cinema quickly became popular among poor Hausa youth and indeed by the mid-1940s cinema-going was stereotyped as a cheap, poor man's entertainment, to be avoided by people in positions of respect. 'The local outlook is as follows,' wrote one colonial official in the early 1950s: 'The intelligent and educated malams (Muslim religious teachers) simply do not go . . . They disapprove of the sort of low-type Hausa that revels in the cinema . . .' (Kano State History and Culture Bureau (HCB); 1954). The low class, mixed sex nature of the cinema theatre meant that it became socially unacceptable for most Hausa women. Those who did attend were seen as *karuwai* ('independent women/prostitutes'), and their presence added significantly to the illicit nature of the arena. Sexual availability and sexual activity within the cinema meant that pleasure and desire were to be found both on and off the screen, the erotic pleasures of one context feeding off the other.

Cinema-going became established as a social activity, an experience that was always much more than the viewing of the film itself. 'Among a large youthful class of Kano City, Fagge and Sabon Gari,' the Kano Resident Featherstone remarked in 1948, 'it has become quite the thing to go to the Cinema quite regardless of whether they understand what they see or hear or not' (Kano State History and Culture Bureau (HCB); Resident of Kano E. K. Featherstone, 1948). Featherstone's paternalistic disapproval of Hausa audiences misses the importance of cinema-going as a social, as well as a visual, event. One viewer told Featherstone that although he did not always understand the films being shown, 'he went regularly to the cinema to be seen and to see his friends.' This social activity was taking place in a particular social space that drew its moral aura from its social and moral place on an urban landscape in the process of transformation. One educated Hausa man who went regularly to the cinema in the late 1940s told me that cinema-going involved leaving the safe confines of the old city and crossing from a moral to an immoral space (the Sabon Gari). For him this was an intentional act that involved a radical attitude toward Hausa authority and Islamic orthodoxy. Defined as undesirable by the values of orthodox Hausa Islam, the pleasure of going to the cinema was thus highly local, an intimate experience of illicitness that framed the spectacle of watching the film and which derived from the peculiar nature of Hausa colonial urbanization.

Religious questions about the ontology of the cinematic apparatus itself contributed to the wariness with which this colonial technology was greeted in mainstream Hausa society. Since the early days of British conquest, part of what Barkindo (1993) has termed the 'passive resistance' of conservative Islamic teachers to colonial rule had taken the form of intense resistance to the new commodities introduced by colonialists. Hiskett (1984) relates that elderly Muslim moralists condemned to hell-fire Muslims who used hurricane lamps, battery flashlights, starch, or wore buttons on their shirts. Nasiru Kabara, a prominent Kano sheikh who served on the first colonial censorship board

similarly told me that 'local malams' (by which he meant poorly educated, neighborhood Islamic teachers) condemned cinema because
they were unsure whether the images on screen were true or false.
According to their logic, if someone was killed in a film they thought
he might actually be dead. If not, then film was magic and because
Islam was against magic then film was *haraam* (forbidden) (Sheikh
Nasiru Kabara, 1995). Many also believed that cinematic representation contravened the Islamic prohibition on the creation of images
and idols.[12]

For Kabara this religious insistence on the blasphemous, magical
nature of the rational technology of cinema was a mark of ignorance
of both the world at large and Islam in particular. But the early Hausa
names for cinema—*majigi*, derived from the word magic,[13] and *dodon
bango*, literally, 'evil spirits on the wall'[14]—reveal how popular the
sense of the enchantment of cinema was. It reveals powerfully the symbolic layers that saturated cinema so that it could only be experienced
through its associations with Christianity, paganism, and colonial rule.

In the segregated world of colonial Kano, cinema-going was a
transgressive activity for Hausa viewers. It was one of the few leisure
activities shared by both Europeans and Africans, a fact that was greeted with ambivalence by Europeans (Larkin, n.d.) and Hausa alike.
While actual performances were segregated as a matter of general
colonial practice, the day following a European performance, African
audiences filed in to watch the same film in the same venue. This
allowed African participation in a form of leisure activity that was originally designed to be for Europeans only and was a marked contrast to
the colonial clubs and sports events from which Africans were effectively excluded. Cinema also became defined by Hausa as part of *bariki* culture, marked by *iskanci* or dissoluteness. *Bariki* derives from the
English word barracks and refers to a moral complex of activities from
pagan spirit possession (*bori*), to male and female prostitution, and
dancing and alcohol consumption. These practices became associated
with the new barracks that were constructed to house young migrant
workers to the North resulting in a new transgressive cultural form.

The spatial and social context of the emergence of cinema theatres
in Kano created an illicit aura, which dovetailed nicely with conservative Hausa distrust of European technologies.

The Palace, El Duniya, and the Maintenance of Hausa Moral Space

The introduction of cinema theatres in Kano intervened in an ongoing conflict over the moral definition of urban space under colonialism.[15] How cinema theatres were to be built, what they were to show, and whether they could sell alcohol were all issues of formal regulation by which the transformative spatial and social ideologies of colonialism were embodied and enacted. Conflicts within the Hausa community over where theatres were to be located and who could attend them are best seen as attempts at the moral reterritorialization of an urban space that was rapidly expanding outside of Hausa control. Appadurai (Appadurai, 1996) has referred to this process as the 'production of locality' which, he argues, involves the assertion of socially organized power over places that are potentially chaotic. The mediation of cinema as a moral space was an attempt to reassert the Muslim basis of Hausa life in opposition to the encroachment of non-Muslim (both European, and southern Nigerian) cultural and religious values. Cinema theatres became markers of neighbourhoods, embodying the moral qualities that allowed those neighbourhoods to exist. For urban Hausa the cinematic experience was (and is) embedded in the history of ongoing debate over the nature and regulation of urban public space.

In 1949, a Lebanese cinema distributor wrote to the Resident, Kano Emirate, asking for permission to build a cinema, The Palace, within the old city, in Jakara quarters, next to Kurmi market. When the application for the Palace was received, cinema-going was well established in Kano; many Hausa regularly left the old city to travel to one of two cinemas located outside in Waje. The uniqueness of this application was that the Palace was to be the first cinema theatre constructed within the confines of the old city. I can date the application and the opening of the Palace from the colonial archives in Kaduna that contain copies of the application file. However the story of the Palace I engage with rests on rumours and prejudice, stories and memories that do not provide an objective history of the Palace as much as they reveal the social place that it and other cinemas occupy in the social imagination. Rumours about cinemas, stories that have come down from parent to child, are a form of local hermeneutics. They are quasi-religious allegories by which people divine the 'real' motives underlying phenomenal events.

The Emir's decision to allow the construction of the Palace cinema provoked a strong backlash in different sections of the Hausa community. Kano *ulama* (religious leaders) were outraged by the penetration of this disruptive, sexual arena into the Islamic space of the old city. The more conservative among them issued a *fatwa* (religious teaching) forbidding the showing of films and citing the religious injunction on the creation of images as evidence that the technology itself was *kafirai* (pagan). According to a story I was told, this *fatwa* was overruled when it came before the Emirate council despite the fact that the Kano Emir at the time, Abdullahi, was widely known to be socially conservative. Abdullahi's decision then sparked its own set of rumours including one that Abdullahi was forced into the decision as a result of pressure from the British Resident (Adamu, 1996).

In 1951, while the controversy over the Palace was raging, but before the cinema was actually open, matters were brought to a symbolic head when the El Duniya cinema burned down killing 331 people[16] in an audience of 600. The government enquiry that followed established that the cause of the fire was flammable nitrate film that caught fire in the projection room and spread along the ceiling. Hausa complicity in the tragedy was reinforced by the fact that 82 percent of the cinema audience during the afternoon performance were Hausa, not Southern Nigerian or European. The youngest was only nine years old.

The rational, functional explanation of the colonial state for why the disaster occurred was accepted by Hausa as explaining how but not why the disaster occurred. In the context of the growing controversy over the Palace it was widely believed by many that the fire was direct divine retribution for Hausa participation in illicit and immoral activity. The tragedy became seen as a judgement about the growing westernization of Hausa society and a series of rumours emerged to explain the tragedy. Most common, and still widely believed, was the accusation that the film being screened that night in the El Duniya contained the image of the Prophet Mohammed, the colonial technology of representation being harnessed for blasphemous ends.

Others believed that during construction of the theatre people passing every day cursed (*tsine*) the theatre and the theatre was engulfed not just by flames but by the combined magical force of these curses.[17]

In a religious society such as Kano, where God's divine intervention in the material world is an everyday occurrence, rumours and stories become part of a critical discourse in which everyday events are interrogated. Stories about the El Duniya represent conflict and ambivalence about the western cultural arena that was infiltrating the Hausa moral world. They underscore the profane nature of cinematic representation, making it guilty of the heresy of representing Mohammed. These rumours grew so strong that the colonial government was forced to take official notice and counter them over the radio. Twice daily for two days in four different languages, the Radio Diffusion Service announced there was no truth to the stories that the people handling the bodies of El Duniya victims died, or that Native Authority Warders who helped in the tragedy had all gone mad, or that prisoners from Kano prison (who helped in handling the corpses) could not eat for days afterwards (Nigerian National Archives). Stories about the El Duniya became part of the informal moral economy that regulated the evolution of cinema in Kano.

On 2 July 1952, a year after the El Duniya burned down, the Palace finally opened after months of controversy. When the opposition to the cinema turned violent, the Emir was forced to call in the police to arrest youths who were demonstrating against the opening (Adamu, 1996). Three months later, the British Superintendent of police reported that ever since the Palace opened, youths outside the open-air theatre had been regularly stoning patrons inside. What was worse, he complained, was that the *alkali* (Muslim judge) to whom the cases were being reported was letting the youths go free and that it was difficult for the police to ensure 'good order' during cinema performances (Nigerian National Archives). Ironically, or perhaps inevitably, the Palace became the immoral social space that its opponents feared. It became a notorious place where, as one friend said to me, men would go to drink alcohol, take drugs and engage in sex with women and other men ('There! There! Right there in the seat next to you!'). In the early 1980s the governor of Kano State, Sabo Bakin Zuwo, who came from Kano's old city and who was a veteran of the anti-Palace campaign, closed down the cinema and, in a grand populist gesture, converted it into a hospital clinic. Since that time no cinema theatre has been opened in the old city[18] and to this day hundreds of Hausa youths travel nightly through the mud gates marking the city's boundaries to cinemas that lie outside in Sabon Gari, Fagge and Nassarawa.

The attempt to resist the construction of the Palace cinema represents an effort by Hausa Muslims to re-establish the moral, spatial equilibrium of urban Kano society. The growth of a metropolis *outside* of what formerly constituted the city, the shift in economic and political balance from the Old City to the Township and Waje, and the rise of a substantial migrant population of 'native foreigners' who owed little allegiance to existing political structures (some of whom openly mocked local religious and cultural practices), helped to create a situation where the assertion of Hausa control over a political and social world under threat became increasingly important. When the Palace as a foreign, immoral, and potentially irreligious institution was built within the Old City, it threatened to erode the carefully produced social, religious and political division between the Old City and Waje, collapsing two very different moral spaces and making protest almost inevitable.

After the controversy over the Palace, Lebanese entrepreneurs never attempted to situate a theatre in the Old City again. As a compromise, two theatres were built *just* outside the city walls: the Orion in Kofar Wambai and the Plaza in Fagge. This construction is a testimonial to the fact that since the 1950s Hausa people have made up the dominant cinema-going population in Kano. Despite the fact that cinema theatres occupy an ambiguous moral position in Hausa society, certainly much more than they do in Yoruba or Ibo society, cinema-going has never waned in its popularity for Hausa youth. To go and see Indian films at the Marhaba or at Plaza is recognized by Ibos, Lebanese and even Indian expatriates, as a Hausa form of social activity.

Conclusion

Cinema theatres in Kano are not discrete buildings but integrated nodes in an urban environment from which they draw their significance and, indeed, which they help to define. As the site for screening fantastic texts of love and adventure, cinema theatres project Hausa audiences into the imagined realities of American, Indian and British culture (see Larkin, 1997). Here my focus has been on the place of theatres as part of a wider urban materiality produced by, and thus expressive of, transformations in colonial modernity. Their social significance cannot be divorced from the other technologies and public spaces produced under colonial rule. Cinema theatres in Kano came into being only twenty years after the construction of the Kano-Lagos railroad and were built in the areas created for the masses of male migrants brought into Kano; they were sited alongside the new colonially constructed markets marking out the borders and moral qualities of the new colonially constructed metropolis; and they formed part of the construction of new modes of sexual and ethnic interaction produced by the transformation in urban public space. Encoded in the physical space of the theatre, in the dirty bricks and broken lights, and in the walls that divide the arena, are traces of history of colonial rule and colonial urbanism. My aim has been to move away from the taken-for-granted quality that so often makes the cinema theatre seem like second nature, an accepted and already understood site that disappears from analytic view as the lights are turned down and the films are projected. Instead, I analyse the materiality of the theatre itself, theorizing its significance for an anthropology of the media which situates technologies within the wider social realms from which they take on meaning.

Notes

This essay is a revised version of 'Theaters of the Profane: Cinema and Colonial Urbanism' published as part of a special symposium I edited in *Visual Anthropology Review* (Larkin, 1999a; b). I thank the AAA for permission to reprint it here. Research for this essay was funded by the Wenner-Gren Foundation for Anthropological Research and a Research Grant from New York University. My research in Nigeria was dependent on the generous institutional support of the Kano State History and Culture Bureau and Arewa House Centre for Historical Documentation in Kaduna. The essay was revised in response to comments by Meg McLagan, Faye Ginsburg, T. O. Beidelman,

Lila Abu-Lughod, Brian Edwards and the anonymous reviewers of *Visual Anthropology Review*.

1 In the 1930s, 1940s and 1950s, Kano mainstream cinemas were dominated by British and American films. In the 1950s cinemas began screening the odd Egyptian and Indian film. By the mid-1960s Egyptian films had disappeared and Indian films had emerged as the most popular film genre (in northern Nigeria at least) though American and some English films were still highly popular. In the 1970s Hong Kong films began to gain in popularity. When I conducted my research in the 1990s Indian films were shown five nights a week at cinemas with one night for Hong Kong films and one night for American films (mostly cheap action films). African films have rarely been shown regularly in mainstream cinemas (the notable exception to this in Nigeria is the case of Yoruba films—a small 'imperfect' cinema which emerged from the Yoruba travelling theatre tradition. For the most part these films were not screened in mainstream theatres but in rented halls formerly used for theatrical performances.

2 The Russian film historian Yuri Tsivian (1994) provides an elegant account of cinema-going as a sensory activity paying attention to the temperature of the auditorium, the placing of the projector, the quality of light and the nature of aural and visual interference.

3 'It is probably true to say that if an African sought admission on one of these [European] nights and was prepared to pay 3/6d he would not be refused admission but the number of Africans who would wish to pay 3/6d admission when they can attend exactly the same performance on another night for 2/-, or 1/- or 6d is very small' (Nigerian National Archives and M.I.A.,). Informal segregation by pricing was a common practice in South India also (Stephen Hughes, personal communication). This raises the question of whether the practice was an Empire-wide means of keeping races separate while avoiding the negative ideological connotations of hardline racial segregation.

4 It could be argued that these names could refer to the Hausa monarchical system both pre- and post-Islamic. It is probably true that the names were chosen for the multiple references: to British imperial splendour and local Hausa authority, but tellingly the names are in English rather than the local equivalent: the Latin Rex (the term emphasizes the connection with the British royal family) instead of *Sarki*, Palace, instead of *Gidan Sarki*, and Queen, instead of *Sarauniya*.

5 In 1946, the Kano District Officer, C.W. Rowling reported in his survey of Kano Land Tenure that the area to the East of the Emir's compound 'still reveals a clear picture of pre-British custom: family compounds, long occupied and still in individual shares, no renting, little pledging and sale only to a local family member needing more house room . . . by one who is dying out' (Frishman, 1977:116-117).

6 T. S. Rice, Memorandum on Segregation and Town Planning, 1921. KNA Kanolocauth 5/2 142/1923 (Frishman, 1977).

7 The Resident Alexander of Kano in a speech to the Conference of Residents in 1926 coined this phrase, which may well sum up the entire symbolic value of Sabon Gari in the eyes of Kano Hausa (Resident Alexander of Kano, 1927 cited in Allyn, 1976:138)).

8 In keeping with this philosophy, European companies were not allowed to trade within the Old City, Christian missionaries were restricted in their activities in the North, and the Kano Emir retained political control over the Northern Muslim areas of Kano (the Old City and Fagge, a traditional trading area to the north of the city).

9 British colonial officials operating in northern Nigeria were often contemptuous of southern Nigerians who they saw as rejecting their 'African' heritage while not quite becoming 'European'. The hierarchical structure of Islamic northern Nigeria was much more amenable to British prejudices and consequently efforts were made to preserve it. 'We want no violent changes,' wrote one Governor-General of Northern Nigeria, 'no transmogrification of the dignified and courteous Moslem into a trousered burlesque with a veneer of European civilization. We do not want to replace a patriarchal and venerable system of government by a discontented and irresponsible democracy of semi-educated politicians.' (Bell, 1910/1911 cited in Allyn, 1976:51)).

10 Sabon Gari is an exemplary illustration of Simmel's (1950) theory of the stranger. Simmel argues that the stranger, who is often a trader, embodies the conflictual principles of nearness and remoteness, that while being outside, he or she is always 'an element of the group itself' (Simmel, 1950:402).

11 This mode of exhibition mimics the history of film in the United States and Britain where the first films were often shown as part of a wider programme of burlesque (see Hansen, 1991), or vaudeville (see Chanan, 1996), sandwiched between singers, comedians and dancers so that they were only one element of the evening's entertainment.

12 Although the Qur'an itself does not explicitly forbid the making of representations, the *hadith* (the sayings and deeds of the Prophets) are explicitly negative about the status of artists (see Bravmann, 1974; Grabar, 1973).

13 Later the name began to be applied mainly to the British Government mobile cinemas that travelled the cities and rural areas screening educational and propaganda films.

14 Both terms were later replaced by the more neutral *sinima* or *silima*.

15 In using 'moral' I refer to two things. Cinema in Kano is defined as an immoral, sexualized space, one that (unlike in the United States) never achieved social legitimation. On another, underlying level, I follow Beidelman's (1993) concept of morality as the set of images and practices through which people both comprehend their world and act within it in ways that conform and subvert their moral understanding. Space, for Beidelman, is a 'moral metaphor', a social product that encodes the imagined order of society and personhood and reveals basic ideas about, and conflicts between, the individual and society. Beidelman's assertion of the active presence of the imagination in moral space has the advantage of foregrounding the concept of space as formed by human action, as something *produced*.

16 See, Nigerian National Archives and Justice Percy E. Hubard. See also, Nigerian National Archives.

17 The power to curse (*tsine*) is a powerful magical attribute in Hausa society as elsewhere in Africa. Certain people are believed to have the magical power to make their curses come true, though if they are not evil people, they may have this ability and not realize it. One person explained the rumour to me by saying that so many people were cursing the construction of the El Duniya that the combined weight of all these curses brought the theatre down.

18 In Sani Mainagge, the Kano State History and Culture Bureau (HCB) operates an open air theatre which it uses for cultural performances such as plays and dances by the famous Koroso dance troupe. When it is not being used by the HCB, videos of Hausa dramas and Indian and Hong Kong films are screened there through a projection unit, making it something like a cinema but with the patina and authority of a government institution.

References

Adamu, Alhaji (1996), interviewed by Brian Larkin in April.

Allen, Robert C. (1983), 'Motion Picture Exhibition in Manhattan, 1906-1912: Beyond the Nickelodeon', in J. L. Fell (ed.), *Film before Griffith*, University of California Press, Berkeley.

Allyn, David Edley (1976), *The Sabon Gari System in Northern Nigeria*, Ph.D. dissertation, UCLA.

Appadurai, Arjun (1996), 'The Production of Locality', in A. Appadurai, *Modernity at Large: Cultural Dimensions of Globalization*, University of Minnesota Press, Minneapolis.

Armbrust, Walter (1998), 'When the Lights Go Down in Cairo: Cinema as Secular Ritual', *Visual Anthropology*, 10: 413-42

Arora, Poonam (1995), 'Imperilling the Prestige of the White Woman: Colonial Anxiety and Film Censorship in British India', *Visual Anthropology Review*, 1:2, 36-49

Barber, Karin (1997), 'Preliminary Notes on the Audience in Africa', *Africa*, 67:3, 349-62

Barkindo, Bawuro M. (1993), 'Growing Islamism in Kano City since 1970: Causes, Forms and Implications', in L. Brenner (ed.), *Muslim Identity and Social Change in Sub-Saharan Africa*, Indiana University Press, Bloomington.

Barthes, Roland (1972), *Mythologies*, Paladin Books, London.

Beidelman, T. O. (1993), *Moral Imagination in Kaguru Modes of Thought*, Smithsonian Institution Press, Washington.

Benjamin, Walter (1978), *Illuminations*, Schocken Books, New York.

Bowser, Eileen (1990), *The Transformation of Cinema, 1907-1915*, History of the American Cinema, 2, Scribner, New York.

Bravman, Rene A. (1974), *Islam and Tribal Art in West Africa*, African Studies Series no. 11, Cambridge University Press, Cambridge.

Buck-Morss, Susan and Walter Benjamin (1989), *The Dialectics of Seeing: Walter Benjamin and the Arcades Project*, Studies in Contemporary German Social Thought, MIT Press, Cambridge, Mass.

Chanan, Michael (1996), *The Dream that Kicks: The Prehistory and Early Years of Cinema in Britain*, Routledge, London.

Friedberg, Anne (1993), *Window Shopping: Cinema and the Postmodern*, University of California Press, Berkeley.

Frishman, Alan (1977), *The Spatial Growth and Residential Patterns of Kano*, Ph.D. dissertation, Northwestern University, Nigeria.

Fuglesang, Minou (1994), *Veils and Videos: Female Youth Culture on the Kenyan Coast*, Department of Social Anthropology Stockholm University, Stockholm.

Grabar, Oleg (1973), *The Formation of Islamic Art*, Yale University Press, New Haven.

Griffiths, Alison (1996), '"Journeys for Those Who Cannot Travel": Promenade Cinema and the Museum Life Group', *Wide Angle*, 18:3, 53-84

Hansen, Miriam (1991), *Babel and Babylon: Spectatorship in American Silent Film*, Harvard University Press, Cambridge, Mass.

Himpele, Jeffrey D. (1996), 'Film Distribution as Media: Mapping Difference in the Bolivian Cinemascape', *Visual Anthropology Review*, 12:1, 47-66

Hiskett, M. (1984), *The Development of Islam in West Africa*, London: Longman.

Hughes, Stephen P. (1999), 'Policing Silent Film Exhibition in South India', in R. Vasudevan (ed.), *Making Meaning in Indian Cinema*, New Delhi: Oxford University Press.

Kano State History and Culture Bureau (HCB), Films and Film Censorship (1948), *Simple list of files removed from Cabinet R918*, Kano.

— (1954), *Minutes by M.H. (?), 20/10/54, in response by a letter from the Director of Education, Northern Region 15/9/54 requesting an assessment of censorship*, Kano.

Kirby, Lynne (1997), *Parallel Tracks: The Railroad and Silent Cinema*, Duke University Press, Durham.

Koszarski, Richard (1990), *An Evening's Entertainment: The Age of the Silent Feature Picture, 1915-1928*, History of the American Cinema 3, Scribner, New York.

Kracauer, Siegfried (1998), *The Salaried Masses: Duty and Distraction in Weimar Germany*, Verso, London, New York.

— and Thomas Y. Levin (1995), *The Mass Ornament: Weimer Essays*, Harvard University Press, Cambridge, Mass.

Kuhn, Annette (1998), *Cinema, Censorship and Sexuality, 1909-1925*, Cinema and Society, Routledge, London.

Larkin, Brian (1997), 'Indian Films, Nigerian Lovers: Media and the Creation of Parallel Modernities', *Africa*, 67:3, 406-40.

— (1999a), 'Introduction to Media and the Technologies for Modern Living', *Visual Anthropology Review*, 14:2, 11-13.

— (1999b), 'Theaters of the Profane: Cinema and Colonial Urbanism', *Visual Anthropology Review*, 14:2, 46-62.

— (n.d.), *White Prestige and the Immoral, Subversive Problem of Film: Moral Panic and Colonial Authority*, n/a

Lugard, Lord (1922), *The Dual Mandate in British Tropical Africa*, W. Blackwell and Sons, London.

Martin, Phyllis (1995), *Leisure and Society in Colonial Brazzaville*, African Studies Series 87, Cambridge University Press, Cambridge.

Miller, Daniel (1997), 'Why Some Things Matter', in D. Miller, *Materializing Culture: Why Some Things Matter*, University of Chicago Press, Chicago.

Mitchell, Timothy (1991), *Colonising Egypt*, University of California Press, Berkeley.

Musser, Charles (1990), *The Emergence of Cinema: The American Screen to 1907*, History of the American Cinema 1, Scribner, New York.

Nigerian National Archives, Kaduna (1934), *Kano Prof. 1391. Kano Township Annual Report 1934*, Kano.

Nigerian National Archives, Kaduna and Justice Percy E. Hubard *Report of the Commissioner appointed by His Excellency the Governor to enquire into the circumstances in which a fire caused loss of life at, and destroyed, the El-Dunia Cinema, Kano, on the 13th day of May 1951, Zaria Prof. vol.II./ EDU/5 Cinema Cinematographs, Cinema Office, (2) Mobile Cinema Routine Correspondence*, Kano.

Nigerian National Archives, Kaduna and M.I.A. *Kaduna 2nd collection, R.1493, Cinematograph Audience 1932-1952*, 2, Kano.

Nigerian National Archives, Kaduna *Kano Prof 4430 (Mr. J. Green Mbadiwe: Application for permission to erect a hotel and cinema at Kano)*, Kano.

Nigerian National Archives, Kaduna *Kano Prof. 6945/Jakara Palace Cinema/Letter to S.D.O.K. from Senior Superintendent of Police, Kano N.A. P.G.F. Sewall. 6/9/52*, Kano.

Nigerian National Archives, Kaduna *Kano Prof. 7564, El Dunia Disaster. Colonial Office (CO)583/317/8. Cinema Disaster at Kano, 1951*, Kano.

Nigerian National Archives, Kaduna *MOI/55/Broadcasting, Radio Diffusion Service and BBC*, Kano.

Resident Alexander of Kano (1927), 'Record of the Proceedings of Conference of Residents, Northern Provinces, 1926', Paper presented to the workshop 'Proceedings of Conference of Residents, Northern Provinces, 1926', Lagos.

Sheikh Nasiru Kabara (1995), interviewed by Brian Larkin in November.

Simmel, Georg (1950), 'The Metropolis and Mental Life' in K. H. Wolff (ed.), *The Sociology of Georg Simmel*, Free Press, Glencoe, Ill.

Sklar, Robert (1975), *Movie-made America: A Social History of American Movies*, Random House, New York.

Tahir, Ibrahim A. (1975), *Scholars, Saints, and Capitalists in Kano 1904-1974. The Pattern of Bourgeois Revolution in an Islamic Society*, Ph.D dissertation, Cambridge University, Cambridge.

Thompson, Elizabeth (2000), *Colonial Citizens: Republican Rights, Paternal Privilege, and Gender in French Syria and Lebanon*, History and Society of the Modern Middle East Series, Columbia University Press, New York.

Tsivian, Yuri and Richard Taylor (1994), *Early Cinema in Russia and Its Cultural Reception*, Routledge, London, New York.

Ubah, C. N. (1982), 'The Political Dilemma of Residential Segregation: The Example of Kano's Sabon Gari', *African Urban Studies*, 14: 51-70

Watts, Michael (1996), 'Place, Space and Community in an African City', in P. Yeager (ed.), *The Geography of Identity*, University of Michigan Press, Ann Arbor.

THE POLITICS OF URBAN SEGREGATION AND INDIAN CINEMA IN DURBAN

VASHNA JAGARNATH

The need for cheap labour on the sugarcane plantations of Natal led to the importation of indentured labour from India: Between 1860 and 1911, 150,000 indentured workers arrived in Natal from India. Mainly they arrived from areas in the northwest of India, the south-eastern coast of India where Tamil and Telugu is mainly spoken and from the northeastern areas of Bihar and Uttar Pradesh.

In spite of the low wages, long hours and strenuous working conditions the majority of them had to accept at the outset, the Indian community of modern South Africa managed to develop a very rich culture. It is a unique culture in many ways due to the many different influences coming together in it—each with its own idea of India or what it means to be Indian.

An important influence on the development of Indian identity as well as ideas and imaginings of India itself was the Indian film. It is usually an overlooked contribution to Indian culture in South Africa, but a vital one which played an important role not only in the field of visual expression, but in music as well.

In this essay I look at the politics of urban segregation and the history of cinema reception in the public space, and its influence on the lives of a particular group of Indians settled in Durban.

Visual entertainment has been a part of the South African Indian community for most of their history. It has taken many different forms, from dance to drama. Hence, the advent of the Indian cinema industry was quick to make an impact on South African Indians. It was not long after India started producing its own films that they made their appearance in South Africa. This was mainly in the form of short silent films, usually shown on a projector set-up in a particular area, and the entire community would turn up to see the moving pictures.

The projector was usually set up in the building that was known as the temple, but was actually a school during the day and a place were community meetings were held. There seem to have been two early cinemas catering to Indian audiences during the days of silent films before 1940, but the first proper cinema to be opened by non-whites in Durban was the Avalon theatre, owned by Kajee and Moosa (Moosa, 2001).[1]

Although mainly Indians frequented these early cinemas, people of other races also patronized them, but mostly when English films were screened. The owners of the new cinemas were keen to open them up to other races and made formal proposals to the government to allow African and Coloured people to attend their film shows. South African segregation policies, however, meant that Indian film did not gain the appeal across race boundaries that it has in other parts of the world where there is an Indian diaspora.

The importation of movies was difficult. As early as 1936, the Indian government tried to export films to South Africa. There was much correspondence between the government of India and the government of South Africa, between parliamentary officials, immigration and customs officers of the two countries. The Indian government requested the lowering of duties on the importation of Indian films. They argued that due to the small population of Indians in South Africa, high import taxes would mean that films could not be imported.

Another argument was that South African Indians were as a whole very poor before 1960. 'A survey as late as 1943/44 estimated that 70.6 per cent of Indians lived below the established Poverty Datum Line' (Freund, 1995:40). On 29 September 1939 the Immigration and Asiatic Affairs office provided these statistics (figures in thousands) of the number of Indians residing in South Africa as of 1936, who were either first generation Indians or Indians born here (Immigration and Asiatic Affairs, 1939):

Cape	10.508
Orange Free State	29
Transvaal	25.493
Natal	183.661
Total Population	219.691

Although the South African government recognized the low population of Indians, it did not agree to the request from the Indian government. The main reason given was that it would show preference to one community over others—the South African government would then have to reduce taxes on all imported films (Secretary Board of Trade and Industries of South Africa, 1940). The other reason was that 'Indian films appear to be purely a money-making matter and not for the education of the Indian community'.[2] This, however, did not mean the end of Indian film imports into South Africa as the opening of the Avalon cinema in 1940 indicates. A further complication arose in 1948, with the coming to power of the National Party government in South Africa and the introduction of formal apartheid, following which the Indian government introduced sanctions, including a prohibition of the export of Indian films to South Africa.

The ways in which Indian films managed to travel to South Africa in spite of everything are both interesting and complicated. They are also steeped in controversy as they were seen by some as being illegal; in most cases it was mainly a matter of finding a loophole in the system. In my interview with Mr A. B. Moosa, he denied any suggestion of the importation of Indian films into South Africa having been illegal. He claimed that the importing of film was 'perfectly legal'.

The actual process of importing worked as follows. The Indian government as far as it was concerned exported films all across the world except to South Africa, Rhodesia and the Portuguese territories.[3] Therefore the films would go to distributors in London, Singapore, Hong Kong, Beirut and the Fiji Islands, and South African cinemas would buy the films from any of these sources.

There were several problems with this way of acquiring films. One was that the South African distributors ended up paying twice as much for the films as they would have if they acquired them directly from India. A distributor interviewed by *The Graphic* newspaper is quoted as saying, 'We are paying through our noses for second rate stuff' (*The Graphic*, 1969).

A second problem was that once a South African distributor had bought a film he could not be assured of exclusive rights over the film in South Africa. If one distributor bought a film from an agency in London, a different South African distributor might buy the same film from a distributor in Singapore, and there was no agency in South Africa to protect the rights of the distributor. A third problem was the irregularity of delivery due to this system of importation, which meant that distributors often had no idea which film they would receive when.

The 1950s witnessed a rise in the opening of cinemas not only in Durban but also in other parts of South Africa. The Kajee-Moosa group did not have a monopoly in the film market, and different people opened other cinemas. Ramnikal Goshalia opened the Naaz Cinema in 1953 when the Victoria Picture Palace's lease expired. The Rajab Brothers established the Shah Jehan Cinema in 1956.

The Rajab brothers opened their second cinema on 26 April 1968, the Shiraz that was housed in the new Rajab Centre in Victoria Street.[4] Twenty years after the Rajab Brothers had established the Shah Jehan they embarked on the launch of a new movie theatre, the Isfahan. It was opened on 4 November 1976. The Isfahan seated a maximum of 700 people. This cinema has recently regained its popularity, and many people frequent it to watch Indian films.

Although all of the cinemas mentioned above have been based in the centre of Durban, many cinemas sprang up also in the other parts of Durban such as the Mayville cinemas and the Avalon cinema in Pietermaritzburg. Mr. Valli Mohammed was the 'man behind this scheme'(*The Graphic*, 1969). He was also the director of the company that ran the Avalon cinema in Johannesburg.

The cinema complexes themselves were large and grand. They came to be a very important part of the architecture of their areas at the time as spaces where people would come together. The grandeur of each cinema became something of a marvel and would be featured prominently in advertisements (*The Graphic*, 1969).[5] The Avalon cinema in Pietermaritzburg boasted that its ladies' powder room would have music relayed into it during show time *(The Graphic,* 1969).

The cinemas were often large and would seat up to one thousand people. Names were in keeping with the grandeur and splendour of the cinemas—Shah Jehan, Isfahan, Raj, and Shiraz. They all aimed at linking themselves with an Indian past of royal dynasties, and Mughal extravagance; and the luxurious interiors of the cinema houses would be made to resemble the rich halls of the Mughal palaces. The walls were adorned with rich carpetry, usually in colours of deep red and royal blue. There were little kiosks within the cinemas that provided sweets and chocolates.

This linkage with the Mughal past was probably made stronger by the fact that South African Muslims owned many of the cinemas, but it also has to do with the cultivation of a very particular idea of the past. In Orientalist representations, the Mughal era has been developed into the general idea of India's history, and it is interesting that not only in the diaspora, but also in India itself there has been an urge to cling to the Orientalist vision of the past (Said, 1978).

An instance of this can seen in the development of nationalist discourse in India from the 1920s onwards—a discourse which made its way to South Africa and became part of the life world of South African Indians and which would include prominently Orientalized notions of India (Prakash, 1995). Another, more down-to-earth reason for the 'dynastic' naming of the cinemas could be that they were seen and meant to be seen as palaces of excess and enjoyment—cinemas did indeed come to represent this in the lives of the many Indians in Durban.

A similar notion of grandeur and extravagance seems to have been attached to cinemas in Nigeria in the form of names like the Palace and the Queen's theatre, but in this case through seeking a linkage with the British Empire. This was the case in Kano where cinemas in a similar way were aiming to introduce an experience of splendour into the lives of audiences there.[6]

Most of the cinemas in Durban showed Hindi movies, but they also showed English films, as black Africans under apartheid regulations were not allowed to attend the various white-owned cinemas where such films would otherwise be shown. Hence, some movie houses would also have a separate hall in the building showing English films alongside those where Hindi movies were screened (*The Leader*, 1969).

Hindi movies would be mainly shown from Monday to Saturday. The most popular shows were the Saturday five o'clock and seven o' clock shows. Although the films were in Hindi, Indians of other language groups went to watch Hindi films as did Indians of different religious backgrounds. This was due to two factors—first, that cinemas did not import films made in other Indian languages as they were more difficult to come by, and secondly, that the languages of Urdu[7] and Gujarati are similar to Hindi, and therefore Hindi was fairly understandable to the language groups that were most prominent in Durban and South Africa.

Another reason for the exclusive importation of Hindi films was of course their popularity, as Bombay is the centre of popular film production, and Hindi is the language of the Bollywood film. Thus, its being in Hindi became part of what made a film popular—even today when copies of films in other Indian languages are more easy to obtain, it is very rare to see an Indian movie screened in Durban which is not in Hindi. Films by Satyajit Ray or even Mani Ratnam may only be glimpsed at an occasional film festival.

The Tamil language is very different from Hindi, therefore the understanding of Hindi films was more difficult for the Tamil speakers, but many of them still went to watch Hindi films. It is strange that Tamil films were not being shown to a greater extent, as the Tamil speaking population is very large among the Indians in South Africa. In Durban, the early cinemas did not show any Tamil films, and it was only with the opening of the Naaz cinema by Mr Goshala in 1953 that Tamil films came to be billed at all. 'These were a hit instantly' (Naidoo, 2001). 'Naaz would run a Tamil film for four shows a day and the film would run for up to four or five weeks continuously, Monday to Saturday. These shows were always well attended'[8]

The first Tamil talkie to come to this country was called *Vanmohini* and one of the stars of the film—called Pandharibhai—is still alive.

Initially when Tamil films were not being shown in South Africa, people would put on shows in the cinema halls in Tamil which tried to imitate stories from films. These shows would have a set of musicians playing music as well as dance acts—this form of entertainment in the Tamil language ended when the screening of Tamil films in South Africa began (Naidoo, 2001).

During World War Two, there was a dip in the screening of Tamil films as they became more difficult to obtain. Hindi films, however, were still shown on a regular basis. The decline in the screening of Tamil films and the demand for them led to the formation of a new company importing Tamil films. This set up competition for the Naaz Company.

The new cinema company was called Mayville Theatres and was owned by the Pathar Brothers. Mayville Theatres challenged the Hindi movie world by showing Tamil films and met with a very positive response.[9] It became like a pilgrimage to go to watch them—especially on Sundays when people used to travel from all areas of Natal—from Chatsworth (which was then still a farming community), from Tongaat and the city of Durban (Naidoo, 2001).

The screening of Tamil films led to an increase in the interest in Tamil music. 'Through the movies people would learn new songs and then they would go to Goshalia's music shop to buy gramophone records which sent Ramnikal's record sales up'.[10] Tamil record selling began to make serious money for the Goshalia family, and the imports of music records from India went up. At the time, records available were all 78 rpm which meant that songs had to fit the format of the shellac record, which was three minutes, and became the standard for both Hindi and Tamil film songs. In this way, Tamil film music gained a great influence also on musicians and singers in South Africa.[11]

The success of the screening of Indian movies in South Africa from the 1950s to the middle of the 1970s was quite phenomenal. Every Saturday the cinema owners were guaranteed a full house—many people would book a week in advance to see a film. At times, it would not matter what film was showing, and the owners themselves often had no idea as to which film would be on at the end of the week. When this occurred the film was termed a 'surprise feature', and people would go to watch a film only to find out what the title of the film was when it began.

The popularity of Indian cinema also affected the type of films being imported, which were mainly commercial and mainstream movies. This tended to create a one-sided view of the Indian film industry in South Africa as people did not get to see instances of the art cinema which was also being produced in India. A director like Satyajit Ray is almost unknown in South Africa, partly because he worked in Bengali. In South Africa, only the Bombay film industry received attention, and later Madras with the screening of Tamil films.

The arrangement of space within the cinema house and the dynamics that were involved in the arranging of the seating were often quite complex. Primarily, cinemas aimed at attracting the Indian population of South Africa as their main patrons but this does not mean that they were not also interested in other customers.

Due to the Group Areas Act, the area in which the theatres were situated would determine the race of people that patronized it. Problems arose as there were no cinemas built in the urban areas to service the African Coloured population. Africans were supposed to travel a long distance to view a film in the townships—if at all a township cinema existed.

Although Indian-owned cinema houses in Durban were situated in the predominantly Indian areas of Grey Street, Victoria Street and Queen Street, Africans and Coloured people were also allowed to occupy certain spaces within that part of the Central Business District. In fact, the relationship between the Indian and the Coloured communities of Durban has been one of fluidity. The interaction between Indian and Coloured people led to many different forms of inter-racial relationships, and many Coloured families lived in Indian areas and Indians in Coloured areas.[12]

The cinemas found that it was almost impossible not to allow Coloured people into their theatres as many Coloured women and men were married to, or in a relationship with, Indians. Finally, on 8 December 1958, a permit was issued to allow Chinese, Indians and Coloured to attend the same cinemas, but the permit was refused to Africans.

The owners of the various cinemas aimed at attracting an African, Coloured as well as Chinese audience with the English films they screened. In fact, there are many records of applications to the Secretary for Bantu Affairs by the Indian cinema owners[13] to be allowed to bring African, Coloured and Chinese audiences into the cinemas. Coloureds and Chinese were granted permission to patronize certain cinema houses but Africans were consistently denied entry.[14]

On 7 November 1959 a report with recommendations was submitted by the Chairman of the Group Areas Board concerning permission to give Africans access to cinemas. At the same time, the Scala Cinema was granted permission to build a theatre on a plot of land near the Indian trading area. It was located on the corner of Mansfield Road and Warwick Avenue.

This became the only cinema at the time to cater to a black African audience—it was screening films from 9:00 am to 10:00 pm, and its patrons were made up of 70% Indian, 10% Coloured, and 20% black African people. When the Avalon Cinema in Victoria Street also opened its doors to people of other races, it only did so in the afternoon and evenings. Chinese people were not allowed to attend these types of cinemas, as there were no separate seating arrangements available.

The cinemas claimed that they were providing a service for the Group Areas Board who were against 'natives' loitering around the streets, by providing a place for them to go to at night when waiting for buses; and it claimed to aim at attracting the many African and Coloured people who used to hang around there all day (NTS).

The above-mentioned applications, rejections and, finally, the acceptance and approval of the screening of films to members of different races at the same time illustrate the rigid control over space and movement that the state in those days exerted over the urban population.

There was a lot of concern about how to keep the 'idle native' occupied. The Indian cinema owners used this to their advantage, making money out of the state's problem by providing a way to take the Africans off the streets and into the enclosed spaces of the cinemas. However, for Africans to be allowed into the cinemas, there had to be separate seating arrangements, an example being the seating arrangements of Shah

Jehan. It had two thousand seats, but only three hundred and eighty seats would be made available to 'natives only'.

In addition to this, the cinemas had to provide separate entrances and exits as well as separate toilets. Just as the architecture and structure of other cinemas in Africa were being influenced by colonial conditions, these Indian-owned cinemas were being influenced by the condition of Apartheid. In Nigeria, for example, similar divisions of space in the theatres were not uncommon with certain seats being reserved for 'whites only'.[15]

More informal and discreet were the mechanisms of gender segregation, which meant that it was very rare for female Indian cinemagoers to ever go to watch an English film where they might be exposed to both immoral content and the company of an audience of predominantly non-Indian males. While in Lamu in Kenya, Indian cinemas had formalized 'ladies' nights', this segregation in Durban along gender lines seems to have been effected more informally.

The increase in petitions to have access to wider audiences illustrates the importance of cinema in both promoting Indian culture in Durban and also as a means of creating economic wealth. Cinema helped to create a specific class of prosperous Indian businessmen and led to the establishment of further businesses that depended for their prosperity on cinemas and moviegoers. The increase in business for buses that would now gain an extra route on the weekends to the cinemas, for the many record companies that sprang up and for the fashion retail industry was spectacular. The sari shops had a steady stream of customers always looking for the latest saris worn by the film stars.

The cinema houses of Durban were thus not only a communicative tool that allowed for the passing on of ideas from India, but also a vehicle that created economic growth which was vital for the maintenance and transformation of notions of Indian identity.

Notes

1 There seems to be conflicting reports on the dates of the first cinema opened and whether it was actually Avalon cinema or the silent movie cinema. The other issue is whether the silent movie cinemas were cin-

emas in the conventional sense or just rooms that were used to show movies. From my interview with A. B. Moosa he seems to think that the Avalon cinema was the first non-white owned cinema in South Africa. I will try to investigate further.

2 Interview with Board of Censors 28 August 1939.

3 The trade sanctions on Rhodesia (present-day Zimbabwe) and Portuguese territories are probably because they were still colonies.

4 See, http://www.sahistory.org.za/pages/specialprojects/greyStreet/cinemas.htm, Title: Grey Street, Durban: Cinemas—the "Silver Screen".

5 In this issue of *The Graphic* an article describes the grandeur of the cinema as well as providing an artist impression of the cinema.

6 Cf. Brian Larkin in the present volume.

7 Many South African Muslims speak Urdu; however many Muslims also speak Gujarati.

8 www.sahistory.org.za/pages/specialprojects/greyStreet/cinemas.htm, Title: Grey Street, Durban: Cinemas—the "Silver Screen".

9 Those Tamil people who went to watch Hindi film when there were not many Tamil films being screened could now go and watch Tamil films, and this would have led to a decrease in numbers. Nevertheless, Indian film was in such demand that I doubt if it really affected the Hindi film market.

10 www.sahistory.org.za/pages/specialprojects/greyStreet/cinemas.htm, Title: Grey Street, Durban: Cinemas—the "Silver Screen".

11 Gujarati and Urdu speakers mainly watched Hindi film in cinemas and only with the advent of television and the video machine could they watch Gujarati and Urdu films. With the advent of the Global Asian channels such as Sony, B4U and ZEE TV Urdu and Gujarati speakers get to view more of their language films, though this is also kept to the minimum as Gujarati and Urdu films are usually aired around once a week.

12 The areas that were designated Indian and Coloured under the Group Areas Act no longer exist.

13 By Indian cinema owners I mean that the owners of the cinemas were Indian. This reference does not denote the type of films screened.

14 See NTS for applications submitted between 1959-1960 by the Raj Cinema.

15 See Brian Larkin in the present volume.

References

Freund, Bill (1995), *Insiders and Outsiders: The Indian Working Class of Durban, 1910-1990*, University of Natal Press, Pietermaritzburg.

Graphic, The (1969), 15. August.

Moosa, A. B. (2001), interviewed by Vashna Jagarnath on 19 September.

Naidoo, T. P. (2001), interviewed by Vashna Jagarnath on 24 September.

NTS *6657 29/313Y (8)*, n/a.

Prakash, Gyan (1995), *Writing Postcolonial-Orientalist Histories of the Third World: Perspectives from Indian Historiography*, Princeton University Press, Princeton.

Said, Edward W. (1978), *Orientalism*, Routledge & Kegan Paul Ltd., London.

Leader, The (1969), 8 August.

THE EXHILARATION OF DREAD: GENRE, NARRATIVE FORM AND FILM STYLE IN CONTEMPORARY URBAN ACTION FILMS

RAVI S. VASUDEVAN

Some crucial transformations occurred in the city of Bombay in the early 1980s. There was the epochal failure of the Bombay textile strike of the early 1980s and a basic reordering of political economy, with shifts away from the factory system into more dispersed forms of production, and an undercutting of labour's presence in public political life. This moment precipitated a crisis for leftwing perspectives, and was paralleled by the emergence of a powerful Hindu chauvinistic politics at the local and national levels. The Shiv Sena acquired political presence in the state and this right wing regional movement linked up with the nationwide Hindu political mobilization under the Bhartiya Janata Party and its radical wings, leading to the devastating attacks on the city's Muslim population in 1992-93. A few months later, bomb blasts in the city were seen as revenge attacks associated with a Muslim underworld. Alongside these political upheavals, Bombay, like many other metropolises in India, became the object of various programmes for urban reorganization, in keeping with the imperative of inviting large-scale foreign investment. The drives to clear urban space fell most heavily on the subordinate sections of Indian cities, vendors, hawkers, small workshops and artisanal units.

We can see well enough how a cinema of urban anxiety has ample sources to develop its scenarios from the life world of the city and the nation. Indeed, the cinema produces a sense of turbulence and transformation, but to seek linkages between one phenomenon and the other may be to fail to engage with the range of forms, energies and social vistas that compose the cinematic experience of the city. In this essay, I seek to address the specifics of film narration, form and history, with a particular concern for how a sensorium related to the city exists in the cinema and can be identified and explored.

By choosing the urban action film for reflection, I will dwell on the mechanisms of story-telling, of excitement and astonishment which accompany tales of fear and danger. The paradoxical relationship of audiences to such entertainment suggests the duality posed by such genres, where the audience is invited to enjoy the pleasures of heightened kinetic engagement and perception while entering fraught narrative worlds governed by a gathering sense of anxiety. This then is a cinema which conveys to us the exhilaration of dread, with all the ambivalence that phrase is designed to convey.

The Transformation of Narrative Structures

One of the most significant transformations wrought in this genre, and more broadly in the contemporary cinema, is the transformation of narrative structures away from older binaries. Moinak Biswas notes that there is in these fictions an effective end to the old lexicon: east/west, country/city, police and criminal underworld, perhaps even, we may add, to the opposition between public and private domains. To explore the sensibility of the period, Ranjani Mazumdar, for example draws upon one node, that of the depressed and dystopian urban subjectivity that defined the Bombay of the mid-1980s (Mazumdar, 2001). Such a mood is only able to conjure up the most fleeting of residual utopian energies in its references to a country idyll as object of longing for the doomed characters of Vidhu Vinod Chopra's *Parinda/Pigeons* (1989). Shohini Ghosh articulates another depletion of binary symbolism in her analysis of mythic archetypes in the structuring of narrative logics and worlds. She notes the shift from the characteristic *Karan-Arjun*, legitimate/illegitimate oppositions in the construction of the hero. There is the emergence of a more directly ambivalent and tortured rather than split self, in the persistence of Karan and the emergence of Abhimanyu as distinct figures in the landscape of the contemporary (Ghosh, 2001). The latter is of course particularly pertinent, legitimate and yet a victim for his inability to gain the full knowledge which would enable him to move from secured, stable and legitimate territories into dangerous and hostile zones and back again.

The particular confusion and continuity between spaces designated as opposed, such as in the relationship between public and private, conveys a sense of the contemporary urban imaginary as a kind of maze. One of the most interesting popular films of the 1990s, *Baazigar/The Player* (dir. Abbas-Mastan, 1993) approaches this question through a scenario of subaltern masquerade and entry into upper class society. While the objective is to expose the cut-throat underpinnings of legitimate wealth, the strategy of class exposé opens the protagonist to an amoral, instrumental logic, and finally to death and self-destruction. There is no doubt that the contemporary imaginary of cinema is, at its most productive, devoted to such senses of an unstable and dangerous subjectivity. This allows us to capture a fluidity of symbolic space and poses, in turn, a problem for spectator empathy and identification.

New Forms of Knowledge

Apart from the broad symbolics of narrative structure, there are issues relating to the nature of cognition and forms of knowledge which define the fictions of urban anxiety. How does one account for the distribution of narrative attention amongst various characters, in ways which appear to reside within but perhaps fundamentally stretch melodramatic binaries? These films displace focus from good/evil oppositions, or at least suggest that this frame does not provide adequate explanations. In the process, they may actually help us understand that terror reduces everyone to vulnerability, and perhaps this has something to do with the way life is imagined in the city. A discussion of *Parinda* shifted focus from the overt, morally calibrated central characters to the villain, the Tamil gangster Anna (Nana Patekar), a figure whose psychosis invites audience fascination in very distinctive ways. Interestingly, a careful reading of the film will suggest that the key event which defines the psychosis—the burning of Anna's wife and son—is contradictorily rendered. We do not know if Anna enacted the horror, or was witness to it, whether it was an expression of psychosis, or whether the horror in turn precipitated Anna's madness, punishing him for the will to survive and dominate others. (In this sense we have here the dystopian rendering of another tale of Tamil immigration and violent assertion, Mani Ratnam's 1987 *Nayakan/Hero*, but now in a manner where the issue of Tamil subalternity in the city is suppressed). Ultimately, as Jeebesh Bagchi suggests, the locus of authority shifts to an opponent, Moosa, astute in manipulating the weakness of others, but otherwise so marginal and almost phantom-like in characterization that he is not so much character as presiding intelligence. Of course, this is only another level of narrative authority identifiable in the diegetic world. For there is always the extra-diegetic, the position which constructs the space-time of the narrative world and assigns functions to its inhabitants. Whether we call this by the name director, generic convention or its transmutation, or whether we call it the position which emerges from a self-reflexive critical discussion about the dominant epistemologies which organize perception in the narration of terror, one thing is clear: this intelligence appears to assume that the source of terror in the city always slips away, beyond the field of full knowledge, and into some cavernous other space.

The Perception of Space

This leads us directly onto another thematic, how symbolic narrative dimensions and narrational mechanisms can be conceived of in terms of the links between key and recurring spaces in the cinematic exploration of urban being: police stations, courts of law, the space of the criminal organization, the home, and the cluster of *mohalla*, bazaar and street that often provide crucial coordinates for the way the 'social' domain in the cinema of urban action and revenge is rendered. Crucial to the mise-en-scene of urban terror is the premise that characters are rarely able to conceal themselves from some overarching gaze, that all spaces are vulnerable to surveillance, and characters are liable to receive messages and other intimations of danger in the most sacrosanct of spaces.

Mazumdar's spatial analysis of *Parinda* indicates an almost schematic rendering and opposition between a domestic space already infiltrated by the criminal history of an elder brother, and the criminal underworld, Anna's factory. As Mazumdar shows, a super-ordinate terror continuously threatens the melodramatic space of romantic possibility, weaving itself into the sentimental construction of domestic bliss. The young couple Karan and Paro's idyll is constantly interrupted by anonymous intrusions and ultimately by death. However, the film redefines space, extending it to character interiority. Terror intrudes into the very psychology of the primary assailant, visiting on Anna irrupting visions of past traumas and premonitions of doom. Mazumdar points out that Anna's garlanding of a photograph of himself and his dead family at the outset of the film seems to cast him in the role of a wraith, a figure already from the beyond whose cold ruthlessness covers an interior world governed by his own escalating fears.

Ira Bhaskar draws our attention to the importance of gothic scenarios to the mise-en-scene of terror. Anna's factory draws on the gothic lineage of dark dungeons and cobwebbed attics, spaces that disclose the inner logic of their narrative worlds. The factory circulates drugs under the guise of oil production, but is primarily intelligible as an assembly line for dead bodies. We enter this space to look at this processing of death, the secret spectacle that constitutes the inner reality of the city. Here, bodies are mutilated by drills, churned along with kernels, and flushed down waste disposal chutes. Ultimately, however, the bodies return, or persist, as elements of the uncanny. The corpse of Anna's lieutenant, Abdul is propped up in a sepulchral coffin as if to leer at Kishan. Framed alongside the coffin, the hero's body contorts with a realization of the ultimate destiny of a life started at the margins of the city and now manifest in the annihilation of his brother. The hero knows this space, his instincts are bound up with a knowledge of its precincts and practices. But he desires another destiny for his brother. However, the factory of death comes to be recognized fatalistically, sickeningly, as the resting place, ultimate home in this homeless world. Thus might Freud have construed this uncanny *unheimlich*, so remote, so other, and yet so undeniably and dreadfully home.

In these abstract spaces the narrative world is pared down to certain essential units of meaning. But these scenes are also stylistically elaborate and draw upon international generic codes. Mazumdar develops interesting comparisons between this narrative of doom and the post-war American genre of film noir (Gopalan, 2002). Spaces wreathed in shadows, a night city empty of people or populated by anonymous crowds, a soundtrack filled with the portent of danger by the constantly ringing phone from some demonic source, all these suggest a rather self-conscious drawing on of codes generated elsewhere, but, as I will suggest, historically available for the contemporary. Here fate, and its manifestation as an ever receding and untraceable authority, would appear to function as the other side of a social domain that has been swept away to reveal its underbelly.

A Cinephiliac History

Here the question of history comes to face us as part of the history of cinephilia. In ongoing work on the analysis of this context, Lalitha Gopalan has suggested that this period signalled a new availability in India of a global cinema. She sites as important to this context the renewed import of US cinema after a long embargo, the circulation of films through the video market, and the induction of graduates from the Film and Television Institute of India into the industry (Mazumdar, 2001). It would be important to distinguish different moments in such a global circulation of the cinema; surely we have such an interactive discourse right from the beginning of the cinema, and in ways which do not reduce the global to American cinema. Nevertheless, the emergence in particular of a certain film-technical cinephilia with the arrival of the FTII graduate in the industry suggests a more precise node of transformation. In this context, film noir is not a historically remote phenomenon, but part of a synchronically available filmic resource.

The history of Bombay cinema is punctuated by formal transformations such as these. In the 1970s, the emergence of a character and an urban subjectivity which could not be recovered within legal and social hierarchies was accompanied by a transformation in filmic representations of Bombay. Hitherto iconically indexed by the establishing shot of Victoria Terminus, Marine Drive or the High Court, the city extends into a kaleidoscope of visual fields. Rather than a realistically evoked space, the cinematic city becomes a stage for the working out of new types of conflict, rhythms of existence and subjectivity. A new aesthetic composes the city in terms of the elaboration of backgrounds, something that the contemporary period takes over and transforms into a tactile field that suffuses the subjectivity. To get to a sense of what I mean here by a tactile field, I will oppose it to the theatrical notion of the prop or the painted background, as something which shifts registers from a presentational to a more dynamic, virtual aesthetic. Rather than positioning us as external viewers of figures cast against a background, our look is drawn in and flows amongst objects and figures within the space-time of the fictive world.

Let me use *Deewar/The Wall* (dir. Yash Chopra, 1974) to describe the earlier form. A black and yellow cab rank provides the background to a debate about morality and pragmatism between two brothers. While this famous sequence draws on new iconic frames of reference, character relationship to setting is rendered statically, and the scene crucially depends on zoom shots and declamatory dialogue for its effects. Mazumdar's analysis of this scene draws upon Benjamin's notion of the ruin to understand the way in which an object or a space may be invested with memory or meaning that is fragmentary and is threatened with dissolution by the tyranny of history's onward march (Mehta, 2001). Here the narrative is brought to a halt, becomes spatialized and is opened to a rhetorical and melodramatic appeal to memory which transcends the impetus of the present moment.

This is a suggestive reading of the scene, one which we may juxtapose with an urban mise-en-scene from Priyadarshan's *Gardish/Celestial Turbulence* (1994). Shiva (Jackie Shroff) is being chased by the hatchet men of the villain, Billa Gilani. The chase takes place across the roofs of cabs caught in a traffic jam. Figures thud across rooftops and collide with each other as Shiva pushes his assailants off him and counter attacks only in order to evade them. Here objects and characters impact on each other, transposing dialogue to a discourse of bodies in space. Urban space is present to the characters who inhabit it, it is integral to the articulation of being. This is not to argue that one form is superior to the other, but that there is a braiding of urban elements with filmic techniques so that the filmic affords a new imagination for inhabiting the urban.

Other instances of a cinematic tactility of urban being abound, as for example in the way Bombay is defined by the monsoon. Black umbrellas provide for an extensive metonymization of the city in *Arjun* (dir. Rahul Rawail, 1986), as they unfold en masse, glistening in the rain, and provide a textured space for violent pursuit and killing. It is an index of the self-consciousness of the cinema of this period that Rawail's film quotes here from an audacious motif in Hitchock's *Foreign Correspondent* of 1940.

Most important here is the railway station, and the railway tracks. In *Zanjeer/The Chain*, (dir. Prakash Mehra, 1973) we are provided a sense of the everyday vulnerability of the massified city to the railway accident, as when a key witness to a gangland killing falls from his precarious perch on a crowded commuter train. Here villainous design precipitates the accident, as the assailant plunges his cigarette into his target's hand, thereby loosening his hold and despatching him to his death. But the documentary-like structures of the scene suggest something more precarious posed within the domain of contingency and chance in everyday urban life. Nevertheless, this scene, with its emphasis on close-ups to designate villainy, and its recourse to the studio for the shots of the train's interior, continue to inhabit a static, tableau rendition of its subject.

The railway track captures liminality and transience, and provides intimations of impending dislocation as the existential condition of the urban. In *Zanjeer* we notice that the policeman hero, who will be framed and expelled from the police force, lives next to the railway track, and later he is beaten and cast down on the railway tracks from an overhead bridge. However, later, these symbolically significant backgrounds are transformed into features of subjectivity. In *Hathyar/The Weapon* (dir. J. P. Dutta, 1988), the violent, emotionally unstable protagonist accompanies his family to Bombay, where they take up residence in a tenement overlooking the railway track. As he listens to his parents in conversation with neighbours, his look is involuntarily drawn to the railway tracks. The character's distracted, edgy look integrates the space into the mise-en-scene of his neurotic subjectivity.

The films of the 1970s generated their own cinephilia, variously drawing on certain populist strands in Hollywood such as the work of

Capra and Kazan, and international genre developments, such as Italian appropriations of the American western, as with Sergio Leone. But the particular highlighting of the cinematic apparatus as a body of techniques, and a fluency of their deployment, seems to be of more recent vintage. *Gardish* is notable for its use of steadicam, and in Ram Gopal Varma's *Satya* (1998), for example, a gang fight is orchestrated via a highly self-conscious camera. A massive crane movement sweeps down the length of an apartment block to meet a gang as they exit from a lift. Subsequently, character and camera movement parallel each other, creating a dynamic doubling of presence, culminating in a top angle pan from the rooftops as we look down on the chase in the streets below. In a particularly resonant segment, the chase climaxes on an overhead suburban railway bridge, quoting from Friedkin's *The French Connection* (1971), and then reaching a crescendo via Scorsese's De Niro/Pesci double gun burst in *Goodfellas* (1990) as the protagonists Bhiku and Satya dispatch their opponent Guru Narayan. The scene is cast against the backdrop of the train hurtling below. Apparatuses of cinema and everyday urban speed double each other, referencing the moment through a kind of world cinema parallax. Characters and actions shadow each other in phantom relay, the baton of form being carried into another territory of social experience. We have here an act of transposition of form where the experience of cinematic looking is not merely self-referential and auto-erotic but enabling of a heightened perception of reality.

One of the issues here is squarely posed by Moinak Biswas, when he asks us to think about the relationship between the cinematic sensorium and the urban sensorium. Rather than simply catalogue parallels between the body of sense impressions that cascade from screen and the urban everyday—sounds, sights, senses of speed and volume and depth and surface—he asks to consider the limits of this sensorial flow, the way the senses are subject to disciplines of frame, narrative structure, rhythm and duration.

Realism/Reality Effects

Biswas goes onto argue that to deploy the category of realism to this new form in the 1980s would be to void it of explanatory force. He deploys the terms 'reality effect', even 'realism effect' to capture the 'realist gain', in the sense of an augmentation of object perception and perception of space, of volume and flow, that emerges in the cinema of this period. He situates this in the emergence of television and the new, global traffic in images of late capitalism and in the fluidity of post-modernist sign systems. In this argument, such heightened perception remains on the surface, and does not engage us in narrative depth. However, we have seen the impact of such formations elsewhere, and they are highly differentiated in the way they configure themselves in relation to local and global audiences. For example, in France, the 'cinema du look', with its avowed subordination of narrative content to style, overlaps in a film such as Kassovitz' La Haine/Hate (1996) with the 'cinema du banlieu', the cinema of the ethnic suburbs, films dealing with a sense of ethnic marginality and struggle.

Within the Indian industry, certain trends in the diaspora family film of the 1990s—which Monika Mehta's research into the industry has uncovered as the category of the 'family love story' (Mehta, 2001)—acquires a particular virtuality of appearance, place abstracted into a non-identifiable space of the globalized imagination. Films such as Parinda, Gardish and Satya emerge from a rather different matrix of production and exhibition. The urban action film has not been such an important vector of the film trade in the lucrative markets of the US and Britain, though there is no lack of a global traffic of images and, indeed, sequences, in the way they are put together. In these films, there is a strong orientation to local constructions of the city, of course inflected by the way Bombay functions as part of a national imaginary. Their 'reality effects' occasionally gesture to modes of observation associated with the documentary essay. The pro-filmic, the space organized for the camera, may be rendered in terms of a significant density of incidental activities which appear to have a logic which carries on irrespective of the actions of the main characters; until, of course, an action scenario emerges to bring a halt to the everyday pattern of events. The reality effect, as opposed to realist procedure, affords us an enhanced perception of this incidental space. For example, in Gardish, a washer-man's space in the market is indexed by the increased volume of the sound of clothes being beaten against the stone, and by a visual enhancement, sprays of water cascading upward in the frame.

As with *La Haine*, we may have something in the way of a hyperrealist form, perception being enhanced through but beyond the commonplace everyday, and with a certain deliberation. The reality effects of *Satya* are such that there is both recognition and a strange sense of hyper-location in the way the film privileges the spectator with perceptions about how the everyday social world and the world of terror are contiguous and threaten to overlap. A top-angle shot on a bar terrace above a crowded Bombay street allows us to see goons mercilessly beat down on Satya as an unaware everyday concourse streams by on the street below. As Bhiku, Satya and their gang torture an opponent in a basement, we see Satya's beloved, Vidya, through a skylight which opens out onto the street above, as she walks along, unaware of what we are privileged to see. The systematic deployment of the steadicam, of seamless bodily movement and character focalization, essayed by Varma earlier as an abstract formal exercise notionally yoked to the horror genre in *Raat* (1991) is in *Satya* recurrently deployed to problematize the inside/outside world in the city. Here the camera's bodily pursuit of a character highlights how privatized spaces may be rapidly infiltrated, often with violent results. Such a hyper-location, braiding the spectator into spaces that are differentiated, draws upon the omniscient conventions of classical narration. Separated spaces can be figured as adjacent, as collapsing into each other, and as rapidly negotiable, via that key apparatus of contemporary communication, the mobile phone.

This is where we may consider that realism is still very much an issue in the contemporary action film, especially in the bid of this cinema to build a coherent spatio-temporal universe dominated by notions of verisimilitude. In a film such as *Satya*, we can see how this is very specifically a Hollywood strategy of exercising a limit, as Biswas might call it, in the sense of building continuity, where a highly consistent narrative dovetailing of sequences is developed. However, the popular format of the Bombay cinema ensures that other registers of play and performativity can be drawn upon to complicate such an agenda, if consciously harnessed to infiltrate the overall structure. Here we need to continue to focus on the multi-diegetic composition, indeed, spaces of multiple narrations, of Indian popular cinema to understand the way the spectator is inserted into the cinematic imagining of the city.

Ravikant points out that in some of the key song sequences, especially 'Goli maaro bheje mein', the comic and parodic outlook of the male student hostel and 'bachelor party' is evoked to provide a particular spectatorial access to the gang world. Realism is displaced by a scenario which allows us imaginative access to the point of production, the way perhaps script writer Saurabh Shukla, *Satya's* Kalumama, fabricated the group dynamics of the film's narrative world, through group interaction and performativity. This gesture to off-screen narrative worlds gives us a particular entry point for *Satya*, and in ways which periodically distance us from its narrative drives. This is not of the mode exactly of Brechtian realism, or the Iranian director Makhmalbaf's perspectivist strategies which stress the importance of perception for an engaged response to reality, for the rest of the narrative abides by a relentless generic drive. However, it nevertheless suggests a movement between distance and immersion in the way spectatorial stances are mobilized, and the layered spaces through which the cinema engages the city.

I will conclude these reflections on the contemporary cinema of urban anxiety by, for the moment, only gesturing to the question of politics. There are ways in which contemporary political transformations are echoed in these films, as in the phenomenon of the extended male group, founded on neighbourhood ties and united by a perceived sense of deprivation based on fallen status. Such fictional focuses certainly become more obvious in terms of character formation in the cinema of this period, and echo the worldview of the Shiv Sena in Bombay. This is especially so of the work of N. Chandra, as in *Ankush/The Goad* (1986), but is observable in a host of other films. Such discourses were to acquire a national frame of reference with the high caste investment in a resurgent political Hinduism in this period, crucially crystallizing around reactions against the V. P. Singh government's attempt to implement the Mandal Commission report on reservation for backward castes in 1990.

However, the overall political framing of experience through the cinema is probably more complicated. Can we come back to the political through the play of sounds and images that compose our relationship to the genre? Let me end by pointing to a motif in *Satya*, which may be construed as a cinephiliac intervention in contemporary forms of political spectacle. Satya, determined to avenge his comrade Bhiku, arrives at the Ganesh chaturti on the beach, an urban spatial practice associated with over a century of nationalist mobilization, and a crucial cultural form in contemporary Shiv Sena and Hindutva politics. Bhiku's assassin, Bhau Thakre, the gangster successfully turned politician, presents himself and his followers before the deity. As Satya moves in, the camera focuses on the red cloth which he has swathed around a knife. The red sheath bobs along in the crowd, reminding us of a similar scene in Coppola's *The Godfather, Part II* (1974) in which Vito Corleone moves through Roman Catholic festivities to target the local gang leader. Satya stabs Bhau Thakre to death, and as the scene dissipates in chaos, we are left with a haunting image. The camera is positioned at the lofty elevation of the deity, looking down on the solitary figure of the dead villain as the ebb and flow of the tide tugs at his body. His followers dispersed, his command over spectacle voided, his rag doll body is offered up for a view that at once assumes the cosmic perspective of the deity, and the cultural momentum of a cinephiliac camera that enframes it. We do not need to recognize the cinematic reference to be caught in the allure of the moment. It is as if the film invites us to be carried along by the rush of a sensorium specifically composed by our investment in the cinema. The energy of that very particular compact between screen and audience is then channelled as an intervention into the contemporary, disembowelling one form of political spectacle by our heady engagement with another.

Notes

This article follows on from discussions at the Sarai workshop on this theme, held at Sarai, CSDS from 29 November to 1 December 2001. References to arguments by Moinak Biswas, Ravikant, Ira Bhaskar and Jeebesh Bagchi are to their oral interventions at the workshop.

References

Ghosh, Shohini (2001), 'Streets of Terror: Urban Anxieties in the Bombay Cinema of the 1990s', Paper presented to the workshop 'The Exhilaration of Dread', Sarai, 29 November–1 December.

Gopalan, Lalitha (2002), *A Cinema of Interruptions*, MS, n/a.

Mazumdar, Ranjani (2001), *Urban Allegories: The City in Bombay Cinema 1970–2000*, New York University, New York.

Mehta, Monika (2001), *Selections: Cutting, Classifying and Certifying in Bombay Cinema*, Ph.D thesis, University of Minnesota, Minneapolis.

VIGILANTISM AND THE PLEASURES OF MASQUERADE:
THE FEMALE SPECTATOR OF VIJAYASANTHI FILMS

TEJASWINI NIRANJANA

In the first sequence after the credits in the Telugu film *Streetfighter* (dir. B. Gopal, 1995), we are shown a top-angle shot of a street blocked by dozens of *bindas*.[1] The hero is lying on the vessels, head cushioned on one arm, right ankle casually crossed, surrounded by the multi-coloured plastic *bindas*; we can see the jeans and shirt, the sports shoes. The water tankers drive up. The coloured vessels block the road with the women lined up behind them, sari pallus tied around their waists. The tankers come to a halt. We see a pair of shoe-shod feet plant itself on the ground. Camera moves slowly up from shoes to trousers to flowered shirt knotted over an orange T-shirt. The face of the hero is covered with a brass vessel which is about to be thrown at the tankers. In the next shot the vessel goes crashing through a wind-screen. The tanker drivers jump out of their cabins and demand to know what's going on. 'How dare you do that? Who are you?' they ask. Camera pans to Vijayasanthi's ponytailed face as she produces a few cheeky aliases. 'Do you know whose tankers these are?' one driver asks. She replies that the tankers belong to the builders who are illegally diverting the water meant for her locality to their construction site. 'Give us the water or else . . .' Vijayasanthi thumps the vessel menac-ingly. The drivers turn hosepipes on the women, and then the fight breaks out. Somersaulting and kicking, jumping on top of parked cars, Vijayasanthi disposes of the men, two at a time. A young man on a bicycle comes by, and places his camera to his eye to record the scene; he later appears as the besotted suitor of the star. The dramatic entry of the 'hero'—with the camera tracking from feet to face, followed by the eruption into action—is in no way different from the entry of a male star into the cinematic narrative. Other Vijayasanthi films too follow this convention with minor variations.

My interest in Vijayasanthi dates back to discussions over the last decade in women's groups about film and media, to our embarrassment about weepy women, anger against the 'degradation' of female bodies, and our discontent regarding female stereotypes. Our reaction was to seek positive images of women, to read for character and plot, which would 'empower' women viewers. Our attention was drawn to the popularity of the Vijayasanthi figure, and we wondered if our applause for a woman beating up the villains would be wholly unqualified. We noticed that both feminist and non-feminist women spectators for different reasons felt some discomfort at watching Vijayasanthi, and were confused about the compulsion to celebrate vigilantism. My paper is an attempt at exploring the reasons for that discomfort (did it have to do with the replication of male violence, or with the fluidity of sexual identity in the films?). Are characters and plot the most interesting aspects of these films? Or would a focus on the problems of spectatorship yield a more nuanced reading of our admittedly ambivalent responses?

Masquerade

In this paper my main concern will be to work out a theory of masquerade, which can account for both representational issues and those of spectatorship in the 1990s vigilante films of Vijayasanthi. While this paper will desist from making claims about empirical spectators of these films, having not (yet?) embarked on the more properly ethnographic enterprise that would yield information about such spectators, it will however suggest that an analysis of the spectator positions created by the films extend, even challenge, in interesting ways the theories of female spectatorship put forward by writers like Laura Mulvey and Mary Ann Doane. Mulvey has famously asserted that in classic Hollywood cinema the gaze of the camera is congruent with the male gaze, and that the spectator position of popular narrative film is a masculinized one (Mulvey, 1975). This assertion is premised on the to-be-looked-at-ness and glamorous/seductive framing of the female star. Doane takes this argument further in her 1982 essay 'Film and the Masquerade', pointing out the close relationship between theories of the image and theories of femininity, and calling for a dissection of 'the *episteme* which assigns to the woman a special place in cinematic representation while denying her access to that system' (Doane, 1991:19).

Drawing on the work of the psychoanalysts Joan Riviere and Jacques Lacan (and those writing in the wake of Lacan, such as Luce Irigaray and Michele Montrelay), Doane talks about how theories of femininity constantly foreground the almost 'claustrophobic closeness' of the woman to her body/image, a closeness that has severe implications for the ability to see herself. The necessity of creating a distance between self and image allows for the possibility of understanding femininity as masquerade. The masquerade is seen as a reaction against the persistent female desire to be a man, a desire at the heart of the cultural construction of femininity, according to Doane via the psychoanalysts (Doane, 1991:25). The excessive femininity represented by masquerade is seen as a form of 'resistance to patriarchal positioning' (Doane, 1991:25). Thus, by 'flaunting femininity', the woman is creating a distance between herself and her image, denying their seeming convergence. As Doane rightly points out, in her case this analysis is still at the level of the cinematic representation, and needs to be extended in the direction of the spectatorship question. Let us stay with the first level for a while and see what is happening there in the Vijayasanthi films.

The screen image of Vijayasanthi in the films studied here is hardly one of masquerade as feminine excess; on the contrary, it appears to disavow almost every aspect of the socio-cultural construction of Indian femininity. Given that Vijayasanthi is shown as a biological woman dressed in men's clothing (but not passing for a man), there is clear evidence here of the presence of masquerade, defined not as pretending to be something other than what one is, but behaving contrary to public expectations (here, those expectations attaching to one who appears to be female). Perhaps we can consider defining masquerade, then, as consisting in this case of the disavowal of femininity.

Even as I attempt to put forward a theory of masquerade, I will assemble the kinds of information that might help us contextually historicize the vigilante female figure in male clothing. This information is varied, ranging as it does from data about Vijayasanthi's career to more general issues relating to Telugu cinema. Vijayasanthi is a six-time Nandi Award winner (the Andhra Pradesh State award for best acting) , as well as the winner of the National Award for Best Actress for her acting in *Kartavyam* (dir. A. Mohan Gandhi, 1990). Speculations about her imminent political career have been rife. She campaigned for the right-wing Bharatiya Janata Party in the 1998 general elections and is likely to consolidate eventually a political future with that party. In the 1999 general elections Vijayasanthi was supposed to contest for the BJP if Sonia Gandhi, President of the Congress (I), announced her candidacy in Cuddapah in Andhra Pradesh. There was also speculation that she would oppose Priyanka Gandhi, Sonia's daughter, in Bellary (a border district in Karnataka State with a substantial number of Telugu speakers) in the by-election of 2000. Some of her audience consider this career with a right-wing party at variance with her screen persona in the enormously popular 'Naxalite' films, *Osey Ramulamma* (dir. Dasari Narayana Rao, 1997), and *Adavi Chukka* (Dasari Narayana Rao, 2000).[2]

Vijayasanthi's career in Telugu films is nearly two decades old. In the 1980s she played both heroine and 'sister' roles. There are many films where Vijayasanthi played the glamorous, hip-shaking, utterly feminine heroine. In the late 1980s, Vijayasanthi was associated with T. Krishna (*Neti Bharatam, Pratighatana,* both 1989) from Ongole in Andhra Pradesh, a director with strong connections with the Communist Party of India (Marxist). Krishna was known for his social criticism films, concerned with the exposure of corrupt politicians and the criminal underworld. Here we find the early version of the female vigilante figure: in these films she is still modestly sari-clad, the good woman roused to anger by attacks on her chastity or her *mangalsutra*. With the untimely death of Krishna, Vijayasanthi moved on to work with directors such as A. Mohan Gandhi, Kodi Ramakrishna and others in the 1990s. It is not until after *Kartavyam* (1990), then, that the distinctive woman-in-male-clothing becomes the central image of Vijayasanthi's films.

What makes Vijayasanthi a phenomenon in Telugu cinema? The popular journal *Sivaranjani* dated 29 July 1994, carries an article with the title—'"Mr" Vijayasanthi—Confined to "Magaraayudu" Roles?'[3] The article went on to quote sources in the Telugu film industry which said she 'lays claim to an image which could hitherto not be imagined'. The sources felt that '. . . The kind of image that a "top command hero" has in terms of business (referring to the film industry) Vijayasanthi too has. Her films have the same drawing power.' A producer called her Mr Vijayasanthi: 'Vijayasanthi herself is the hero of my film. Going by the kind of business interest there is in both Telugu and Tamil in this film, anyone would call her Mr.Vijayasanthi.'

In a more recent article in the Telugu film magazine *Number One*, dated 2 July 1999, the writer eulogizes Vijayasanthi's career: 'She has grown from the kathanayika (heroine) image to the kathanayaka (hero). Our screenplay writers have had to write new stories for her.' Vijayasanthi is seen to have 'overcome the competition from hero-oriented films', and the reasons for her success are obviously that '. . . there are spectators to watch her films. There are producers to make her films. There are "buyers" to purchase the films. There are exhibitors to show her films.' The article mentions how the star is pursued by producers who feel that she is the main cause for a film doing well at the box-office: '. . . At a time when a film without a hero is thought of as a low-budget film, just on the basis of Vijayasanthi's image producers who are willing to get suitable stories written for her and invest crores of rupees are waiting for her call sheets.'

The above quotes are meant to illustrate the star-value of Vijayasanthi for the Telugu film industry. The rest of the paper, focusing on four key Vijayasanthi films, will speculate on the reasons for her success, and for the popularity of the vigilante figure, by situating the films in a specific historical context. The films chosen are *Kartavyam* (dir. A. Mohan Gandhi, 1990), where Vijayasanthi plays a police officer, *Aasayam* (dir. A. Mohan Gandhi, 1993), in which she is student turned cabinet minister, *Police Lock-Up* (dir. Kodi Ramakrishna, 1993), where she is a Central Bureau of Investigation officer/housewife (double role), and *Streetfighter* (dir. B. Gopal, 1995), where she takes on the role of a neighbourhood tough.

Other important films starring Vijayasanthi include *Neti Bharatam* (dir. T. Krishna, 1989), where she becomes a Physical Education teacher in a school, *Bharatanari* (dir. Muthyala Subbiah, 1989), where she runs a school in a slum, *Pratighatana* (dir. T. Krishna, 1989), where she is a college teacher,[4] *Osey Ramulamma* (dir. Dasari Narayana Rao, 1997), where she is a rural dalit, and *Bharataratna* (dir. Kodi Ramakrishna, 1999), where she is an army officer/petty thief (double role). In 2000, she acted in *Adavi Chukka* (dir. Dasari Narayana Rao) as a demure middle-class urban housewife with a tribal/Naxalite past.[5] Also in 2000 was released *Vaijayanthi* (dir. K. S. Nageswara Rao), where the star plays an 'orphan' separated from her family by wicked feudal lords, becoming first a soldier and later an undercover officer for the Home Ministry.

Genealogy of the Vigilante

I give below a brief listing of the diverse representational strands that feed into the construction of the female vigilante in the Vijayasanthi films:

—the social reform woman, the transformative force: e. g., the good daughter-in-law, as in *Ardhangi* (dir. P. Pullaiah, 1955), and other films from the 1940s and 50s; the nationalist (as in *Malapilla*, dir. Gudavalli Ramabrahmam, 1938); Mahila Mandali films; the heroine-as-teacher films.

—the cowgirl: *Rowdy Rani* (dir. K. S. R. Doss,1970); *Korada Rani* (dir. K. S. Rami Reddy, 1972); *Rowdy Rangamma* (dir. Vijayanirmala, 1978).[6]

—the bandit/costume drama: *Oka Nari Vandha Thupakulu* (dir. K. V. S. Kutumba Rao, 1973).

—masquerade gender reversal: *Jambalakidipamba* (dir. E. V. V. Satyanarayana, 1992).

—Ramoji Rao's Ashwini Nachappa films, with the main protagonist being an athletic champion in real life (1980s and 90s).

—the male star/hero/vigilante of Hindi, Telugu and Tamil films—all circulating in the cinema-viewing space of the Telugu audience, in the case of Tamil—in dubbed versions or re-makes (Amitabh Bachchan, Chiranjeevi, Rajnikant).

—the Hollywood male star as vigilante, e.g., Clint Eastwood, Sylvester Stallone.

—the Hong Kong martial arts film: first Bruce Lee and then Jackie Chan are hugely popular with male audiences in Andhra Pradesh.

Of course, these antecedents cannot be traced in linear fashion, and we have to keep in mind the many criss-crossings and borrowings, and consequent transformations, which produce the Vijayasanthi star-persona.

Situating the Female Vigilante

The historical context is that of the late 1980s to the 1990s, a period in India when the vocabularies of dominance include as their central feature a kind of neo-nationalism. This is a nationalism, which, as I have shown elsewhere, depends in its cinematic representations on the figure of the male lover as exemplary citizen (as in the films of Mani Ratnam through the 1990s). I have argued that the new nationalism of the 90s was premised on a leaving behind of the national-modern, on a refiguring of modernity to include the newly valorized 'ethnic' (often displayed by the female body), and on the private citizen taking over the functions of the inefficient welfare state (Niranjana, 2000). Central to this nationalism was also the formation of the conjugal bond and the creation of the private sphere of the nuclear family. But here we have a different kind of narrative. In the Vijayasanthi films, the focus is not on romance or the citizen-lover, but on the citizen-in-arms, engaged in doing what the state has failed to do, that is, usher in the modern.

Here the citizen is female, and being female she cannot be both lover and citizen, since that particular subjectivity is gendered male (the lover-as-citizen, the citizen-as-lover). Vijayasanthi is always portrayed as an austere figure—she does not show much emotion vis-a-vis men interested in her. I refer specifically to the films discussed here— *Kartavyam, Streetfighter, Police Lock Up, Aasayam*—unlike the earlier *Neti Bharatam* and *Bharatanaari* where the loss of the lover is what spurs the heroine to attack the criminals. An aspect of this austerity is to be seen in her clothing: we always see Vijayasanthi in white sari, police uniform, army uniform, pants and shirt, or tracksuit.[7] The camera does not linger on her bosom or behind like in other commercial films. While watching her daredevil stunts and martial arts sequences, one sometimes even suspends knowledge of the sexed identity of the persona, concentrating instead on appreciating her sheer strength and grace.

Why is it that this phenomenon can be observed only in Telugu cinema? Kannada, Tamil and Hindi have a few films like this, but their success is not on the scale of that achieved by the Vijayasanthi films in Telugu. One can only speculate that Naxalism from the 1970s on, and the availability of a broadly leftist popular critique of feudalism, combined with a powerful and visible women's movement in Andhra Pradesh and its contribution to the popular understanding of female empowerment are some of the factors relevant to an understanding of how the Vijayasanthi persona is constructed. Clearly the films present anti-feudal narratives, and locate themselves specifically within urban landscapes. In their depiction of the vigilante's attempt to cleanse (and/or form) civil society, they embark on what might be called a cinematic re-figuring of the feudal.

In the ruralist melodrama of early Telugu cinema (eg. *Rytu Bidda*, dir. Gudavalli Ramabrahmam, 1945), or in the new wave (eg. *Maa Bhoomi*, dir. Goutam Ghosh, 1980), or in the pro-ML films of R. Narayanamurthy (1980s to the present, e. g. *Ardharaatri Swaatantram* (1986), *Lal Salaam* (1992), *Dandora* (1993), *Errasainyam* (1994)), or in Maadaala Ranga Rao's films *Viplava Sankham* (1982), *Yerra Mallelu* (1981) the feudal—presented as the canker at the heart of the nation—is (a) situated in the rural, (b) viewed through its individualized representatives (the zamindar, the good peasant, the revolutionary), (c) sought to be addressed in public modes (political organization, insurrection, execution, confrontation in the fields). In the more familiar idiom of the family sentiment films (eg. *Rowdygari Pellam*, dir. K. S. Prakash, 1991), the attempt of the heroine is to reform the alcoholic or wayward husband, the bad-tempered father-in-law, the corrupt brother, etc. The feudal is re-sited here within the family (although often in an urban location), and therefore needs to be overcome or transformed only in that space. In the re-figured feudalism of the Vijayasanthi films, the family is no longer central to the narrative, although the Vijayasanthi figure is often part of an extended, troubled or dysfunctional family (in *Aasayam*, Vijayasanthi and mother are rejected by her corrupt brother and sister-in-law; in *Kartavyam*, Vijayasanthi's father has remarried and his second family dislikes his closeness to his first daughter). Vijayasanthi's marginality in the family narrative seems to enable her to perform other functions elsewhere. Earlier, the reforming woman worked within the family; now her aim is to transform society itself.

What is interesting about the Vijayasanthi films is the re-representation of the problem—the feudal is now at the centre of urban life (corruption of the bureaucracy, the judiciary, the police force, the politicians, and the whole of civil society; the arch-villain Muddukrishnayya in *Kartavyam* says he has both truth and justice with him, since the Circle Inspector and an important criminal lawyer are in his pay). The feudal is also that which is illegal (not just a family problem), against the law (when the law is good, it is on the side of modernity; when it is not, it sides with the feudal). We are shown repeatedly the courtroom scenes where justice is denied due to the manipulation of the judge by the lawyers. The citizen-vigilante addresses the problem in public, out in the street, but only sometimes in public modes (demonstration, dharna, or speech). The more common resolution is the single-handed pursuit of the criminals.

I would like to connect the discussion of masquerade from the earlier part of this paper with the question of feudalism by referring to the centrality of the female vigilante in the various Vijayasanthi films. Although involving different scriptwriters and directors, the films appear to have a similar frame of reference, hinging as they do on the star-persona of Vijayasanthi and the cinematic memories of her films which audiences bring to each new viewing. The historical moment which makes this representation of violent individual agency possible relates, as I suggested in 'Nationalism Refigured', to the dismantling of the functions of the developmentalist post-colonial nation-state in the age of liberalization. The nation-state which set out to abolish feudalism could only produce its contemporary versions. The horrors of the feudal, imaged repeatedly (in the Naxalite films in particular) as what it does to women, are sought to be countered by one who is unwilling to be its victim. The masquerading vigilante is clothed in such a way as to confound our sense of her gender identity, since it is only by slipping away from womanliness and into its antithesis that the feudal can be challenged and overcome.

Given the centrality to the narrative of the female vigilante, it is important that this challenge to the feudal not be confined to spaces defined as conventionally private. Much of the action, therefore, takes place in the public gaze. There are very few encounters in enclosed spaces, except the lockup, the interrogation chamber, or courtroom. And even these are not private spaces. Witness for example the ubiquitous lockup and courtroom scenes where the vigilante is sought to be thwarted in her pursuit of justice by those who claim to uphold the law. Or the courtroom, as in *Police Lock Up*, where we see the manipulation of the judiciary by lawyers, and where the fighter for justice is framed as a criminal. Or the interrogation chamber in *Aasayam*— where false accusations and torture turns a justice seeker into a criminal. Interestingly, in most instances the crooked lawyers and police accuse the character played by Vijayasanthi of being a Naxalite (asking questions like 'Which forest are you from? Which is your "squad"?').

The public spaces of this society in transformation form the representational staple of the Vijayasanthi films. We have the street (*Streetfighter, Kartavyam, Aasayam*) for fights and processions, the latter associated with conventional modes of democratic protest, and the former with individualist vigilantism, the lower middle class urban neighbourhood (*Streetfighter*), carparks/basements of highrise buildings (*Police Lock Up*), parks (where Vijayasanthi goes jogging, conventionally a male activity in most Indian cities, as in *Aasayam* or *Police Lock Up*), the Tank Bund in Hyderabad (where Vijayasanthi stages a dharna with hundreds of fellow students in *Aasayam*), the mansions and living rooms of the politicians and criminals, the rooftops of chase sequences, the rooftop restaurant where Vijayasanthi confronts the villains (*Police Lock Up*), the public platform, the courtroom, the lockup, the police station, and the hospital. The most memorable aspect of the representation of these public areas is the visibility they afford to the female vigilante, practically showcasing her effortless negotiation of urban space.

We should remark here on the secularism of these urban spaces— Vijayasanthi's 'modern' clothing, her occasional use of English, her occupation, references to family background (her father is a joint-collector, a bureaucrat, in *Aasayam*, and a public prosecutor in *Kartavyam*).

Of course this is a secularism of class: her caste and community are not known, or rather remain unmarked, although the latter can be guessed more or less accurately from the social mobility available to her. Unlike in the 'family sentiment' films, we never see the female star praying, standing in temples or puja rooms, expressing devotion to the gods. On the contrary, in *Aasayam* she says at the end, after losing her husband, that she will 'live for this three-foot flag' (we see her face framed against the national flag).

The good citizen is herself pure, incorruptible, because female (the good policemen in *Kartavyam*, for example, are often feminized—the young cop Suribabu who is seen as slightly mad, and the older man who has lost his legs and is confined to a wheelchair). To remain incorruptible, and in order to remain mobile in the pursuit of justice, she cannot have any ties. In *Kartavyam* and *Aasayam*, she emerges from within the family and moves away and above; in the first, she handcuffs her would-be lover for murdering the arch-criminal who tried to kill her; in the second, her husband dies in a bomb-blast at a political rally and she swears eternal loyalty to the national flag, which is what she wants to live by; in both films, her father is killed by the villains.

Does the Vijayasanthi persona have a private life? Except in *Streetfighter*, she is alone at the end, usually moving on to higher things. Her lover/husband is dead or imprisoned. Her other family members, if any, are either dead or invisible. Also, there are either no song and dance routines at all, or they do not involve the star, except for *Streetfighter*, with Vijayasanthi doing a Holi dance in her customary male clothing. In *Police Lock Up*, she is a completely lone figure. She comes out of nowhere, authorized by the state to solve the crime, and goes back after the task is done. Sometimes she shows grief at the loss of a father (*Kartavyam, Aasayam*), a friend (*Police Lock Up*), a sister (*Streetfighter*); but this emotion is almost immediately transformed into rage, leading to the pursuit of the villains and their eventual decimation.

How does one understand this apparent isolation and lack of emotion on the part of the vigilante? If the character's subjectivity is an issue for feminist criticism, and if the conventions of psychological realism allow for the cinematic characterization of female subjectivity by representing the inner life of the protagonist, this is clearly not a feature of the Vijayasanthi films. Here it is precisely the absence or negation of a private life that produces the character's subjectivity/agency. If the private sphere is equated in the common-sense of our times with questions of sexuality and sexual identity, and this is usually counterposed to the public sphere, what happens to the sexual identity of a protagonist who does not inhabit the private realm at all, except fleetingly?

The Spectator and Masquerade

Here the de-sexing of Vijayasanthi through her clothing and move-ments actually draws our attention to the conventionality of modes of female sexualization. Just as excessive femininity draws attention to how femininity is constructed, so does the negation of femininity 'nat-uralized' in the Vijayasanthi films. Nowhere is this double process more obvious than in *Police Lock Up*, where the norm itself is shown up as masquerade. The coy and flirtatious Santhi—behaving like most Telugu cinema heroines—comes across as engaged in masquerade as much as the tough CID officer Vijaya.

Moving now to the question of female spectatorship, we can spec-ulate on another kind of disavowal that manifests itself in discussions with actual viewers. (This reference is not meant to suggest any ethno-graphic fullness but merely to provide an additional bit of data for the larger argument about spectatorship.)[8] Curiously, the star's presence on the screen—overwhelmingly not feminine by conventional stan-dards—invokes a kind of refusal even to acknowledge the actual cloth-ing of the actress. Spectators seem to be engaged in a disavowal, there-fore, of the star's femininity. Randomly selected interviewees, all of whom were women, said that Vijayasanthi wore a sari only once in *Kartavyam*, the film which in a sense inaugurates the genre for which she is now famous. A quick count indicates that in fact she appears in saris, although mostly in semi-private situations, upto *seven* times! This impression is counterpointed by the star's own disavowal of mas-culinity, as in her *Sivaranjani* interview (*Sivaranjani*, 1994), where she continually proffers an alibi for why she dresses like a man: Replying to a question about the dress and image of the star—'In all three films (*Magaraayudu, Streetfighter, Lady Boss*) you wear pants and shirt . . .' Vijayasanthi answers: 'In *Magaraayudu*, I don't wear pants and shirt in the first half; until the interval I wear a sari and appear as an innocent lady doctor. After the interval, after the dead hero's spirit enters into the heroine's body, she starts behaving and dressing like the hero. But you don't see the star Vijayasanthi on screen; you see the hero in Vijayasanthi's body. No matter who plays that role, she has to wear pants and shirt. Coming to *Streetfighter*, when there are several girl children in a middle-class family, we notice that the last girl is dressed like a boy and pampered. I play one such girl, who then—just as a boy would—tries to avenge the wrong done to her family.'[9]

'Pleasure' of the Female Spectator?

The argument made by Doane seeks to complicate Mulvey's assertion of the masculinization of the spectator-position in the cinematic apparatus by showing how masquerade (defined by Doane as the production of feminine excess) can perhaps undermine that position, thereby providing for the female spectator an alternative to passive identification. The idea of the masculine spectator-position is based on the over-visible image of the woman (to be looked at, to be acted upon); what happens, then, when the woman's image at the heart of the film is no longer that of the feminine female but the almost anti-feminine Vijayasanthi? What then is the spectator-position in relation to the masquerade, since this is a different kind of masquerade? Would it be appropriate to talk about the de-masculinization of the spectator-position of classic narrative cinema? (A far more complicated question of course, which I am not yet competent to deal with, is that of the non-approximation of the Indian cinemas to the classic model.)

What happens, then, in the case of Vijayasanthi? Take the example of *Kartavyam*. If there is a matching of the look with male subjectivity in the feminist film theory referred to so far, we have to deal with a different kind of problem here. We do see the policewoman played by Vijayasanthi always *looking*—at her father, at the slack cops, at the series of villains. There are both spectator and point-of-view shots showing this. The film, of course, is alluding to the spectator-cinema relationship, as in other scenes of looking in the cinema in general. But here we find not a simple reversal as a reaction to the voyeurism and fetishism of the male gaze; here there is no simple claiming of the pleasure of the female gaze vis-à-vis male figures. The classic scenario is confounded because of who looks (not a 'woman' instead of a man, but a woman in man's clothing). If feminist film theory suggests that agency in looking confers a male subjectivity on the looker, this argument would not be able to make sense of the film in question. The drama of subjectivity is far more complicated in this instance. Vijayasanthi's is not a gaze of power. But it is precisely her helpless gaze which reveals the scenes as reeking of corruption (the rapist cutting his birthday cake—the politician hailing the rapist as a leader with a bright future—the police 'controlling' the crowds).

Within what subject position, then, are women viewers of these films located? If—since the hero is female—what is no longer available to them is the masochistic identification with the male hero, a process that requires a trans-sex movement or transvestism (Mulvey on *Duel in the Sun*), how does one describe the psychic processes at work here (Mulvey, 1989)? We look at Vijayasanthi knowing she is woman. But the prohibited female body is not represented in such a way as to enforce what Doane calls the rules of prohibition (a combination of revelation and disavowal) (Mulvey, 1989:19-20). So if 'spectatorial desire' is conventionally only voyeurism or fetishism, neither would work for male *or* female spectators of the Vijayasanthi films.[10]

For men, given the representation of Vijayasanthi's body-in-action in crucial fight sequences, for instance, the voyeuristic gaze cannot quite come into being (compensatory processes may include the occasional representations of her sari-clad, feminized body; and therefore the double knowledge of her as woman-but-not-woman, like-but-unlike other women). For women, by definition voyeurism and fetishism do not obtain; however, the same double knowledge does obtain. But if women have to bring to bear on the Vijayasanthi image the same desiring gaze they would bestow on the male star (one of envy?), they would need to engage in masquerade too. The process of creating the 'distance between oneself and one's image' (Doane, 1991:26)—if this is indeed what the female spectator of Vijayasanthi films is doing—is enabled by the film not just by clothing Vijayasanthi like a man, but displaying to us her strength and mobility.

'Women can't be like this. But she is a woman'. It is precisely this disavowal on the part of the spectator which involves masquerade. The disjuncture produced between the frame and the spectatorial gaze here manifests itself as masquerade, leading, I suggest, to a de-masculinization of the spectator-position. To recapitulate the argument: Mary Ann Doane's formulation about masquerade as feminine excess countered the supposed stability of the to-be-looked-at female image from classic feminist film theory; extending this idea to include the reframing of the masquerade question as one involving not the display of femininity but rather its opposite would show up the screen-image of Vijayasanthi as unstable on both counts. Contributing to this process would be the representations of the male lover, as in *Streetfighter* or *Aasayam*; and the representations of other women which counterpoint the representation of Vijayasanthi, as in *Kartavyam* or *Police Lock Up*. Both, I would argue, draw attention to the masquerade at the level of representation.[11] Both destabilize the normed spectator-position, the gaze as male.

As Doane points out in the context of the masquerade involving the excessively feminine, but which applies also to the kind of masquerade displayed in the Vijayasanthi films, 'Masquerade . . . attributes to the woman distance, alienation, and divisiveness of self (which is constitutive of subjectivity in psychoanalysis) rather than the closeness and excessive presence which are the logical outcome of the psychoanalytical drama of sexualised linguistic difference' (Doane, 1991). One of the key functions of masquerade, then, is to point to the instability of the feminine, to show up the norm itself as a disguise. Here lies perhaps one of the causes for women's discomfort in watching the films of Vijayasanthi: in that the female image is not offered up for the narcissistic gaze but instead stages the visual confusions of gender identity. As Vijayasanthi in *Streetfighter* dances her vigorous Holi dance in jeans and sports shoes and bandanna tied round her leg, as the men and women of the locality swirl around her in their 'ethnic' clothes, as her bespectacled suitor stares on bemusedly, they solicit the off-screen spectator's participation in the detachment of masculinity and femininity from bodies biologically male and female.

Notes

1 *Binda* is Telugu for the vessel, made of metal or plastic, that holds water.

2 The 'Naxalite' films are hugely popular commercial films claiming inspiration from the revolutionary Naxalite armed struggle. These films, made by mainstream Telugu filmmakers and using the idiom of the commercial cinema, are often criticized by the ideologues of the revolutionary parties for what they contend are distorted representations of the movement.

3 The reference is to the film *Magaraayudu* (Mr. Son) (dir. E. V. V. Satyanarayana, 1995) starring Vijayasanthi.

4 The genealogy of this teacher figure can be traced back through the narratives of the social reform movement and through nationalist discourse in India.

5 *Deccan Chronicle*, the local English-language newspaper, carried full-page advertisements in colour purporting to be letters written by Vijayasanthi to her female fans: 'My sweetest wishes to the overall set of audience, in particular to the respectable women who adore me and hold me in high esteem' (*Deccan Chronicle*, 2000).

6 There is a reference to 'Rowdy Rani', played by her real-life aunt Vijayanirmala, by Vijayasanthi in the opening scenes of *Streetfighter*, when the truck-drivers ask her who she is, and she replies that they can call her what they will, like Rowdy Rani for example.

7 Vijayasanthi is almost always, with very few exceptions, a state functionary (police officer, army officer, criminal investigator, cabinet minister). The vigilantism does not result from a rejection of her state-enabled role but is enhanced by it. Among the films I analyse, it is only in police lock-up that she is actually (and as it turns out, mistakenly) arrested by the police in spite of being an investigating officer. She escapes from jail and carries out her task of punishing the evil doers.

8 The remarks about the 'actual' spectators of Vijayasanthi films are based on a sample set of interviews done by L. Chaitanya in different regions of Andhra Pradesh during the research for the workshop on Telugu cinema and politics conducted by the Centre for the Study of Culture and Society, Bangalore, and Anveshi Research Centre for Women's Studies, Hyderabad, in August 1999.

9 Why she needs an alibi: Vijayasanthi is not a cosmopolitan figure, and therefore the narrative is required to provide reasons as to why the

'good Indian woman' should wear western clothes. Note that the star does not wear Indian—i.e., non-western—men's clothes. This detail serves to mark her modernity. Another common connection is made between militancy and male clothing. In her Naxalite films, Vijayasanthi makes the transition from rural dalit or tribal woman's blouse-less sari to khaki pants and shirt, and red bandanna.

10 Voyeurism: desire to look at an object outside the subject (Freud); object of the look is outside of and distanced from the subject, no punishment for looking, no reciprocity (Metz); the spectator's look stands in for the look of the camera (Mulvey). Fetishism: unpleasurable aspects of looking have to do with the castration anxiety; this anxiety is dealt with by turning woman into fetish—through lingering close-ups, glamorous costumes, settings, lighting around female star. This interrupts the flow of the narrative, and constitutes woman as spectacle. The excessive idealization of the female star-image is fetishization (Mulvey, 1989).

11 Suribabu in *Aasayam* is told sarcastically by his grandmother that he is the 'server', not lover, of his object of affection. He is always shown not in the centre of the frame when Vijayasanthi is present, but in the margins—as helper, not initiator of the action. The besotted photographer in *Streetfighter* is a similar figure. In *Kartavyam*, we have the figure of the teenaged Karuna who has been raped, and who comes to Vijayasanthi the policewoman seeking help in bringing the criminals to justice. In *Streetfighter*, we have the lower middle-class neighbourhood women in homely saris who demand water, posed against the 'hero' in her jeans and bandanna. In *Police Lock Up*, there are the sequences of CID officer Vijaya with Santhi the housewife, played by Vijayasanthi herself.

References

Doane, Mary Ann (1991), 'Film and the Masquerade', in *Femmes Fatales: Feminism, Film Theory, Psychoanalysis*, Routledge, London.

Mulvey, Laura (1975), 'Visual Pleasure and the Narrative Cinema', *Screen*, 16:3, Autumn.

— (1989), 'Afterthoughts on "Visual Pleasure and Narrative Cinema" Inspired by *Duel in the Sun*', in L. Mulvey (ed.), *Visual and Other Pleasures*, Indiana University Press, Bloomington.

Niranjana, Tejaswini (2000), 'Nationalism Refigured: Contemporary South Indian Cinema and the Subject of Feminism', in P. Chatterjee and P. Jeganathan (ed.), *Community, Gender and Violence*, Columbia University Press, New York.

ABBAS, Khwaja Ahmad (1977), *I Am Not an Island : An Experiment in Autobiography*, Vikas Publishing House, New Delhi.

ADAMU, Alhaji (1996), interviewed by Brian Larkin in April.

ALLEN, Robert C. (1983), 'Motion Picture Exhibition in Manhattan, 1906–1912: Beyond the Nickelodeon' in J. L. Fell (ed.), *Film before Griffith*, University of California Press, Berkeley.

ALLYN, David Edley (1976), *The Sabon Gari System in Northern Nigeria*, Ph.D dissertation, UCLA.

ANDERSON, Benedict (1983), *Imagined Communities: Reflections on the Origin and Spread of Nationalism*, Verso, London.

APPADURAI, Arjun (1990) 'Disjuncture and Difference in the Global Cultural Economy', *Public Culture*, 2:2, 1–24.

— (1996), 'The Production of Locality' in A. Appadurai, *Modernity at Large: Cultural Dimensions of Globalization*, University of Minnesota Press, Minneapolis, Minn.

— (1997), *Modernity at Large: Cultural Dimensions of Globalization*, Oxford University Press, New Delhi.

— (1998), 'The Politics of Repetition: Notes on the Reception of Indian Hit Films', Paper presented at the Workshop on Media and Mediation in the Politics of Culture, Centre for

Studies in Social Sciences, International Globalization Network, Calcutta, March, pp. 4–7.

ARMBRUST, Walter (1998), 'When the Lights Go Down in Cairo: Cinema as Secular Ritual', *Visual Anthropology*, 10, 413–42.

ARORA, Poonam (1995), 'Imperilling the Prestige of the White Woman: Colonial Anxiety and Film Censorship in British India', *Visual Anthropology Review*, 1:2, 36–49.

BABB, Lawrence and Susan Wadley (eds.) (1995), *Media and the Transformation of Religion in South Asia*, University of Pennsylvania Press, Pennsylvania.

BAKHTIN, Mikhail (1968), *Rabelais and His World*, MIT Press, Cambridge, Mass. and London.

BALÁZS, Béla (1948), *Filmkultura. A Film Müvészfilozofiája*, Szikra Kiadó, Budapest.

— (1972), *Theory of the Film: Character and Growth of a New Art*, Arno Press and The New York Times, New York (first published 1952).

— (1976), *Der Film. Werden und Wesen einer neuen Kunst*, 5, Globus Verlag, Vienna.

— (1984), 'Der Geist des Films [1930]', in H. H. Diederichs and W. Gersch (ed.), *Béla Balázs: Schriften zum Film*, Carl Hanser Verlag, Munich.

BALZAC, Honoré de (1971), *Lost Illusions* [1837–43], Penguin, Harmondsworth.

BANDYOPADHYAY, Samik (1991), 'Calcutta Cinema: The Early Years', in S. Chaudhuri (ed.), *Calcutta, the Living City*, Oxford University Press, Calcutta and New York.

BANKER, Ashok (2001), *Bollywood*, Penguin Books, Harmondsworth.

BARBER, Karin (1997), 'Preliminary Notes on the Audience in Africa', *Africa*, 67:3, 349–362.

BARKINDO, Bawuro M. (1993), 'Growing Islamism in Kano City since 1970: Causes, Forms and Implications', in L. Brenner (ed.), *Muslim Identity and Social Change in Sub-Saharan Africa*, Indiana University Press, Bloomington.

BARTHES, Roland (1972), *Mythologies*, Paladin Books, London.

BASU, Shrabani (2002), 'Dimple's Designer Home on View at Selfridge's', *The Telegraph*, Calcutta, 8 February.

BBCI (2002), www.bbc.co.uk/asianlife/film/indiansummerindex/shtml

BEDELL, Geraldine (2002), 'World Wide Webber', *Life: The Observer Magazine*, Indian Summer Special issue, 7 April, pp. 10–12.

BEIDELMAN, T. O. (1993), *Moral Imagination in Kaguru Modes of Thought*, Smithsonian Institution Press, Washington.

BELL, Sir Hesketh (1910/1911), 'Recent Progress in Northern Nigeria', *Journal of African Society*, 10.

BENJAMIN, Walter (1936), *Das Kunstwerk im Zeitalter seiner technischen Reproduzierbarkeit*, Suhrkamp Verlag Frankfurt am Main, Frankfurt.

— (1977), *Illuminationen: Ausgewählte Schriften*, Suhrkamp Verlag Frankfurt am Main, Frankfurt.

— (1978), *Illuminations*, Schocken Books, New York.

BERMAN, Marshall (1983), *All That Is Solid Melts Into Air: The Experience of Modernity*, Verso Editions, London (first published 1982).

BHABHA, Homi (1994), *The Location of Culture*, Routledge, London and New York.

BHARUCHA, Rustom (1994), *A Question of Faith*, Oxford University Press, New Delhi.

BHATTACHARYA, Malini (ed.) (1988), *Selected Stories*: *Manik Bandyopadhyay*, Thema, Calcutta (second revised edition 2003).

BHATTACHARYA, Pradyumna (1976), 'Samajer Matra Ebong Tarashankarer Upanyas: 'Chaitali Ghurni', *Ekshan*, Calcutta.

— (1998), 'Rajnaitik Upanyas: Swarupyer Sandhane?', in P. Bhattacharya, *Tika Tippani*, Papyrus, Calcutta.

BISWAS, Hemango (1998), 'Gananatya Andolon o Loksangeet', in *Ganer Bahirana*, Papyrus, Calcutta.

BOWSER, Eileen (1990), 'The Transformation of Cinema, 1907–1915' in *History of the American Cinema*, vol. 2, Scribner, New York.

BRAVMANN, René A. (1974), *Islam and Tribal Art in West Africa*, African Studies Series no. 11, Cambridge University Press, London.

BUCHIGNANI, Norman (1980), 'The Social and Self-identities of Fijian Indians in Vancouver', *Urban Anthropology*, 9:1.

BUCK-MORSS, Susan and Walter Benjamin (1989), *The Dialectics of Seeing*: *Walter Benjamin and the Arcades Project*, Studies in Contemporary German Social Thought, MIT Press, Cambridge, Mass.

BURCH, Noël and Ben Brewster (1990), *Life to Those Shadows*, University of California Press, Berkeley.

Businessworld (2000), 'Hot New Dot.coms', January 24.

CHAKRABARTY, Dipesh (2002), *Habitations of Modernity*, Chicago University Press, Chicago.

CHAKRABARTY, Satyesh C. (1991), 'The Growth of Calcutta in the 20th Century', in S. Chaudhuri (ed.), *Calcutta, the Living City*, Oxford University Press, Calcutta and New York.

CHAKRAVARTY, Sumita S. (1993), *National Identity in Indian Popular Cinema 1947–1987*, Texas Film Studies Series, University of Texas Press, Austin, Texas.

CHANAN, Michael (1996), *The Dream that Kicks: The Prehistory and Early Years of Cinema in Britain*, Routledge, London.

CHATTERJEE, Partha (1984), 'Gandhi and the Critique of Civil Society', in Ranajit Guha (ed.), *Subaltern Studies III*, Oxford University Press, London.

— (1993), *The Nation and its Fragments: Colonial and Postcolonial Histories*, Princeton Studies in Culture/Power/History, Princeton University Press, Princeton, NJ.

— (1995), 'Religious Minorities and the Secular State— Reflections on an Indian Impasse', *Public Culture*, 8:1, 11–39.

— (1997), *The Present History of West Bengal: Essays in Political Criticism*, Oxford University Press, New Delhi.

— (1997a), 'Beyond the Nation? Or Within?', *Economic and Political Weekly*, 32,1–2.

— (1997b), 'Our Modernity', in P. Chatterjee, *The Present History of West Bengal: Essays in Political Criticism*, Oxford University Press, New Delhi.

— and G. Pandey (eds.) (1992), *Subaltern Studies VII : Writings on South Asian History and Society*, Oxford University Press, New Delhi.

CHATTERJI, Joya (1994), *Bengal Divided : Hindu Communalism and Partition 1932–1947*, Cambridge University Press, Cambridge.

CHOPRA, Anupama (1997), 'Bye-bye Bharat', *India Today*, 1 December.

CORMACK, Michael J. (1994), *Ideology and Cinematography in Hollywood 1930–39*, St. Martin's Press, New York.

CUNNINGHAM, Stuart and John Sinclair (eds.) (2001), *Floating Lives: the Media and Asian Diasporas*, Rowman and Littlefield, USA.

DAS, Arvind N. (1998), 'Reels of Indian Reality', *Biblio: A Review of Books*, September–October.

DAS, Dhananjay (ed.) (1992), *Bangla Sanskritite Marxbadi Chetanar Dhara*, Anustup, Calcutta.

DAS GUPTA, Chidananda (1968), 'The Cultural Basis of Indian Cinema', in C. Das Gupta, *Talking About Films*, Orient Longman, New Delhi.

DAVIES, John (2000), 'On the Sources of Interethnic Conflict in Fiji', *Peace Initiatives*, 6:1–3.

DEAN, Michelle (1996), 'Foucault, Government and the Enfolding of Authority', in A. Barry, et al. (ed.), *Foucault and Political Reason: Liberalism, Neo-liberalism, and Rationalities of Government*, University of Chicago Press, Chicago.

Deccan Chronicle (2000), July 4.

DERNÉ, Steve (1995), 'Market Forces at Work: Religious Themes in Commercial Hindi Films' in L. Babb and S. Wadley (eds.) *Media and the Transformation of Religion in South Asia*, University of Pennsylvania Press, Pennsylvania.

DIAWARA, Manthia (1992), *African Cinema: Politics and Culture*, Indiana University Press, Bloomington.

DIEDERICHS, Helmut H. (1997), 'Béla Balázs und sein Beitrag zur formästhetischen Filmtheorie' (lecture at Freie Universität Berlin, Institut für Theaterwissenschaften, 20 November 1997), quoted from http://www.sozpaed.fh-dortmund.de/diederichs/texte/balazsvo.html

DIMITROV, Georgi (1945), *The United Front against Fascism: Speeches at the Seventh Congress of the Communist International, August 1935*, Current Book Distributors, Sydney.

DOANE, Mary Ann (1991), 'Film and the Masquerade', in M. A. Doane, *Femmes Fatales: Feminism, Film Theory, Psychoanalysis*, Routledge, London.

DONALD, James (1995), 'The City, the Cinema: Modern Spaces' in Chris Jenks (ed.) *Visual Culture*, Routledge, London.

DYER, Richard (1986), *Stars*, British Film Institute, London.

EDEL, Leon (1992), 'Novel and Camera', in J. Harrison (ed.), *Salman Rushdie*, Twayne Publishers, New York.

FLAVELL, John (1970), *The Developmental Psychology of Jean Piaget*, Van Nostrand Reinhold, New York.

FOUCAULT, Michel (1986), 'Of Other Spaces', *Diacritics*, 16:1, 22–27.

Frankfurter Zeitung (1926), 'Kult der Zerstreuung: Über die Berliner Lichtspielhäuser', March 4.

Frankfurter Zeitung, (1927), 'Die Photographie', October 28.

Frankfurter Zeitung, (1928), 'Die heutigen Film und sein Publikum', November 30 and December 1.

FREUND, Bill (1995), *Insiders and Outsiders: The Indian Working Class of Durban, 1910–1990*, University of Natal Press, Pietermaritzburg.

FRIEDBERG, Anne (1993), *Window Shopping: Cinema and the Postmodern*, University of California Press, Berkeley.

FRISHMAN, Alan (1977), *The Spatial Growth and Residential Patterns of Kano*, Ph.D dissertation, Northwestern University, Nigeria.

FUGLESANG, Minou (1994), *Veils and Videos: Female Youth Culture on the Kenyan Coast*, Department of Social Anthropology, Stockholm University, Stockholm.

FULLER, Thomas (2000), 'Indian Movies Speak to a Global Audience', *International Herald Tribune*, 20 October (Hague edition).

GANGAR, Amrit (1995), 'Films from the City of Dreams', in S. Patel and A. Thorner (ed.), *Bombay: Mosaic of Modern Culture*, Oxford University Press, Bombay.

GANGULY, Keya (1992), 'Migrant Identities: Personal Memory and the Construction of Selfhood' *Cultural Studies*, 6:1, 27–50.

GESCHIERE, Peter and Birgit Meyer (1998), 'Globalization and Identity: Dialectics of Flow and Closure', *Development and Change*, 29: 601–15.

GHATAK, Ritwik (1987), 'On Subarnarekha', in A. Rajadhyaksha and A. Gangar (ed.), *Ghatak: Arguments/Stories*, Screen Unit, Bombay.

GHOSH, Nimai (2003), 'Prasanga *Chhinnamul* O Anyanya: Nimai Ghosher Sakskhatkar', in S. Basu and S. Dasgupta (ed.), *Chhinnamul, Nimai Ghosher Prabandha Baktrita Sakkhatkar, Ebong Tar Jiban o Kaj Samparke Alochona*, Cine Central o Monchasha, Calcutta.

GHOSH, Shohini (2001), 'Streets of Terror: Urban Anxieties in the Bombay Cinema of the 1990s.' Paper presented to the workshop 'The Exhilaration of Dread', Sarai, 29 November–1 December.

GHOSH, Sugata (1998), 'Industry Status: Cinema May Find Itself Going Round Trees', *The Economic Times*, May 12.

GIDDENS, Anthony (1990), *The Consequences of Modernity*, Polity Press, Oxford.

GILLESPIE, Marie (1995), *Television, Ethnicity, and Cultural Change*, Comedia, Routledge, London; New York.

GOLDBÆK, Henning (2002), *Nye Drømme - Postmoderne Æstetik*, Dagbladet Information, 25 July, Copenhagen (Review of A. R. Rahman's and Andrew Lloyd Webber's *Bombay Dreams*).

GOPALAN, Lalitha (2002), *A Cinema of Interruptions*, MS, n/a.

GRABAR, Oleg (1973), *The Formation of Islamic Art*, Yale University Press, New Haven.

GRIFFITHS, Alison (1996), 'Journeys for Those Who Cannot Travel: Promenade Cinema and the Museum Life Group', *Wide Angle*, 18:3, 53–84.

HALLPIKE, C. R. (1979), *The Foundations of Primitive Thought*, Clarendon Press, Oxford.

HANSEN, Miriam (1991), *Babel and Babylon: Spectatorship in American Silent Film*, Harvard University Press, Cambridge, Mass.

HANSEN, Thomas (1996), 'Globalization and Nationalist Imaginations', *Economic and Political Weekly*, 31:603.

HAQ, Rupa (1997), 'Asian Kool? Bhangra and Beyond', in S. Sharma and J. Hutnyk (eds.), *Dis-orienting Rhythms: The Politics of the New Asian Dance Music*, Zed Books, London.

HARRISON, James (ed.) (1992), *Salman Rushdie*, Twayne Publishers, New York.

HAUSER, Arnold (1968), *The Social History of Art*, vol. 4, Routledge and Kegan Paul, London.

HIMPELE, Jeffrey D. (1996), 'Film Distribution as Media: Mapping Difference in the Bolivian Cinemascape', *Visual Anthropology Review*, 12:1, 47–66.

HISKETT, M. (1984), *The Development of Islam in West Africa*, Longman, London.

HOBBS, Renee et. al. (1988), 'How First-time Viewers Comprehend Editing Conventions', *Journal of Communication*, 38:4, 50.

HUGHES, Stephen P. (1999), 'Policing Silent Film Exhibition in South India', in R. Vasudevan (ed.), *Making Meaning in Indian Cinema*, Oxford University Press, New Delhi.

HUTNYK, John (1996), 'Media, Research, Politics, Culture', *Critique of Anthropology*, 16:4, 417–28.

HUTNYK, John and Sanjay Sharma (1997), *Dis-orienting Rhythms: The Politics of the New Asian Dance Music*, Zed Books, London.

Immigration and Asiatic Affairs (1939), *M735*, 28 September, Immigration and Asiatic Affairs, South Africa.

JAYAWARDENA, Chandra (1980), 'Culture and Ethnicity in Guyana and Fiji', *Man*, 26: 430–50.

JHA, Lalit K. (2000), 'Mania for Hindi Movies Sweeps Myanmar', *The Hindu*, 29 February.

KAARSHOLM, Preben (2001), 'The Jungle of the City: London and the Imperialist Imagination c. 1900' in M. Zerlang (ed.), *Representing London*, Spring Publishers, Copenhagen.

KABIR, Nasreen Munni (2001), *Bollywood: The Indian Cinema Story*, Channel 4 Books, London.

Kano State History and Culture Bureau (HCB), Films and Film Censorship, *Simple list of files removed from Cabinet R918*, Kano.

— Films and Film Censorship (1954), *Minutes by M.H. (?), 20/10/54, in response by a letter from the Director of Education, Northern Region 15/9/54 requesting an assessment of censorship*, Kano.

KAVIRAJ, Sudipta (1992), 'The Imaginary Institution of India', in P. Chatterjee and G. Pandey (ed.), *Subaltern Studies VII: Writings on South Asian History and Society*, Oxford University Press, New Delhi.

— (1995), *The Unhappy Consciousness: Bankimchandra Chattopadhyay and the Formation of Nationalist Discourse in India*, Oxford University Press, New Delhi.

— (1998), 'The Culture of Representative Democracy', in P. Chatterjee (ed.), *Wages of Freedom: Fifty Years of the Indian Nation-State*, Oxford University Press, New Delhi.

KELLY, John Dunham (1991), *A Politics of Virtue: Hinduism, Sexuality, and Countercolonial Discourse in Fiji*, University of Chicago Press, Chicago.

— (1998), 'Time and the Global: Against the Homogeneous, Empty Communities in Contemporary Social Theory', *Development and Change*, 29: 839–79.

— (2000), 'Fiji's Fifth Veda: exile, Sanatan Dharm, and countercolonial initiatives in diaspora' in Paula Richman (ed.), *Questioning Ramayanas: A South Indian Tradition*, University of California Press, Berkeley and Oxford University Press, New Delhi.

KIRBY, Lynne (1997), *Parallel Tracks: The Railroad and Silent Cinema*, Duke University Press, Durham.

KOSAMBI, Meera (1995), 'British Bombay and Marathi Mumbai: Some Nineteenth Century Perceptions', in S. Patel and A. Thorner (ed.), *Bombay: Mosaic of Modern Culture*, Oxford University Press, Bombay.

KOSZARSKI, Richard (1990), 'An Evening's Entertainment: The Age of the Silent Feature Picture, 1915–1928' in *History of the American Cinema*, vol. 3, Scribner, New York.

KRACAUER, Siegfried (1965), *Theory of Film. The Redemption of Physical Reality*, Oxford University Press, New York.

— (1972) *Kino. Essays, Studien, Glossen zum Film*, Suhrkamp, Frankfurt.

— (1974a), 'Der Mann mit dem Kinoapparat', in *Kino: Essays, Studien, Glossen z. Film*, Suhrkamp, Frankfurt am Main.

— (1974b), 'Montage', in *From Caligari to Hitler: A Psychological History of the German Film [1947]*, Princeton University Press, Princeton, NJ.

— (1995a), 'Cult of Distraction', in *The Mass Ornament*, Harvard University Press, Cambridge, Mass.

— (1995b), 'Film 1928', in *The Mass Ornament*, Harvard University Press, Cambridge, Mass.

— (1995c), 'Photography', in *The Mass Ornament*, Harvard University Press, Cambridge, Mass.

— (1998), *The Salaried Masses: Duty and Distraction in Weimar Germany*, Verso, London and New York.

— and Thomas Y. Levin (1995), *The Mass Ornament: Weimer Essays*, Harvard University Press, Cambridge, Mass.

KUHN, Annette (1998), *Cinema, Censorship and Sexuality 1909–1925*, Cinema and Society, Routledge, London.

KAARSHOLM, Preben (2001), 'The Jungle of the City: London and the Imperialist Imagination c. 1900', in M. Zerlang (ed.), *Representing London*, Spring Publishers, Copenhagen.

LAL, Brij (1983), '*Girmitiyas*: The Origins of the Fiji Indians', *Journal of Pacific History Monograph*, Australian National Open University, Canberra.

— (1985), 'Kunti's Cry: Indentured Women on Fiji Plantations', *Indian Economic and Social History Review*, 22.

— (1992), *Broken Waves: A History of the Fiji Islands in the Twentieth Century*, Pacific Islands Monograph Series no. 11, Centre for Pacific Islands Studies, School of Hawaiian, Asian and Pacific Studies, University of Hawaii, University of Hawaii Press, Honolulu.

— (1998), Interviews with Manas Ray, May, Canberra.

— (2001), 'Fiji: A Damaged Democracy', in B. Lal, *Coup: Reflections on the Political Crisis in Fiji*, Pandanus Books, Canberra.

LARKIN, Brian (1997), 'Indian Films, Nigerian Lovers: Media and the Creation of Parallel Modernities', *Africa*, 67:3, 406–40.

— (1999a), 'Theaters of the Profane: Cinema and Colonial Urbanism', *Visual Anthropology Review*, 14:2, 46–62.

— (1999b), 'Introduction to Media and the Technologies for Modern Living', *Visual Anthropology Review*, 14:2, 11–13.

— (n.d.), *White Prestige and the Immoral, Subversive Problem of Film: Moral Panic and Colonial Authority*, n/a.

LARSEN, Peter (1993), 'Benjamin at the Movies. Aura, Gaze, and History in the Artwork Essay', *Orbis Literarum*, 48.

— (1997), 'Benjamin, Kracauer, Mass Culture', *Working Papers,* 26, Department of Media Studies, University of Bergen.

LATH, Mukund (1998), *Transformation as Creation*, Aditya Prakashan, New Delhi.

The Leader (1969), 8 August.

LEFEBVRE, Henri (1996), *Writings on Cities*, Blackwell, Oxford.

LERNER, Daniel (1964), *The Passing of Traditional Society: Modernizing the Middle East*, The Free Press, New York (first published 1958).

— (1968), 'Modernization: Social Aspects', in D. L. Sills (ed.), *International Encyclopaedia of the Social Sciences*, The Free Press, New York.

LUGARD, Lord (1922), *The Dual Mandate in British Tropical Africa*, W. Blackwell and Sons, London.

LUKÁCS, György (1963), 'Critical Realism and Socialist Realism', in G. Lukács, *The Meaning of Contemporary Realism*, Merlin, London.

LURIA, A. R. (1976), *Cognitive Development. Its Cultural and Social Foundations*, Harvard University Press, Cambridge, Mass.

LUTGENDORF, Philip (1995), 'All in the (Raghu) Family: A Video Epic in Cultural Context' in L. Babb and S. Wadley (eds.), *Media and the Transformation of Religion in South Asia*, Pennsylvania, University of Pennsylvania Press.

MADSEN, Peter and Richard Plunz (eds.) (2001), *The Urban Life*

World: Formation, Perception, Representation, Routledge, London.

MARSH, Joss (2001), 'Recreating London: Dickens, Cinema and the Imagined City', in M. Zerlang (ed.), *Representing London*, Spring Publishers, Copenhagen.

MARTIN, Phyllis (1995), *Leisure and Society in Colonial Brazzaville*, African Studies Series, 87, Cambridge University Press, Cambridge.

MAZUMDAR, Ranjani (2001), *Urban Allegories: The City in Bombay Cinema 1970–2000*, New York University, New York.

MEHTA, Monika (2001), *Selections: Cutting, Classifying and Certifying in Bombay Cinema*, Ph.D thesis, University of Minnesota, Minneapolis.

MESSARIS, Paul (1993), 'Visual "Literacy": A Theoretical Synthesis', *Communication Theory*, 4.

— (1994), *Visual "Literacy": Image, Mind, and Reality*, Westview Press, Boulder, Colorado.

METZ, Christian (1982), *The Imaginary Signifier: Psychoanalysis and the Cinema*, Indiana University Press, Bloomington.

MILLER, Daniel (1997), 'Why Some Things Matter', in D. Miller, *Materializing Culture: Why Some Things Matter*, University of Chicago Press, Chicago.

MISHRA, Vijay (1979), *Rama's Banishment: A Centenary Tribute to the Fiji Indians 1879–1979*, Heinemann Educational Books, London.

— (1985), 'Towards a Theoretical Critique of Bombay Cinema', *Screen*, 26:3–4, May–August.

— (1992), 'Decentring History: Some Versions of Bombay Cinema', *East-West Film Journal*, 6:1, January.

MITCHELL, Timothy (1991), *Colonising Egypt*, University of California Press, Berkeley.

Moosa, A. B. (2001), interviewed by Vashna Jagarnath on 19 September.

Moshavi, Sharon (1995), 'Bollywood Breaks into the Big Time', *The Economic Times*, 3 October.

Mulvey, Laura (1975), 'Visual Pleasure and the Narrative Cinema', *Screen*, 16:3, Autumn.

— (1989), 'Afterthoughts on "Visual Pleasure and Narrative Cinema" Inspired by *Duel in the Sun*', in L. Mulvey (ed.), *Visual and Other Pleasures*, Indiana University Press, Bloomington

Musser, Charles (1990), 'The Emergence of Cinema: The American Screen to 1907' in *History of the American Cinema*, vol. 1, Scribner, New York.

Naficy, Hamid (1993), *The Making of Exile Cultures : Iranian Television in Los Angeles*, University of Minnesota Press, Minneapolis.

Naidoo, T. P. (2001), interviewed by Vashna Jagarnath on 24 September.

Nandy, Ashis (1995), 'The Intelligent Film Critic's Guide to the Indian Cinema' in A. Nandy (ed.), *The Savage Freud*, Oxford University Press, New Delhi.

— (1998), *The Secret Politics of Our Desires: Innocence, Culpability and Indian Popular Cinema*, Oxford University Press, New Delhi.

Newsweek International (2000), 'Bollywood Goes International', February 28.

Nigerian National Archives, Kaduna, *Kano Prof. 4430 (Mr. J. Green Mbadiwe: Application for permission to erect a hotel and cinema at Kano)*, Kano.

—, *Kano Prof. 6945/Jakara Palace Cinema/Letter to S.D.O.K. from Senior Superintendent of Police, Kano N. A. P .G. F. Sewall. 6/9/52*, Kano.

—, *Kano Prof. 7564, El Dunia Disaster. Colonial Office (CO) 583/317/8. Cinema Disaster at Kano, 1951*, Kano.

—, *MOI/55/Broadcasting, Radio Diffusion Service and BBC*, Kano.

—, (1934), *Kano Prof. 1391. Kano Township Annual Report 1934*, Kano.

— and Justice Percy E. Hubard, *Report of the Commissioner appointed by His Excellency the Governor to enquire into the circumstances in which a fire caused loss of life at, and destroyed, the El-Dunia Cinema, Kano, on the 13th day of May 1951, Zaria Prof. vol.II./ EDU/5 Cinema Cinematographs, Cinema Office, (2) Mobile Cinema Routine Correspondence*, Kano.

— and M.I.A. *Kaduna 2nd collection, R.1493, Cinematograph Audience 1932–1952, 2*, Kano

NIRANJANA, Tejaswini (1994), 'Interrogating Whose Nation? Tourists and Terrorists in *Roja*', *Economic and Political Weekly*, 29:3, 15 January.

— (2000), 'Nationalism Refigured: Contemporary South Indian Cinema and the Subject of Feminism', in P. Chatterjee and P. Jeganathan (ed.), *Community, Gender and Violence*, Columbia University Press, New York.

—, P. Sudhir and Vivek Dhareshwar (eds.) (1993), *Interrogating Modernity: Culture and Colonialism in India*, Seagull Books, Calcutta.

NTS *6657 29/313Y (8)*, n/a.

PANDEY, Gyanendra (2001), *Remembering Partition: Violence, Nationalism and History in India*, Cambridge University Press, Cambridge.

PATIL, S. K (ed.) (1951), *Report of the Film Enquiry Committee*, Government of India Press, New Delhi.

PRADHAN, Sudhi (1979), *Marxist Cultural Movements in India: Chronicles and Documents*, vol. 1, Santi Pradhan, Calcutta (Distributors: National Book Agency, Calcutta).

— (1982), 'Bharatiya Gananatya Sanstha Ebong Bharatiya Chalachchitra', *Chitrakalpa*, July.

PRAKASH, Gyan (1995), *Writing Postcolonial-Orientalist Histories of the Third World: Perspectives from Indian Historiography*, Princeton University Press, Princeton.

PRASAD, M. Madhava (1993), 'Cinema and the Desire for Modernity', *Journal of Arts and Ideas*, 25–26, December.

— (1998), *Ideology of the Hindi Film*: *A Historical Construction*, Oxford University Press, New Delhi.

— (2000), 'What the Other Calls Me', *The Telegraph*, 24 February.

PREMCHAND, Munsi (1979), 'The Nature and Purpose of Literature', in S. Pradhan (ed.), *Marxist Cultural Movements in India: Chronicles and Documents*, Santi Pradhan, Calcutta (Distributors: National Book Agency, Calcutta).

PUDOVKIN, V. I. (2003), 'The Uprooted', in S. Basu and S. Dasgupta (eds.), *Chhinnamul, Nimai Ghosher Prabandha Baktrita Sakskhatkar, Ebong Tar Jiban O Kaj Samparke Alochona*, Cine Central and Monchasha, Calcutta.

— and Cherkasov, N (2003), 'A Letter from V. I. Pudovkin and N. Cherkasov', in S. Basu and S. Dasgupta (ed.), *Chhinnamul, Nimai Ghosher Prabandha Baktrita Sakskhatkar, Ebong Tar Jiban O Kaj Samparke Alochona*, Cine Central and Monchasha, Calcutta.

RAJADHYAKSHA, Ashish (1987), 'The Phalke Era: Conflict of Traditional Form and Modern Technology', *Journal of Arts and Ideas*, 14 and 15.

— (1993), 'The Epic Melodrama: Themes of Nationality in Indian Cinema', *Journal of Arts and Ideas*, 25–26.

— (1997), 'Who's Looking? Viewership and Democracy in the Cinema', *Cultural Dynamics*, 10:2, 171–95.

— and Amrit Gangar (1987), *Ghatak: Arguments/Stories*, Screen Unit, Bombay.

— and Paul Willemen (1994), *Encyclopaedia of Indian Cinema*, British Film Institute, London (second edition 1999).

RAY, Manas (2000), 'Bollywood Down Under: Fiji Indian Cultural History and Popular Assertion', in S. Cunningham and J. G. Sinclair (eds.), *Floating Lives: The Media and Asian Diasporas*, University of Queensland Press, St. Lucia, Queensland.

RAYCHAUDHURI, Tapan (1988), *Europe Reconsidered: Perceptions of the West in Nineteenth Century Bengal*, Oxford University Press, New Delhi.

REDFIELD, Marc (1999), 'Imagi-nation: The Imagined Community and the Aesthetics of Mourning', *Diacritics*, 29:4, 60–82.

RESIDENT ALEXANDER OF KANO (1927), 'Record of the Proceedings of Conference of Residents, Northern Provinces, 1926', Paper presented to the workshop 'Proceedings of Conference of Residents, Northern Provinces, 1926', Lagos.

RESIDENT E. K. FEATHERSTONE OF KANO (1948), Letter to The Secretary of Northern Provinces, 9 January.

ROSE, Nikolas S. (1996), 'The Death of the Social? Re-figuring the Territory of Government', *Economy and Society*, 25:3, 327–56.

ROUSE, Roger (1991), 'Mexican Migration and the Social Space of Postmodernism', *Diaspora*, 1:1, 8–23.

RUSHDIE, Salman (1982), *Midnight's Children*, Picador, Pan Books, London.

— (1991), *Imaginary Homelands: Essays and Criticism 1981–1991*, Granta Books in association with Viking, London.

SAID, Edward W. (1978), *Orientalism*, Routledge and Kegan Paul Ltd., London.

SARKAR, Sumit (1983), *Modern India, 1885–1947*, Macmillan, Delhi.

SECRETARY BOARD OF TRADE AND INDUSTRIES OF SOUTH AFRICA (1940), interviewed by Vashna Jagarnath on 28 March.

SECRETARY NORTHERN PROVINCES (1932), Letter No. 16497.10A, to Chief Secretary Lagos, 6 February.

SENGUPTA, Amalendu (1989), *Uttal Challish: Asamapta Biplab*, n/a.

SENGUPTA, Ratnottama (1999), 'Taalis for the Showman', *The Times of India*, 8 July.

SHEIKH Nasiru Kabara (1995), interviewed by Brian Larkin in November.

SHUKLA, Sandhya (1997), 'Building Diaspora and Nation: The 1991 "Cultural Festival of India" ', *Cultural Studies*, 11:2, 314.

SIMMEL, Georg (1903), 'Die Grosstädte und das Geistesleben', in T. Petermann (ed.), *Die Grossstadt. Vorträge und Aufsätze zur Städteausstellung. Jahrbuch der Gehe-Stiftung Dresden*, Band 9, Dresden. English translation 'The Metropolis and Mental Life', in Kurt H. Wolff, (ed.), *The Sociology of Georg Simmel*, Free Press, Glencoe, Ill.

— (1950), 'The Metropolis and Mental Life', in K. H. Wolff (ed.), *The Sociology of Georg Simmel*, Free Press, Glencoe, Ill.

Sivaranjani (1994), 29 July.

SIVATHAMBY, K. (1981), *The Tamil Film as a Medium of Political Communication*, New Century Book House, Madras.

SKLAR, Robert (1975), *Movie-made America: A Social History of American Movies*, Random House, New York.

SOUTHALL, Aidan and Peter C. W. Gutkind (1957), *Townsmen in the Making: Kampala and Its Suburbs*, East African Institute of Social Research, Kampala.

SPENCER, Neil (2002), 'Bollywood Blockbuster', Indian Summer Special issue, *Life: The Observer Magazine* (2002), 7 April.

SPIEGEL, Alan (1976), *Fiction and the Camera Eye: Visual Consciousness in Film and the Modern Novel*, University Press of Virginia, Charlottesville.

SRINIVAS, S. V. (1996), 'Devotion and Defiance in Fan Activity', *Journal of Arts and Ideas*, 29: 67.

TAHIR, Ibrahim A. (1975), *Scholars, Saints, and Capitalists in Kano 1904–1974: The Pattern of Bourgeois Revolution in an Islamic Society*, Ph.D dissertation, Cambridge University, Cambridge.

The Economic Times, (1999), 'US Box Office Sways to the Rhythm of *Taal*', 21 August.

The Graphic, (1969), 15 August.

The Indian Express, (1996), 3 October.

The Indian Express, (1998), 'Make Bollywood's India a Reality', 19 April.

The Leader (1969), 8 August.

The New Indian Express, (1999), 'Rajnikant Bowls over Japanese Youth', 10 June.

The Times of India, (1999), 'Interview, Netvamsham!', 18 July.

THOMAS, Rosie (1987), 'Mythologies and Modern India', in W. Luhr (ed.), *World Cinema Since 1945*, Ungar, New York.

THOMPSON, Elizabeth (2000), *Colonial Citizens: Republican Rights, Paternal Privilege, and Gender in French Syria and Lebanon*, History and Society of the Modern Middle East Series, Columbia University Press, New York.

TSIVIAN, Yuri and Richard Taylor (1994), *Early Cinema in Russia and Its Cultural Reception*, Soviet Cinema, Routledge, London and New York.

UBAH, C. N. (1982), 'The Political Dilemma of Residential Segregation: The Example of Kano's Sabon Gari', *African Urban Studies*, 14:51–70.

UNESCO (1981), *Statistics on Film and Cinema 1975–77*, Office of Statistics, Paris.

VASUDEVAN, Ravi (1993), 'Shifting Codes, Dissolving Identities: The Hindi Social Films of the 1950s as Popular Culture', *Journal of Arts and Ideas*, 23–24.

— (1998), 'Cinema and Citizenship in the "Third World" ', Published lecture delivered at Northwestern University, 4 May.

— (1999), 'Review of M. Madhava Prasad ['s] *Ideology of the Hindi Film*' in *Journal of the Moving Image*, 1:117–27.

— (2000), *Making Meaning in Indian Cinema*, Oxford University Press, New Delhi.

WATTS, Michael (1996), 'Place, Space and Community in an African City', in P. Yeager (ed.), *The Geography of Identity*, University of Michigan Press, Ann Arbor.

WILLIAMS, Raymond (1975), *The Country and the City*, Paladin Books, London (first edition 1973).

— (1977), 'A Lecture on Realism', *Screen*, 18:1, 61–75.

WIRTH, Louis (1964), 'Urbanism as a Way of Life [1938]', in L. Wirth (ed.), *On Cities and Social Life: Selected Papers*, The Heritage of Sociology, University of Chicago Press, Chicago.

ZIZEK, Slavoj (1997), 'Multiculturalism, or the Cultural Logic of Multinational Capitalism', *New Left Review*, 225 (September–October).

CONTRIBUTORS

Moinak Biswas is the head of the Department of Film Studies, Jadavpur University, Calcutta, and writes on Indian cinema and culture. He is the author of the Bengali monograph *Chaplin* (1997), and has edited two volumes of writings in Bengali by Hemango Biswas (1989, 1998). He is currently editing a volume of essays on Satyajit Ray for Seagull Books.

Vashna Jagarnath is a graduate student with the Historical Studies Programme at the University of Natal, Durban. Her BA Honours thesis is called 'Filmi very Filmi' and is a social history of the influence of Indian film on South African Indians. Her MA dissertation project is on family photographs.

Preben Kaarsholm is associate professor in International Development Studies, Roskilde University. He has published on Sergio Leone and on transformations of the John Wayne character in the John Ford westerns from *Stagecoach* to *The Searchers*, on theatre and the development of democratic opposition in Zimbabwe, and is currently working on violence, culture and politics in South Africa during the transition from apartheid.

Sudipta Kaviraj is a political theorist at the School of Oriental and African Studies in London. He has written on civil society and democracy in India, on urban development in Calcutta, and in 1995 published *The Unhappy Consciousness: Bankimchandra Chattopadhyay and The Formation of Nationalist Discourse in India*.

BRIAN LARKIN writes on media and urbanization in northern Nigeria. He is co-editor of *Media Worlds: Anthropology on a New Terrain* (with Faye Ginsburg and Lila Abu-Lughod, 2002) and is currently working on issues of piracy and media infrastructure. He teaches anthropology at Barnard College, Columbia University.

PETER LARSEN is professor of media studies at University of Bergen, and has published widely on iconography, visual communications, and semiotics and film theory.

M. MADHAVA PRASAD has been a fellow at the Centre for Studies in Social Sciences, Calcutta and the Centre for the Study of Culture and Society, Bangalore. He is now professor of film theory at the Central Institute of English and Foreign Languages, Hyderabad. He is the author of *Ideology of the Hindi Film: A Historical Construction* (1998).

TEJASWINI NIRANJANA is senior fellow at the Centre for the Study of Culture and Society, Bangalore. She is the author of *Siting Translation: History, Post-structuralism and the Colonial Context*, and co-editor of *Interrogating Modernity: Culture and Colonialism in India*. She is currently finishing a book on gender and race in the subaltern Indian diaspora in the Caribbean.

ASHISH RAJADHYAKSHA is a senior fellow at the Centre for the Study of Culture and Society in Bangalore. He is the author of *Ritwik Ghatak: A Return to the Epic* and (with Paul Willemen) of *The Encyclopaedia of Indian Cinema*.

MANAS RAY is a fellow at the Centre for Studies in Social Sciences, Calcutta, and coordinator of the Centre's Urban History Archive. 'Growing Up Refugee: on memory and locality' (*History Workshop*

Journal, 53, 2002) and 'Nation, Nostalgia and Bollywood' (in *Media of Diaspora: Networking the Globe,* 2003) are his two latest publications.

RAVI S. VASUDEVAN has written on Indian film history, and is currently running a project on the social and cultural history of cinema in the city of Delhi. He is a fellow with the Centre for the Study of Developing Societies in New Delhi, and co-director of the Centre's Sarai programme, which researches contemporary urban and media experience. He has edited *Making Meaning in Indian Cinema* and *Sarai Reader 02: The Cities of Everyday Life*.

MARTIN ZERLANG is associate professor at the Department of Comparative Literature, University of Copenhagen. He has published on literary history, the history of entertainment, magic realism in Latin American literature, urban culture, and literary and filmic representations of London.